I0149816

Rebbe Nachman and The Knights of the Rosh HaShanah Table

The modern-day adventures of people who found their way to Uman

Compiled by
Debbie Shapiro

Published by
Breslov Research Institute
Jerusalem/New York

Copyright © 2009 Breslov Research Institute
ISBN 978-1-928822-29-5
All rights reserved

*No part of this book may be translated, reproduced, stored in any retrieval system
or transmitted, in any form or by any means, electronic, mechanical, photocopying,
recording or otherwise, without prior permission in writing from the publisher.*

First edition

For further information:
Breslov Research Institute, POB 5370, Jerusalem, Israel
or:
Breslov Research Institute, POB 587, Monsey, NY 10952-0587

e-mail: info@breslov.org
Internet: www.breslov.org

Cover design: Ben Gasner

Printed in Israel

The Breslov Research Institute
extends its deepest gratitude and thanks to

Yehudah and Chayah Levinson

for their self-sacrifice and beneficence
to disseminate the teachings of

REBBE NACHMAN OF BRESLOV

In the merit of Rebbe Nachman,
may they be worthy of
good health and success
and stability with security,
and tremendous nachat
from all their children
and grandchildren

"Yoh essen nit essen, yoh shlofen nit shlofen, yoh davenen, nit davenen—abi du zolst bei mir zein oif Rosh HaShoneh!"

"Whether you eat or don't eat; whether you sleep or don't sleep; whether you pray or don't pray [i.e., with the proper concentration]—just make sure to be with me for Rosh HaShanah!"

REBBE NACHMAN OF BRESLOV

Contents

Defining Moments

My Heart Is In The "East"

Publisher's Foreword

"Many stories will be told about my followers—stories and stories about each one of them."

This book took over twenty years to be written.

It started in 1988, when the Soviet Union allowed 250 Breslover chassidim to spend Rosh HaShanah at the *tziyun* (gravesite) of Rebbe Nachman in Uman. This was the first Rosh HaShanah gathering to take place in Uman in nearly twenty years. It was also the first in over seventy years in which chassidim living outside the Soviet Union were able to travel to Uman, and the first time those in Russia were able to travel there without fear of being thrown into prison—or worse. For most of the chassidim who came that first year, it was the fulfillment of a lifelong dream.

The following year, Rosh HaShanah 1989, the Soviet regime flung open its gates and allowed 1,000 chassidim to enter. Each succeeding year, the numbers increased, until as of last Rosh HaShanah 2008, the city of Uman (population 80,000) was flooded with some 25,000 chassidim (including many non-Breslovers), Litvaks, curiosity-seekers and hippies, along with all types of hair or no hair, jeans, shorts and everything in between!

I was privileged to be among the 1,000 men who traveled to Uman for Rosh HaShanah 1989. We stayed in a hotel that could only be described as "minus three stars." (There are plenty more colorful descriptions in the accounts that follow.) A few of us English-speakers from England, Canada, the United States and

Israel ate our Yom Tov meals together. Despite the gravity of the day and the austerity of the meals, the atmosphere was festive. We were overwhelmed with a combination of joy tinged with awe that we were privileged to accomplish what many had only dared to yearn for: to spend Rosh HaShanah with our Rebbe!

In those early years, our group consisted of about ten men. Besides the fact that kosher items were nonexistent in Ukraine in those days, the local foods and drinks which we could have purchased were not fit for consumption, even if they were canned or bottled. It was just a few years after the Chernobyl nuclear reactor disaster, and we had to assume the local produce was contaminated. So we brought all our food from home and pooled our resources.

We brought the challah with us from Israel. By the time Yom Tov rolled around, it was far from fresh, so we supplemented it with matzah. Someone always brought the traditional *simanim*— the apple and honey, beets, carrots, leeks and fish head—that are customarily eaten on the first night of Rosh HaShanah. For the first course, we served tuna fish. Every once in a while, someone brought along a can of sardines, or even chanced bringing an unbroken, well-traveled glass jar of gefilte fish. Most of it made it to our holiday table.

We supplemented these delicacies with *cordon bleu* canned peas and carrots, or corn served straight from the can. The main course, of course, was gourmet salami. (One time, one of our friends brought along a frozen salmon, but lost his luggage in London when changing planes. On the way home, he was able to identify his luggage easily—the stench was unmistakable—but he refused to claim his bag!)

The next year, we felt like we had landed in the lap of luxury: we rented a one-room apartment in a decrepit building that reeked of alcohol. There were nine floors in the building, over a hundred apartments, and an elevator that could lift just three people, or one with luggage. Our apartment was on the fifth floor (luckily, we don't use an elevator on Yom Tov!). The one room had to accommodate six people in addition to the table we set up to eat our meals. But the apartment's location was great, being almost adjacent to the *tziyun*. We continued to rent that apartment for several years. Meanwhile, our little group grew to some fifteen, twenty people.

In the mid-1990s, during our Yom Tov meals, we started going around the table, telling our stories. We told our stories because of what Reb Noson writes in *Likutey Halakhot*, that Rosh HaShanah—the day that commemorates the creation of the world—is a great *chesed* (kindness) from God, since the creation of the world occurred through God's *chesed,* as it is written, "For I have said, 'The world is built upon *chesed*'" (Psalms 89:3). We had so much to be thankful for, especially for the privilege of spending Rosh HaShanah in Uman. What better way to express our gratitude than by relating our stories and sharing the miracles that brought us to the Rebbe!

I began by telling my story, how I was drawn to Breslov by my teacher in grade school, Rabbi Zvi Aryeh Rosenfeld (later, I became his son-in-law), and was privileged to become close to Rebbe Nachman. When I finished telling my story, another member of our group told his. And so we continued around the Rosh HaShanah table, each man relating the details of his spiritual journey.

The following years, we found better lodgings. Our group grew to close to fifty people, although not everyone participated in the communal meals. To alleviate the drudgery of our surroundings, we renamed our apartments after world-famous luxury hotels. The main building, which we dubbed the Waldorf Astoria, was a three-bedroom villa that had a roomy dining area large enough to accommodate some twenty people. Here we squeezed in some thirty to thirty-five people. The other apartments were known by such distinguished names as the Hilton, Sheraton, Hyatt, Inn on the Park, Marriott and Claridge's.

Each year, more and more people joined us for our Yom Tov meals, and guests would tell their personal stories of how they came to Uman. Some tales were simple. Others were exciting. And some were absolutely incredible.

In 2001, we purchased a villa in Uman. We signed the papers on 9/11. We were in the lawyer's office in Uman when we were informed of the terrorist attack on the Twin Towers, and immediately returned to the *tziyun* to *daven*.

After renovations, our villa was so "luxurious" that we named it the Ritz-Carlton. Later on, afraid that we might be sued for using the hotel chain's name, we dubbed it the "Uman Ritz-Carton"!

For the next few years, we ate our Yom Tov meals in a tent that we had set up in the villa's yard. Only recently, we built a permanent roof. Today, between fifty to sixty people eat their meals with us.

Until 2003, everyone brought food from home and we pooled our resources. That year, my son decided to prepare proper, homemade meals for the entire group. We purchased several refrigerators and stoves to store and cook all the food. My son's wife wrote down several recipes and he simply multiplied the ingredients by sixty. And God, in His ever-loving kindness, guarded everybody from food poisoning and helped us all to survive those meals. Since then, the food has improved considerably. (It's comforting to know that if things ever get tough, my son can always find work as a professional chef!)

But the food was never the main attraction. It was, and still is, the stories of personal growth and redemption that are told around our Rosh HaShanah table. With the increasing number of people coming to Uman each year, we hear more and more amazing stories of spiritual journeys to Breslov, and of the impact that Rebbe Nachman's teachings have had on people's lives.

Though the majority of these stories were told around the table of the Uman Ritz-Carton, we've included several from members of the Côte Saint-Luc Breslov Centre in Montreal, Quebec. This Centre began as a result of a few members finding the publications of the Breslov Research Institute and beginning study sessions in them under the directorship of Rabbi Saadia

Elhadad. This led to a strong connection between the French-speaking Moroccan community and the English-speaking Breslov Research Institute.

Over the years, people suggested that we collect these stories and make a book out of them. *Knights of the Rosh HaShanah Table* is that book. We hope you enjoy it. And perhaps next year, you will join us and tell us your story.

Chaim Kramer
Menachem Av 5769
August 2009

Compiler's Note

When Chaim Kramer first approached me about this project, I never dreamed of the impact it would have on my life. Then, just a few weeks before I flew to the United States to conduct the initial interviews for this book, I was privileged to make my own journey to Uman. After that experience, words that might have rung hollow now struck a deep chord of recognition. I listened to grown men choke back tears as they tried to describe the spiritual impact of their journey. While outwardly remaining the impartial "reporter," I identified with them completely. After all, I, too, had been there. With each person I interviewed, my appreciation and connection with Breslov grew deeper. I found myself on fire with Breslov!

I would like to thank Chaim Kramer and the Breslov Research Institute for presenting me with this opportunity. May they continue to spread the light of Rebbe Nachman to the world.

It is my sincere hope that these interviews convey the quiet heroism of the many who overcame the obstacles and made the journey. May God grant me the privilege of continuing to support my husband in his spiritual and physical journey to Uman for many, many more years to come, and may we be granted much *Yiddishe nachat* from our children, grandchildren and all future generations.

Debbie Shapiro

Tammuz 5769
June 2009

Acknowledgments

This book contains personal stories from individuals around the world. Often, the principals who tell their stories have a connection or two with others who relate their memories. We have included an alphabetized list of contributors in Appendix A as a handy cross-reference. We also include a list of Breslov personalities quoted in this book, with brief biographies, in Appendix B.

Many people who learn Torah in English, Spanish, French, etc., invariably end up peppering their speech with Hebrew and Yiddish idioms that are not easily translatable. To preserve the flavor of our storytellers' words, we've retained their bilingual style and provided a glossary of terms at the end of the book.

WE EXTEND OUR DEEPEST APPRECIATION TO Mrs. Debbie Shapiro, the wife of our esteemed colleague, Rabbi Dovid Shapiro, for her efforts in collecting and organizing these stories for publication.

Also, many thanks to S. Brand and Y. Hall for their laborious editing efforts, working under the perennial pressure of the tyrannical head of the Breslov Research Institute to complete their work and meet our deadlines.

And to all of the "Knights of the Rosh HaShanah Table," kudos for your cooperation. Our Sages teach, "One mitzvah leads to another mitzvah" (*Avot* 4:2). May the trips you made to Uman inspire others to do the same, increasing your "mitzvah base" many times over. May we all merit to see the Coming of the *Mashiach*, the Redemption of the Jewish Nation and the Rebuilding of the Holy Temple, speedily and in our days. Amen.

The Promise

"I have accomplished, and I will accomplish!"
(*Tzaddik* #126)

The Jewish world is filled with them—new leaders, new ideas, new approaches. Some innovations have not been so positive, leading Jews away from the pure waters of Torah and into the murky depths of secularism, atheism and assimilation. The better innovations have enriched and broadened our connection to God and Torah. But all these new movements have one thing in common: when their leader passes away, everyone acknowledges the "end of an era." Sometimes, the leader's son or close disciple manages to recapture some of the spirit or fire of the originator, but in most cases, succeeding generations must settle for a watered-down version of the original.

Breslov Chassidut is unique in the annals of new movements. When Rebbe Nachman passed away in 1810, few believed that his influence would continue to spread as far or as strongly as it did.

Born in 1772, Rebbe Nachman was only eighteen years old when he first began to attract a following. Many of his chassidim were outstanding scholars and kabbalists in their own right, some of them far older than he. The Rebbe taught them the path of faith, simplicity and joy; of looking for the good points; and of how to develop a close, personal relationship with God.

But the Rebbe also saw his mission extending far into the future, even after his earthly sojourn was over. "I have accomplished, and I *will* accomplish!" he declared. He made a similar statement: "*Mein fierel vet shoin tluen biz Moshiach vet koomen*—My fire will burn until the *Mashiach* comes!" (*Tzaddik* #126).

Standing on the verge of the modern age, which would introduce both an industrial revolution that would totally transform the way people lived, and an ideological revolution that would shake the entire framework of beliefs and assumptions on which people had based their lives for centuries, Rebbe Nachman said, "I'll tell you a secret. A great wave of atheism is about to enter the world" (*Rabbi Nachman's Wisdom* #220). One of the Rebbe's main objectives was to throw out spiritual life rafts to those who would become engulfed in the impending ideological torrent.

Rebbe Nachman had a profound grasp of the alienation, anguish and despair so characteristic of the modern age. Hero after hero in his stories spends years wandering through vast forests, deserts, wildernesses and the like, searching and searching. Again and again, Rebbe Nachman addresses contemporary issues such as anxiety, frustration, depression and existential conflict. He saw clearly that further sophistication was not the answer. "The greatest wisdom of all," he declared, "is to be simple." "*Gevalt!*" he cried. "Don't give up!"

Today, nearly 200 years after the Rebbe's passing, we see the truth of Rebbe Nachman's vision, and eagerly grab hold of the lifeline that he extends to twenty-first-century humanity. Every year, the numbers of people who discover his books and read his stories and lessons grows. Every Rosh HaShanah, the number of people who flock to Uman to be with the Rebbe increases. His lessons, conversations, parables and epigrams electrify and inspire as he expresses the wisdom of the Torah in a totally original way, opening up entire new vistas for every aspect of life. Rebbe Nachman's optimistic message, "Serve God with simplicity and joy," strikes a deep chord in many who have found themselves on the fringes of the Jewish people, as well as those born and raised in observant homes. Indeed, the Rebbe has accomplished...and will continue to accomplish!

Destination: Uman

AS LONG AS REBBE NACHMAN WAS ALIVE, hundreds of chassidim would travel to be with him for Rosh HaShanah. On his last Rosh HaShanah in Uman in 1810, the Rebbe made his strongest statements ever about the importance of coming to him for Rosh HaShanah. "No one should be missing," he said. *"Gohr mein zakh iz Rosh HaShanah*—My very essence is Rosh HaShanah!" (*Tzaddik* #403).

Eighteen days later, on the fourth day of Sukkot, Rebbe Nachman passed away. According to the normal scheme of things, it should have been only a matter of time before the Breslov movement disappeared. In most Chassidic groups, when one rebbe dies, a new one is chosen to succeed him, but Rebbe Nachman did not leave a "successor" as such. To his followers, Rebbe Nachman was a figure without parallel. There was no one to compare with him. Therefore, one might have expected the Rebbe's followers to eventually drift apart and go their separate ways.

Which indeed they might have, had it not been for Reb Noson, the Rebbe's closest disciple and scribe, who was only thirty years old at the time of the Rebbe's passing. After the Rebbe's burial that Sukkot of 1810, all the chassidim who had been with him in Uman journeyed back to their hometowns, pondering, among other things, why the Rebbe had spoken so much that year about the importance of coming to him for Rosh HaShanah, since he must have known it was going to be his last one in this world. It was Reb Noson who spelled out what Rebbe Nachman meant.

As the weeks passed, all kinds of statements that the Rebbe had made over the years kept running through Reb Noson's mind. Rebbe Nachman had been most emphatic that his followers travel to him for Rosh HaShanah. "Although many other chassidim traveled to the *tzaddikim* for Rosh HaShanah, there was no one who was as insistent about the matter as Rebbe Nachman," Reb

Noson wrote (ibid., #23). The Rebbe said, "My Rosh HaShanah is completely new. ...God gave me the gift of knowing what Rosh HaShanah is" (ibid., #405). On Rosh HaShanah, the Rebbe said, he was able to help people in certain ways that were beyond his ability during the rest of the year (ibid., #406). And the Rebbe stated that anyone who has the privilege of being with him on Rosh HaShanah is entitled to be very, very happy throughout the coming year (ibid., #403).

Reb Noson realized that the Rebbe meant that just as his chassidim had come to him for Rosh HaShanah during his lifetime, so they should come to his gravesite in the future.

To that end, Reb Noson organized a pilgrimage to the Rebbe's *tziyun* in Uman for the following Rosh HaShanah. Though only about sixty out of the hundreds who had previously journeyed to Uman joined that Rosh HaShanah pilgrimage, it was enough to convince Reb Noson that the Rosh HaShanah gathering, or *kibutz* as it come to be called, would continue. Indeed, with each passing year, the numbers grew.

Rebbe Nachman had made another promise, an extraordinary one. About seven months before he passed away, the Rebbe called for two of his closest followers, Rabbi Aharon, the *Rav* of Breslov, and Reb Naftali of Nemirov, and asked them to act as witnesses for a most unusual vow.

He declared: "When my days are over and I leave this world, I will intercede for anyone who comes to my grave, recites the Ten Psalms of the *Tikkun HaKlali*, and gives a coin to charity. No matter how serious his sins and transgressions, I will do everything in my power to save him and cleanse him. I will span the length and breadth of the creation for him. By his *peyot*, I will pull him out of Gehinnom!" (*Rabbi Nachman's Wisdom* #141). "It makes no difference what he did until that day, as long as he undertakes not to return to his foolish ways from now on" (*Tzaddik* #122).

This declaration was revolutionary. No other *tzaddik* had ever made such a promise. And because of the magnitude of this promise, Rebbe Nachman's followers throughout the centuries have yearned to make the journey to Uman to pray at his gravesite. One who fulfills these three conditions at any time of year receives the same benefit, quite apart from the custom of doing so on Erev Rosh HaShanah.

The Movement Grows

THANKS TO REB NOSON'S DEDICATION in publishing the Rebbe's works and teaching other searching souls, the Breslov movement grew. And because Reb Noson and others refused to take the place of the Rebbe, Rebbe Nachman's message was transmitted directly to future followers, giving each person the opportunity to have a direct relationship with the Rebbe. Because of the draw of the Rebbe's *tziyun*, it was natural that Uman would become more and more of a focal point. In Uman, Reb Noson built the first Breslov synagogue, known as the *kloyz*.[1]

After Reb Noson's passing on December 20, 1844, his devoted student, Reb Nachman of Tulchin, kept the Breslov community in Uman alive, turning it into a vibrant center of spirituality and devotion. Reb Noson's *kloyz* continued to host Rosh HaShanah services for Jews who would travel to Uman from all over the Ukraine, White Russia and Lithuania, and from as far away as Poland. By the early 1900s, people were even making the Rosh HaShanah pilgrimage from Israel, where the beginnings of a Breslov community was forming.

Then the gates slammed shut. The Russian Revolution of 1917 sealed the border to foreign tourists. In 1919, successive waves of troops passed through Uman, perpetrating a series of pogroms in which hundreds of Jews lost their lives. As the Communist regime made every effort to repress Jewish religious life, the chassidim in Poland began to hold their own Rosh HaShanah

---

1 Still standing, the *kloyz* is no longer in use as a synagogue today. To avoid confusion with the "New *Kloyz*" built under the leadership of Reb Michel Dorfman, it is sometimes called the "Old *Kloyz*."

gathering in Lublin. The chassidim in Jerusalem established another gathering. These gatherings were not meant to replace Uman, but to prevent Breslover chassidim from eventually forgetting about "the Rebbe's Rosh HaShanah."

Meanwhile, those who had immigrated abroad established new Breslov communities in Israel and America, and these were expanding rapidly. With all access to Uman completely barred to Jews from outside the Soviet Union, the main Rosh HaShanah gatherings became those held in Israel. In 1936, Rabbi Avraham Sternhartz, a great-grandson of Reb Noson, immigrated to Israel and initiated an annual gathering in Meron at the gravesite of Rabbi Shimon bar Yochai, author of the *Zohar*, citing the deep connection between Rabbi Shimon bar Yochai and Rebbe Nachman, as explained in the Prologue of the *Likutey Moharan*. By the 1970s and 1980s, the gatherings held in Meron and Jerusalem each attracted many thousands, while smaller gatherings took place in New York and, later, in Manchester, England.

The gatherings in Meron and Jerusalem were major events, involving a whole organizational infrastructure to arrange accommodations, meals and so on. But, from time to time during the Rosh HaShanah dancing, a few people would sing the traditional Breslov song, *"Uman, Uman, Rosh HaShanah."* However, the idea of actually being in Uman for Rosh HaShanah was as laughable as Abraham and Sarah having a baby in their old age.

The first chink in the Iron Curtain developed in the summer of 1963, when Gedaliah Fleer, a student of Rabbi Zvi Aryeh Rosenfeld in New York, met with Reb Michel Dorfman in Moscow and told him of his wish to travel to Uman, an impossibility at that time. Nevertheless, Reb Michel agreed to meet the determined young man in Kiev and accompany him to the *tziyun*. Being caught would have meant immediate exile to Siberia. But the trip came off, opening a door to Uman for the first time in over forty-five years.

The following winter, a group of eleven people from the United States traveled to Uman under the leadership of Rabbi

Rosenfeld. More trips followed, but owing to the presence of military installations nearby, the Soviets circumscribed the visitors in every conceivable way. You had to travel all the way to Kiev just to apply for the special visa required to visit Uman, and visas were often as not refused. Even when they were granted, it was forbidden to visit Uman unaccompanied, and certainly not to stay in the town overnight.

Yet the draw of Rebbe Nachman's *tziyun* never lost its grip on the imagination of the Breslover chassidim. By the early 1980s, organized groups were traveling to Uman from the United States, England and even Israel. The Russian authorities turned down all requests to arrange a tour to coincide with Rosh HaShanah— they still wouldn't even allow visitors to stay in Uman overnight— but the Breslovers kept asking...and praying.

Reb Noson once said, "Even if the road to Uman were paved with knives, I would crawl there just so I could be at Rebbe Nachman's grave" (*Tovot Zikhronot*, p. 137). For the most devoted Breslovers, visiting Rebbe Nachman's *tziyun* was the dream of a lifetime. People resorted to all kinds of stratagems to get around the Soviet obstinacy, sometimes putting themselves at considerable risk to travel to Uman even without a visa. One of the main principles of Breslov teachings is that the obstacles to any holy goal are only sent in order to increase one's yearning and determination to achieve it. How many prayers flowed forth in the endeavor to get to Uman! And they were answered.

In 1988, it happened. After protracted negotiations, the Soviet façade cracked and the authorities finally gave permission for 250 people to spend Rosh HaShanah in Uman. Even after agreeing, they kept changing their minds, creating innumerable difficulties along the way. Nevertheless, by a miracle, it came off. Uman's one and only hotel—a shabby, dilapidated building that was more like an army barracks—was inundated with chassidim who sang, danced and poured out their hearts in prayer, leaving the bemused locals to stare at the strange spectacle in their midst.

The following year, 1989, over 1,000 people came. A large, empty factory site was rented some ten minutes' walk from the *tziyun*. The production halls were hastily converted into a synagogue, dining hall and dormitories, and food was flown in from Israel. Elderly Jews who had lived their entire lives in Uman began to emerge out of nowhere to join the festivities. The sight of so many of their emancipated brethren literally dancing in the streets finally convinced them that they could drop the paranoid attitudes that had perforce become second nature during the long years of Stalinist, Nazi and post-Stalinist persecution.

By Rosh HaShanah 1990, the number of visitors had doubled to 2,000 and an even larger factory site was acquired two minutes away from the gravesite. In 2000, over 10,000 visitors were present for the Rebbe's Rosh HaShanah. Five years later, that number doubled!

Future Vision

IN HIS MANUSCRIPT OF *Chayey Moharan* (translated into English as *Tzaddik*), Reb Noson writes that a time will come when people will travel to Uman from all over the world to pray beside Rebbe Nachman's grave on Erev Rosh HaShanah. The gathering will be so large that it will be necessary to hire guards to ensure that visitors do not remain at the *tziyun* too long, so that others will have a place to stand (*Siach Sarfey Kodesh* V, 125).

At the time that Reb Noson made this prediction, it no doubt seemed unimaginable to his followers. Yet we see that we have virtually reached this point today!

We also cherish the words of Reb Shimshon Barski, an influential Breslover chassid in pre-war Uman, who wrote: "I once read an old letter that told of how the Rebbe had predicted the invention of the airplane, stating that this is one of the signs of the Final Redemption. The Rebbe declared: 'Many machines are destined to be invented. And in one of these machines, a great number of people will travel in the air. Thus, a Jew who has a source of distress before praying will decide to fly to Jerusalem to ask the *Mashiach* for advice on how to pray properly—and still have time to return home to recite his prayer.'

"It is well known that the Rebbe's follower, Reb Naftali, said, 'If you should ever hear of such a machine, you should play music and dance in the marketplace!'" (*She'arit Yisrael*, Letters of Rabbi Shimshon Barski #94, excerpted in *Siach Sarfey Kodesh* I, 501).

The hopes and dreams of generations have come true in the wonderful sight of tens of thousands of Jews traveling to Uman every Rosh HaShanah to *daven* by the Rebbe's *tziyun*.

As Rebbe Nachman once observed, "Every year, people say that previous years were better and times are not as good as they were before. But the opposite is true. God now directs the world better than ever!" (*Rabbi Nachman's Wisdom* #307).

The Obstacles, The Triumphs

The extent of a person's desire is primarily determined by the obstacle that Heaven arranges for him. When a Jew needs to do something for his Judaism...an obstacle is arranged for him...When confronted by an obstacle, a person's desire grows even stronger. And the greater the desired objective, the greater the obstacle.

For there are three elements: the desire, the desirer and the desired—that is, the person who desires, the objective that is desired, and the desire that one has for the desired objective. The extent of the desire has to be in proportion to the magnitude of the desired objective. Therefore, when the desired objective is very great, one's desire has to be very great. One is then confronted by an extremely difficult obstacle, through which one's desire becomes particularly greater... (Likutey Moharan I, 66:4).

"The Obstacles Are Just An Illusion"

Chaim Mann

Raised in a non-religious Jewish home in Montreal, Canada, Chaim Mann had already begun observing the Torah before he was introduced to Rebbe Nachman. He studied under Rabbi Saadia Elhadad, founder of the Breslov Centre in Montreal.

I encountered tremendous opposition when I made my initial decision to travel to Uman in 1996. People thought that anyone who traveled there would return a total wacko. My father warned me that if I went to Uman, he would throw me out of our family business. My mother informed me that she would be so hurt that she'd never speak to me again. My wife threatened to divorce me.

I phoned Rabbi Elazar Mordekhai Koenig in Tzefat to ask his advice. I was positive that he would tell me to remain in Montreal. Instead, he said, "No matter what, you must come. The obstacles you are experiencing are just an illusion." I thought, *If he is putting himself out on such a limb to convince me to travel to Uman, something unbelievable must be going on there!*

The other Breslover chassidim had warned me that when a person travels to Uman, he faces many obstacles. The threats were exactly that, because afterward, when I returned home to Montreal, my entire family came to the airport to greet me with open arms. All their threats were just an illusion, a big, fat *yetzer hara* that disappeared the moment I returned.

Since that first trip, I travel to Uman for Rosh HaShanah every year. Each year, Uman is not just an experience. It's a *chidush*, something completely new. I've never been disappointed.

A PERSON COMES TO UMAN completely broken, and then rebuilds himself. To go to Uman, one needs a pure heart and a sincere desire to come close to God. If he doesn't have that, he'll never even make it to the plane! Those two factors—a pure heart and a sincere desire—are the common denominators for all the people who succeed in getting there.

It's not about the money. I've seen people board the plane and then turn around and leave. Either they lose heart or they are overwhelmed by obstacles, sometimes in the form of last-minute phone calls. On the other hand, I've seen men with no money, facing almost unconquerable obstacles, who were burning with the desire to be in Uman—and they succeeded in getting there. A person needs the proper yearning. Uman is all about yearning and wanting to get closer to God.

In Uman, this yearning often expresses itself in song. Tens of thousands of people burst into a song, and the melody seems to emerge on its own, as if Rebbe Nachman himself were whispering this song into our ears, touching us all—together—in a split second. In Uman, so many people join together with one heart, one heartbeat. It impacts the entire world. And it impacts each person personally. When you leave Uman, you are touched in a way that you've never been touched before. The last time I was there, we sang together for over two hours! I'll never forget that. The community was giving expression to its pure essence, its love for God.

ALTHOUGH MY FATHER originally opposed my spending Rosh HaShanah in Uman, eventually he, too, made the journey. He was against it for many years, but when he finally got there, I witnessed the tears in his eyes. He had worked his entire life to build his business, and then he had watched his children turn their backs on his lifestyle and become religious. That was difficult for him.

My father traveled to Uman to pray for my sister. She was still childless after many years of marriage. On Erev Rosh HaShanah, standing next to the Rebbe's *tziyun*, he poured out his heart to God in a way that he had never done before. A month later, my sister joyfully announced that she was expecting!

> Uman is all about yearning and wanting to get closer to God.

My wife, too, eventually accepted my attachment to Breslov. Only after I myself had filtered the Rebbe's teachings and begun to follow his advice, instead of just talking about it, did she start to understand what it was all about. People will only take you seriously if you apply the Rebbe's teachings. When she saw that I had transformed myself, she realized the power of Breslov.

LAST YEAR, IN ADDITION TO TRAVELING to Uman for Rosh HaShanah, I traveled to Uman before Pesach.[2] It was like an intimate meeting with the Rebbe. I felt so connected, like I had attained great spiritual heights.

I view taking my children to Uman as a form of spiritual insurance for their future. It is my hope that the fear of Heaven which we experience there will shed its light on them.

I am privileged to belong to a group of people bound by strong bonds of brotherhood. We all started at the beginning and went through similar spiritual falls and elevations. Our discussions and the encouragement we offer each other have made us unique. I am proud to be part of such a special group of chassidim.

---

2 Our Sages teach that the first day of the Hebrew month of Nisan is the Rosh HaShanah for kings (*Rosh HaShanah* 2a). Rebbe Nachman was born on that day, two weeks before Pesach. Since it is like a "mini" Rosh HaShanah, many chassidim travel to the *tziyun* for the Rebbe's birthday.

Everything Works Out In The End

Dovid Abeles

*Originally from Toronto, Canada, Dovid Abeles is presently
studying in a yeshivah in Tzefat, Israel.*

My family is traditional. Not Orthodox, but very Jewish. My
father even puts on *tefilin* each morning. As a kid, I was
fascinated by my father's *tefilin* and dreamed of being religious.
On my first day at a Conservative Hebrew Sunday school, the
teacher asked, "Do any of you have a Shabbat meal on Friday
night?" I wished that we did; but instead, every Friday night, our
family would go out to eat at a non-kosher restaurant.

At the end of my first day at Sunday school, I proudly
continued to wear my *kippah* instead of removing it like all the
other boys did. My mother, noticing the *kippah*, jokingly asked,
"Well, now that you're so religious, would you prefer going out
to eat at a (non-kosher) restaurant, or buying (kosher) deli
sandwiches for lunch?"

I said that I wanted the kosher deli sandwiches and added,
"From now on, I am going to eat only kosher and I am going to
keep Shabbat."

I was seven years old at the time. My parents were shocked—
and amused. They assumed that this was just another stage that I
was going through. But it wasn't. I continued wearing my *kippah*
all the time. The kids at public school would ask me why I was

wearing a beanie on my head. The adults smiled and thought I was cute. I persevered.

Slowly, I became more observant. When I was nine, I learned about *tzitzit* and wanted to start wearing them. But I didn't actually get a pair until I was eleven.

ALTHOUGH I WAS OFFICIALLY *shomer Shabbat*, when our family was occasionally invited to a celebration on Shabbat, I'd have to go. Of course, that meant being driven there in their car. When I turned thirteen, I informed everyone that from then on, I would never, ever drive in a car again on Shabbat.

I was immediately tested. My cousin in Boston was about to have her bat mitzvah, and the entire extended family expected me, together with my parents, to attend the ceremony that was to be held in a Reform temple on Shabbat. When I told the family that I wasn't going, my aunts and uncles screamed at me that I'd regret it. But I didn't go! I stayed at home. After Shabbat, one of the relatives yelled at my father for allowing me to remain home. My father's response: "My son did the right thing by not traveling on Shabbat. We were the ones who were wrong."

I remained in public school until I turned fourteen. That's when someone told me about a yeshivah high school for boys who had never had the opportunity to learn properly. I drove my parents crazy—all I could talk about was how I wanted to leave public school to learn in that yeshivah. Finally, they relented.

The *rosh yeshivah* was Chassidic, and several of the boys came from *chassidishe* homes. That was my first introduction to Chassidut.

But one year later, the yeshivah closed and I went back to public school. Meanwhile, I had discovered Toronto's Breslov shul. It was a two-hour walk from my parents' home. Despite the distance, I started attending services there on Shabbat, as well as several classes during the week.

HALFWAY THROUGH MY SENIOR YEAR in high school, I decided to transfer to a yeshivah. I spent an entire month looking for the right place to learn. During that time, I traveled to New York and discovered a Breslov shul in Boro Park. I was especially attracted to the Breslov concept of *hitbodedut*. Prayer is a real power, it makes a *real* impact.

While in New York, I decided to join the Breslov group on their weekly outing to do *hitbodedut* in Murray Park. The time that I went was the one and only time that the group was fined for disturbing the peace!

Although I ended up in Morristown Yeshivah,[3] I was more of a Breslover chassid than a Chabadnik. The rabbis at Morristown were upset that I did such strange things as dancing after prayers and going out for *hitbodedut* at night. At the end of the semester, they asked me to leave.

From Morristown, I traveled to Israel to learn in a real *litvishe* American yeshivah. When I returned to the States for Pesach and visited the Breslov shul in Boro Park, one of the chassidim there said, "While you were in Israel, you lost your connection to Breslov. But there are so many Breslov shuls there. You must be strong and continue."

I realized that he was right. When I went back to Israel, I returned to my old routine: getting up at five o'clock in the morning, going to the *mikveh* and doing *hitbodedut* before praying. The rabbis in the yeshivah thought I had gone bonkers.

So how did I get to Derech HaMelech,[4] an American yeshivah with a leaning toward Breslov? Some of the boys from my former yeshivah attended the engagement party of a boy who was learning there. They were amazed—all the boys in that yeshivah were just like crazy Dovid! That night, when they returned to the yeshivah, they told me they had found the perfect place for me and convinced me that I had to go there.

---

3 The Rabbinical College of America, located in Morristown, New Jersey, is a Chabad-Lubavitch yeshivah.

4 A yeshivah founded in Jerusalem in 2005 for young men interested in Chassidut. The yeshivah also has a *kollel* with a rabbinical ordination program.

The following day, I went to see the yeshivah. The boys were both serious about their learning and into Chassidut. There was even a *Likutey Moharan* class after morning prayers. I felt that that this was for me, and transferred to the new yeshivah.

> The rabbis in the yeshivah thought I had gone bonkers.

AFTER ATTENDING DERECH HAMELECH for a few months, I realized that I had to travel to Uman for Rosh HaShanah. One of the men who prayed at the yeshivah was a travel agent. He was selling tickets to Uman for $690. I didn't have $690, but I asked him to reserve a seat for me. He agreed, but warned that I would lose my ticket if I didn't bring him the money by a certain date.

I called my parents and told them that the entire yeshivah was traveling to Uman and that I also wanted to go. "Is Uman that crazy place in the Ukraine?" my mother asked. Although they were not willing to pay for my airfare, they did give me permission to travel there.

I had no idea how I would be able to afford a ticket. I only had 450 shekels in the bank (a little more than $100). I took it out and handed it to the travel agent. He looked at me and laughed. "Dovid," he said, "you're 2,500 shekels short. You'd better bring me the rest of the money by Sunday or you'll lose the seat I reserved for you."

I prayed. I did *hitbodedut*. But I still did not have the money.

On Sunday after morning prayers, the travel agent asked, "Dovid, *nu*? Do you have the money?" When I told him that I didn't, he said, "I'm giving you back your 450 shekels and taking you off the list."

I cannot tell you how hard I prayed. I *mamash* cried to God! *Why aren't You letting me go?* I pleaded. But then I realized that you can never question God's ways. I had done my utmost, but it seemed obvious that it was not meant to be. I was not yet worthy to spend Rosh HaShanah with the Rebbe. I made the decision to be *be-simchah*, to be happy with my circumstances, and prayed that I would be worthy to travel the following year.

I arranged that the travel agent would return my 450 shekels after services the following morning. But the following day, he wasn't well and didn't come to shul.

Just as I was finishing the morning prayers, one of the married men who learned in my yeshivah received a phone call on his mobile phone and walked out of the study hall to answer it. He returned a few moments later carrying an envelope. "A stranger gave this to me," he said, "and asked me to deliver it to you."

I assumed that the envelope was from the travel agent and that it contained my 450 shekels. On the outside of the envelope, someone had written, "Dovid, may all your prayers be answered in Uman. Have a good year and much success."

When I opened the envelope, I was shocked to discover that it contained 2,500 shekels, exactly the amount of money I needed to travel to Uman!

But there were more obstacles ahead. At Ben Gurion Airport, the travel agent told me some bad news: "Someone stole your ticket. You won't be able to go."

I tried to speak with the airline personnel, but to do that, I first had to pass through security, which was impossible without a ticket. It was a catch-22 situation. The plane left without me.

I wasn't the only person facing what appeared to be insurmountable obstacles. There were people whose tickets had been stolen, or whose tickets had been issued in the wrong name. Some gave up and returned to Jerusalem. But I was not ready to admit defeat. I realized that this was just another test and I was positive that I would somehow succeed in traveling to Uman in time for Rosh HaShanah.

I went to the area of the airport where travel agents sell last-minute tickets. Tickets to Kiev via Prague were available for $800. But I didn't have $800!

I secluded myself in a deserted area of the airport to spend some time in *hitbodedut*. At the end of my *hitbodedut*, I returned to the ticket counter and spoke with one of the other chassidim standing there. He said, "Every year, I travel to Uman for Rosh HaShanah. I've never spent the Yom Tov with my wife and children. But this year, the airline issued me a ticket in the wrong name. I can't use it, so I'm returning home."

It was a catch-22 situation. The plane left without me.

Someone who knew about my predicament said to him, "If you're not going to Uman, maybe you could lend this guy over there (pointing to me) $800 so that he can go?"

The chassid examined me from head to toe and asked, "Do you promise to pay me back?"

I told him that I would do my utmost to return the money.

The chassid took out his credit card and bought me a ticket to Uman. Then he said, "Well, if you can go to Uman, I can also go!" He booked a seat on the same flight.

OUR NEW FLIGHT WAS SCHEDULED to leave on the morning of Erev Rosh HaShanah. We arrived in Uman just twenty minutes before the beginning of the Yom Tov. I had no time to put up the tent I had brought with me or to make arrangements for food.

That night, a rabbi invited me to eat the evening meal in his apartment. The following day, I met someone I knew from the Breslov shul in Boro Park. He gave me a ticket to eat that day's meal in the main dining room. The rabbi of the Breslov shul in Toronto gave me a ticket for a seat in the main shul and invited me to join him for the rest of the Yom Tov meals. As for sleeping, a *tzaddik* who spent the entire night in *hitbodedut* let me sleep in his bed.

So in the end, everything worked out—I had food to eat, a place to sleep and a place to pray.

It was an unbelievable experience, the best Rosh HaShanah I have ever had. There were so many different types of people, yet everyone was joined through their connection to Rebbe Nachman. And the joy! There was so much joy!

IT WAS DIFFICULT FOR ME to leave Uman. I felt bad that I ended up having so little time there because my plane ticket was stolen.

In the end, it was decreed from Above that I would remain an additional few days. When I arrived at the Kiev airport, I discovered that my passport had been stolen. I had to postpone my flight for two days until it could be replaced. A *tzaddik* also postponed his flight to stay with me, to make sure that I'd manage to get back home somehow.

Now that I had two extra days in the Ukraine, I returned to Uman and spent the night praying quietly by the *tziyun*. I was so glad that I was able to have that extra time alone with the Rebbe.

The second night, that *tzaddik* and I stayed at a *ba'al teshuvah* yeshivah in Kiev. The next morning, we flew to Prague. The *tzaddik* insisted that I use his business-class ticket while he traveled coach. I felt like a king! We toured Prague's Jewish Quarter. He paid for everything. He even took me out to a restaurant.

I just took the plunge and traveled to Uman, and everything worked out in the end. It was an amazing experience, as if God Himself had raised me up and carried me on His wings to the *tziyun*.

The Light At The End Of The Tunnel
Menachem Herman

Menachem Herman is a popular rock guitarist and songwriter.
He lives in Ramat Beit Shemesh, Israel.

I had what you'd call a culturally-Jewish background, but not very religious; "Jewish Lite," you could call it. My parents were *shomer Shabbat* and they sent me to a Jewish day school. That was about the extent of it.

My family is very musical. My mother is a classical violinist and I play many instruments: drums, accordion, bass guitar and guitar. My first encounter with a religious musician was in 1976, when I was sixteen. Rabbi Yossel Rosenzweig and his brother-in-law, Avraham Rosenblum, came to Winnipeg to play for the kids at the Jewish high school. Imagine, a religious guy with a black beard and a black *kippah* playing rock guitar? For me, that was the big "wow" factor. Seeing a "rockin' rabbi" made a tremendous impact on me—and from then on, I never looked back.

I spent the summer of 1976 in Israel on a six-week tour. One Saturday night, our group made its way through some winding alleyways in the Old City to a courtyard to hear the Diaspora Yeshiva Band[5] play. That same rabbi who had come to my high

---

5 The Original Diaspora Yeshiva Band, formed in 1975 by Avraham Rosenblum and other musicians, was named after the *ba'al teshuvah* yeshivah of the same name (see note 7, p. 24).

school, Rabbi Yossel Rosenzweig, was there playing guitar. He was real! I saw that it's possible to be religious and still play guitar.[6]

At the end of the summer, I returned to Winnipeg, met my wife and got married. We both wanted to live in Israel. We wanted to raise our future children in a place with proper Jewish values.

While packing our things, I discovered Zalman Schachter's translation of Rebbe Nachman's book, *Restore My Soul*, hidden behind the other books on my father's bookshelf. I started reading the book and felt as if the Rebbe were speaking directly to me. The Rebbe spoke about feeling up and feeling down, that it's all part of life and that it's okay. It was exactly what I needed to hear. To this day, whenever I read that book, it sings my song.

In Israel, I studied Torah at the Diaspora Yeshiva.[7] Although I liked what I had read in *Restore Your Soul*, it didn't occur to me to look any further. I didn't know that Breslover chassidim existed in real life. Then one afternoon in the middle of the week, one of the guys at the yeshivah said, "I just had the most amazing experience. I prayed *Minchah* in Meah Shearim."

I had prayed in Meah Shearim before, and I knew that he had also prayed in Meah Shearim before. So why was he was so excited?

"I went to this shul where they really meant what they were saying. It was the Breslov shul."

Suddenly, everything clicked. The book, *Restore My Soul*, and now this. I had been in Israel for an entire year before discovering that there were real live Breslover chassidim living there!

---

6 Later, as a married man, I returned to Israel to learn in the Diaspora Yeshiva, where I became a member of the Diaspora Band. We had our last show in Carnegie Hall in 1991.

7 A yeshivah founded in Jerusalem in 1967 in order to help students from abroad who were searching for their spiritual heritage in the land of their ancestors. Its main teaching facility is on Mount Zion, adjacent to the Jewish Quarter of Jerusalem's Old City.

I WENT TO THE BRESLOV YESHIVAH in Meah Shearim and met some nice, English-speaking Breslover chassidim. They introduced me to the Rebbe's books, to *Likutey Moharan* and *Likutey Halakhot*.

> I saw that it's possible to be religious and still play guitar.

I left the Diaspora Yeshiva to study in Dvar Yerushalayim.[8] The rabbi there arranged for me to study Rebbe Nachman's book, *Hishtapkhut HaNefesh* (*Outpouring of the Soul*), with a Breslover chassid. A few weeks later, though, my wife and I decided to move to Tzefat so that I could learn in the Breslov *kollel* there. Two years later, in 1982, we returned to Jerusalem, where I joined an English-speaking Breslov *kollel*. So as you can see, we were very involved in Breslov. But in 1982, travel to Uman was still a dream.

Around that time, my mother remarried. Her new husband, who was originally from Russia, loved adventure. When we told him that we wanted to travel to Uman, he suggested that we travel via Bucharest.

So my wife and I, another couple, and my mother and her husband traveled to Bucharest, where we applied for a visa to Uman. After that, we were followed by the secret police, questioned, and then promised a visa. But in the end, our request was rejected. Within two weeks, we had used all our money and then some without obtaining the promised visa. We returned to Israel without traveling to Uman.

IN 1985, A LARGE GROUP OF ISRAELI STUDENTS traveled to Uman on false passports. They succeeded in reciting the *Tikkun HaKlali* at the *tziyun* before the Russians caught them and sent them out of the country.

---

8 An outreach yeshivah based in Har Nof, Jerusalem, established by Rabbi Baruch Horovitz from Manchester, England; it originally opened in the Geulah neighborhood of Jerusalem in 1970.

A couple of months later, in May 1985, a few of us with foreign passports—me with a Canadian passport, Elya Succot with an American passport, Moshe Mykoff with an American passport, Yisrael Meir Gabbai with a French passport, and Gavriel Savin with an American passport—attempted to travel to Uman. An Israeli was also planning to travel with us, but he missed the flight out of Israel.

We flew to Bucharest, and from Bucharest we took a train into Russia. At Yfgen, the first train station in Russia, our group—and only our group—was taken off the train. We had no idea what was going on. It was terrifying.

We were taken into a closed room and called in, one by one, to the interrogation room. The interrogating officer spoke perfect English. We had no idea what they wanted from us, but we were foreigners and they were pumping us for information.

The officer asked me a lot of questions: *Is Breslov a political group? What's our political mission? What are we trying to accomplish in the world?* It took him ten minutes to realize that I didn't know any of the details about the large group of Israelis that had traveled to Uman on false passports a few weeks earlier.

At one point, he said, "Did you know that Rebbe Nachman said there's nothing as whole as a broken heart?" I was surprised. I assumed he wasn't Jewish.

Afterward, they made me sign some papers and write that I was happy to be in Russia. I would have been willing to sign anything to get to Uman!

Back in the waiting room, I paced back and forth, singing, "*Mi yitein li eiver kayonah a'ufah tziyun hakodesh Umanah*—If someone were to give me wings like a dove, I would fly to the holy *tziyun* in Uman."[9] It suddenly dawned on me...*tziyun hakodesh*, the holy *tziyun*...My wife was expecting in another month, and if it would be a girl, we'd call her Tziona. The name was not so farfetched.

---

9 Paraphrase of Psalms 55:7.

My late aunt's name was Tzirel Tanya, which sounded like Tziona. I hoped that in the merit of pledging to name a future daughter, Tziona, I would be privileged to reach the *tziyun*.

> Our group—and only our group—was taken off the train.

The interrogation lasted a full twenty-four hours. We were exhausted, hungry and petrified. When it was over, they put us on a train back to Romania. They assumed that we were somehow connected to the previous group that had traveled to Uman on false passports. We never made it to Uman.

We returned to Israel and discovered that the Israeli who had missed the flight and was planning to travel with us on a false passport, actually made it!

IN THE SUMMER OF 1989, I finally succeeded in traveling to Uman. The Russians had given permission for a group of Israelis to travel to Rebbe Nachman's *tziyun*. We were three busloads of men, among them several Americans. I took along my son, who was five and a half at the time.

Since the trip was legal, we had to go through Intourist, the official Soviet tourist bureau. They forced us to visit Kiev and tour the sights, but we just wanted to get to the *tziyun*. For years we had dreamed of being there, and now we were beyond impatient. The Israelis screamed at the Intourist guide, but he was unfazed. It was his job to make sure that we saw every single one of the attractions.

It was strange to finally arrive at the *tziyun*. In those days, it was in the yard of a woman's house, and there was no gravestone over the actual grave. But one of the Israelis had been there before and knew the *tziyun*'s exact location. He was a bit artistic and outlined the Rebbe's *tziyun* with a Magic Marker and wrote inside, "*Poh nitman*—Here he is buried."

It was very humbling to stand in front of the *tzaddik*'s grave. I had received so much spiritual strength through the *tzaddik*'s writings, and now here I was, in Uman! I asked God to help me take the next step, but I wasn't sure what that step should be. I wanted God to help me understand what I should do while standing there, to show me how to connect with the *tzaddik*. I realized that in truth, the *tzaddik* is there to help me bind to God. It's all interrelated; it's all connected like a chain.

Afterward, I helped my son say the *Tikkun HaKlali*. We stayed at the *tziyun* for only an hour. After all, it was an official, guided tour, and we had to move on to see other sights.

THE FIRST TIME I TRAVELED TO UMAN for Rosh HaShanah was in 1991. The following winter, Ukraine declared independence.

The journey was very difficult. Again we traveled through Bucharest, Romania. In Bucharest, we weren't sure if there would be a plane to take us to Kiev. Some people were so nervous that they started yelling and shouting at each other. Others were dancing, while yet others were learning. Each person had his own way of handling the tension. Once we got to Kiev, there was the hassle of finding the baggage. Then we were interrogated. They treated us as if we were spies.

The whole trip was fraught with tension—spiritual tension, emotional tension. We encountered every possible inconvenience and delay. We were trying to accomplish a great spiritual feat, but at every stage of the way, the people around us were doing everything possible to prevent us from accomplishing it. Thank God, we finally made it!

Since that first trip in 1991, I've traveled to Uman every year. Each year, getting to Uman is a tremendous hassle. There's finding the suitcases at the airport in Kiev, shoving to get on the buses from the airport to Uman, finding a place to stay or obtaining the key to my lodgings. As I get closer to the *tziyun*, the tension grows stronger. It's a fear that I won't make it.

And then, finally, I arrive at the *tziyun* and I am overwhelmed with a mixture of joy and relief—unbelievable joy and relief! I feel as if a window within me is being opened to *emunah*—a window that should always remain open.

One year, I took upon myself to pray for a close friend of mine who had not yet been blessed with children. Standing at the *tziyun*, I felt everything inside me open up, and I prayed like I had never prayed before, begging God to have mercy on my

> Standing at the *tziyun*, I felt everything inside me open up.

friend and his wife, both wonderful people who devote their lives to helping their fellow Jews. That same year, my friend's wife gave birth to triplets.

Another time, Rabbi Yaakov Bleich, the *Rav* of Kiev, hired my band to play Jewish rock 'n' roll at a Chanukah concert that he was making for the Jewish community in Kiev. We agreed to come without payment on condition that he would arrange for us to spend Shabbat Chanukah in Uman.[10]

Posters were plastered all over Kiev announcing the event. At least 1,000 people showed up for the concert. For the Russian Jews, it was a powerful experience to see a group of rabbis standing on stage playing rock 'n' roll. After the concert, we traveled to Uman for Shabbat Chanukah. I spent a lot of time at the *tziyun*, praying that my daughter would find her true soul mate.

My daughter was married within the year. Her future husband had gone to Uman that same Rosh HaShanah and had remained until after Yom Kippur to have extra time at the *tziyun* to pray for his soul mate.

The couple married on the fifth of Tammuz. For our family, this is a very significant date. Many years before, I had been in a serious car accident on that date and miraculously survived. Every year on the fifth of Tammuz, our family makes a thanksgiving feast to thank God for saving my life.

---

10 Shabbat Chanukah was one of the three set times when the Breslover chassidim would travel to be with Rebbe Nachman. The other times were Rosh HaShanah and Shavuot.

In addition, the fifth of Tammuz is a significant day for Breslover chassidim. On that day, 30,000 holy Jews were murdered in Uman because they refused to forsake their religion. The Rebbe is buried next to their mass grave.

ONE EREV ROSH HASHANAH IN UMAN, I attended a class given by Rabbi Elchonon Tauber of Los Angeles. He was giving it in the main *kloyz* to a group of about fifty English-speaking men. He said that most of us waste too much time worrying about things we don't need to worry about. For example, we're not worried about whether or not we'll have bread and milk to eat. Instead, we're concerned about which brand of ketchup to buy. All these peripherals are mental baggage that weighs us down. It takes away from our joy in living.

Then he said something that I thought was amazing. The mind is like a muscle. Just like a person who wants to run a twenty-six-mile marathon begins by practicing to run one mile and then slowly builds himself up, we, too, must train our mental muscles. So if we want to be *be-simchah* (happy), we first must make a conscious decision to be happy. Happiness has nothing to do with a person's financial status. There are plenty of miserable wealthy people and miserable poor people. If we slip and forget to be happy, we should flex our mental muscles and pop back into the happiness mode.

The same holds true for *hitbodedut*. A person cannot simply begin speaking to God for an hour a day. (I once heard Rabbi Avraham Yitzchak Carmel of Bnei Brak say that starting out doing *hitbodedut* for an hour a day is a *segulah* to go to sleep!) Someone who is not used to such intense focusing will not be able to handle it. Instead, said Rabbi Tauber, begin with just fifteen minutes. Then, after you've gotten into shape, add a few more minutes until you've worked yourself up to an hour or so. It's a process.

After hearing Rabbi Tauber's *shiur*, I took it upon myself to be happy. That wasn't difficult in Uman. But what kept me going after I returned home? It was the memory of being in Uman for

Rosh HaShanah, of reciting the *Tikkun HaKlali* at the Rebbe's *tziyun*.

That Erev Rosh HaShanah was amazing. Imagine tens of thousands of people standing together to recite *Tikkun HaKlali*. It's a powerful experience and very, very serious. Everyone's

That Erev Rosh HaShanah was amazing.

praying wholeheartedly, begging God to end our troubles and bring the *Mashiach*. When we finished reciting *Tikkun HaKlali*, I expected everyone to run to the *tziyun*, to cry out to God and beg for consolation. Instead, much to my astonishment, there was a tremendous outburst of joy. People started playing drums and guitars, and everyone spontaneously began singing and dancing. When I saw that, I realized that our generation needs joy. Joy is our generation's path in *avodat Hashem*.

In Uman, people are always asking me, "Where's your guitar?" I answer, "Guitar? I came here to recharge my batteries!" Being in Uman is renewal. When things are difficult during the year, I know that there's a light at the end of the tunnel: that I'll be going to Uman!

In The Way A Person Wants To Go, God Leads Him

Tanchum Burton

*Originally from Brooklyn, New York, Tanchum Burton is now a
practicing psychotherapist, rabbi and educator in Jerusalem.*

I had spent two wonderful years in yeshivah in Jerusalem.
Now I was commuting back and forth to Manhattan to a job
that was not suited to me, and spiritually, I was yearning. My
first introduction to Breslov was through Rabbi Schik's inspiring
pamphlets, which I would read while riding the sluggish and
crowded D train. Then one of my friends whom I had learned
with in Israel and who had transferred to the Bat Ayin Yeshivah[11]
visited me in Flatbush, where we were living at the time. He
spoke a lot about Breslov and Rebbe Nachman, and gave me a
copy of *Outpouring of the Soul*. After reading it, I was interested
enough to purchase another book, *Crossing the Narrow Bridge*.
I liked what I read, although some of the things seemed a bit
weird to me.

In particular, I had a lot of difficulty with the concept of
simplicity. I'm a naturally complex person, drawn to abstract

---

11 A small yeshivah that emphasizes Rebbe Nachman's path, founded in 1989
in the moshav of Bat Ayin in the Judean Hills.

ideas, and I wasn't able to understand the profundity of being simple. A lot of the *Yiddishkeit* that had sustained me until that time was very philosophical in nature. But I was not enjoying it anymore. I wanted to do the right thing, to be a *talmid chakham* (Torah scholar). But I was chasing a spiritual high, wanting to feel *Shabbosdik* and spiritual all the time, and I was finding that there were so many opportunities to feel that I wasn't a good Jew because I couldn't cover every last detail in *halakhah* or *minhag*, or do everything according to all opinions.

Then I discovered the beauty of simplicity. Reb Noson mentions *Kiddush Levanah* (the blessing of the New Moon) as an example of simplicity. There is a tendency to want to wait until the moon is one-hundred-percent big and full and the night is crystal clear, without a cloud, to recite *Kiddush Levanah*—to the point that one can miss the *halakhic* time for the blessing. Why should one be so particular when it is permissible, according to the *halakhah*, to recite *Kiddush Levanah* when the moon is visible through thin clouds? Be simple. Do the mitzvah.

MY WIFE AND I LISTENED TO lots of taped classes on Breslov, hosted lectures in our house, and tried to incorporate the ideas that we were learning into our lives. One year, as we were cleaning up from the Pesach Seder at two o'clock in the morning, my wife said, "Let's use the money from our tax rebate to pay for you to travel to Uman this Rosh HaShanah."

I was shocked. Who leaves a wife on Rosh HaShanah? It's incomprehensible! I would never have presumed to make such a seemingly ludicrous request. We are a close family and we like to be together. On the other hand, I was thrilled. Thank God, my wife saved me the dread of having to ask; she actually suggested it!

I was advised to take this encouragement from my wife to go to Uman and put it in my "back pocket," to draw strength from it at some point later in life.

The tax refund ended up being used for necessities, which meant that I still had no idea how I would pay for traveling to

Uman. I decided that if by Tisha B'Av (seven weeks before Rosh HaShanah), I didn't have the money for the ticket, I would forget about the whole idea. Meanwhile, the travel agent was nudging me to finalize my flight plans. He wanted a deposit, but I kept putting him off because if I were to cancel, I would forfeit the deposit. Someone advised me to ask a prominent *posek* if I could use my *ma'aser* money to pay for the trip. That seemed implausible to me, and when I asked the *posek*, he confirmed my suspicions.

Tisha B'Av came and went—and still I did not have the money. I decided to wait until Rosh Chodesh Elul (exactly one month before Rosh HaShanah). Hopefully, by then I would find the resources to travel. Meanwhile, I told all my friends to pray for me. It was a really uncomfortable feeling of suspense, because I knew that the entire thing would depend on faith and prayer, and I was still uncertain why I wanted to go in the first place.

TWO WEEKS BEFORE ROSH HASHANAH, I received a call from a friend of mine whom I had convinced to travel with me to Uman. He had been sitting in his company cafeteria where he told one of his coworkers about his plans for Rosh HaShanah. The coworker's immediate response was, "What kind of nutty thing is that?" My friend remarked that the person who had convinced him to travel to Uman was short on funds and unable to go himself. The coworker asked how much money I needed.

My friend didn't know if he was being serious. This guy just took out his checkbook, wrote out a check for $1,000 and handed it to my friend. "Deposit this check in your bank account," he said, "and write him a check for $1,000. And don't tell him who gave you the money."

But it was not enough—the ticket cost $1,250 and money was really tight. Then I told my father the story of the guy who gave me $1,000. My father was so touched by the Divine Providence evident in the situation that he handed me a check for $250.

BORISPOL AIRPORT IN KIEV was a crazy and crowded place. The line in front of the visa counter was really unpleasant, with everyone pushing and shoving. I kept reminding myself of Reb Noson's comment that he would travel to the Rebbe even if the road to Uman were paved with knives.[12] For me, these were knives. Going to Uman is not a pleasure trip.

> My clothes, my box of food, all of it had disappeared.

On the other hand, it's important to have the correct perspective. While waiting in that crazy line, a friend of mine shared with me the second lesson in *Sichot HaRan*, where Reb Noson talks about how we should give everything over to God and that we should have no expectations when approaching a big event like Shabbat or Yom Tov or, in this case, traveling to Uman. I found that what was most helpful for the experience was to compile a list of the few things one has to accomplish while there: say *Selichot*, immerse in the *mikveh*, give a small coin to *tzedakah* in Rebbe Nachman's name, recite *Tikkun HaKlali* at the gravesite, pray the Rosh HaShanah prayers. That's all.

In the airport, the Ukrainian officials wore these ornate military uniforms and didn't speak a word of English. On that first trip, an official at passport control asked me something in Russian. Of course, I didn't understand her, so I just nodded and said, *"Nyet?"* Thinking that I would understand better, she just screamed louder. After getting through that ordeal, I went to get my bags. But they were not there! My clothes, my box of food, all of it had disappeared. All I had were my *talit* and *tefilin*, a toothbrush and a few Jewish books.

The airport officials noted that my bag had not arrived and informed me that if it were located, then tomorrow night—Rosh HaShanah—it would be dropped off in the middle of Pushkina Street. With the poverty that is rampant in Uman, that was akin to putting a can of tuna in the middle of the street for all the cats in the neighborhood to eat. But there was nothing I could do. Everyone was rushing to the buses, hurrying to get to Uman.

---

12 *Tovot Zikhronot*, p. 137.

I was afraid that the buses would leave without me and that I'd end up stranded in the Ukraine.

I ended up wearing the same clothes for five days straight, which really was not that terrible. It was freezing. Since I didn't have my sleeping bag, I wore my clothing under my gritty blanket. We were renting an apartment from a Ukrainian who kept coming in to turn off the lights because he was worried about the cost of the electricity—even though he was making an entire year's salary from renting the apartment to us for those few days.

Uman is like a wild, flying circus. Crazy things are going on, people are selling all sorts of things like *"segulah* knives," and people you never heard of go around asking for money for a *pidyon*[13] as if they themselves were the central character of the Uman saga. Suddenly, everyone has become a "rebbe"!

And then there's the music. One year on Erev Rosh HaShanah, there was one song blasting through enormous speakers for twelve hours straight, a rip-off of a Romanian rave song with new words. I couldn't get it out of my head the entire Yom Tov.

It was a very tense experience, and I was not really able to process it at the time. There was so much to take in. It was unbelievably transforming, but it wasn't until the following Pesach that I felt happy I had made the journey.

SOMETHING HAPPENS WHEN I ARRIVE in Uman. It's as if I plug into my soul's root. New pathways open up for me; I attain a new sense of self. It's a few days that I am able to distance myself from my life so I can think about it—how to be a better husband, a better father, a better son, a better friend, a better Jew. It's a sense of "I made it! I did this! I got here!" The services are arduous and long but intensely beautiful. The first time the *chazzan* intoned the word *"HaMelekh* (King)" and everyone clapped—I don't know how to explain it—it's not that I didn't

---

13 "Redemption money"; traditionally, one who visits a *tzaddik* with a personal petition gives the *tzaddik* a donation for charity in order to expedite his redemption from his difficulties.

believe in God before, but WOW! At that moment, you realize that God is here and He is running the show. He loves us and takes care of us and helps us get to where we need to go.

> It's a sense of "I made it! I did this! I got here!"

I returned to the States completely burnt out. I had spent five nights on a lumpy mattress covered with that awful blanket. I had been completely at the mercy of my surroundings. But that in itself was another victory. And the truth is that I had exactly what I needed. I had clothes, even if I wore them for five days straight. I had a *minyan*. I had food. I had friends. Rebbe Nachman says, "*Yoh essen nit essen, yoh shlofen nit shlofen, yoh davenen, nit davenen.*" It doesn't matter if there's food to eat or no food to eat, prayers or no prayers, the main thing is to be by the Rebbe for Rosh HaShanah. Nothing was comfortable, but I was there and that was the main thing.

When I came back, I spent a month fighting with Lufthansa trying to get my luggage back. It had obviously gotten rerouted somewhere, and I insisted that they return it to me. Finally, they told me to make an estimate of how much the things were worth so that they could reimburse me. The amount of money they paid me was exactly what I needed to purchase a new *sheitel* (wig) for my wife. And then a few days later, my bags were found and delivered to my house! So in the end, I traveled to Uman for free, got back everything I had lost, and made enough money to buy my wife a new *sheitel*.

Since that first trip, I try to travel to Uman every year. One year, I didn't go because I could not possibly afford it, which is really a poor excuse once you understand the power of *ratzon* (will) the way the Rebbe understood it. But after missing Rosh HaShanah in Uman, I was determined to make it the following year. Each year that I make it is a miracle. Even though it's financially difficult, the money is not the real issue. Once a person decides that he's going, no matter what, God helps him. There are no obstacles in God's way.

Overcoming Obstacles From Without And Within

Dovid Shapiro

Originally from Paterson, New Jersey, Rabbi Dovid Shapiro presently resides in Jerusalem, where he edits Hebrew manuscripts.

When asked how he came to Breslov, Reb Dovid smiles modestly and replies, "God made me into a Breslover chassid. But there were some people who helped me along the way."

After high school, I studied in yeshivah full-time. Although I was progressing rapidly in my studies, I felt depressed. The yeshivah emphasized *mussar*, but I took the *mussar* studies too seriously. Furthermore, my parents, who were not as religious as I, were unhappy about my yeshivah studies.

At the time, I was studying with Reb Shmuel Breines, a member of the yeshivah's *kollel*. He was aware of my difficulties and asked one of the other students to give me a copy of *Meshivat Nefesh* (*Restore My Soul*). Reading *Meshivat Nefesh* gave me a new—and encouraging—perspective on life's challenges. I was especially impressed by the excerpts from Reb Noson's *Likutey Halakhot* that were quoted in this book. Reb Noson explains how we can learn from even the most arcane *halakhot* how to serve God.

During the summer break, I attended a yeshivah in the Catskills, where I became friendly with the Serdehelli *Rav*, Rabbi

Yechiel Weinberger. I asked him how I could find *simchah* (joy). He told me to study Chassidic books. When I asked him about Breslov books, he responded, "Breslov is particularly appropriate for attaining *simchah*!" That reinforced my interest in Breslov. After all, Rabbi Weinberger was a Hungarian *rav*, not a Breslover chassid, yet he looked positively on studying Breslov.

The yeshivah was housed in an old mansion that had enormous closets. I would do *hitbodedut* in the big closet in my dorm room. I decided that I must begin praying even for things that I was planning to take care of myself. I felt that although we must make every natural effort, our main effort is prayer.

At the time, one of my shirts was torn and I was planning to sew it. But meanwhile, I prayed that it be repaired. That week, I mistakenly sent my torn shirt to the laundry together with my other shirts. The laundry repaired it prior to washing it.

But although I was doing *hitbodedut* and learning Breslov books, I still didn't define myself as a Breslover chassid. I was bothered by the fact that Rebbe Nachman was from a previous generation. I had been taught that each generation has its own leaders, so how could Breslover chassidim follow a leader who lived 200 years ago?

I asked my study partner, Reb Shmuel, about this, but he wasn't able to give me a satisfactory answer. He put me in touch with Reb Hershel Wasilsky, who eventually had a strong influence on me. But he, too, could not satisfy me.

Reb Shmuel suggested that I travel to Israel to ask my question to the Breslov elders there. The trip cost $450, and I was a penniless yeshivah student.

At the time, my parents were planning a trip to Europe in honor of their twenty-fifth wedding anniversary. I told them that rather than joining them in Europe, I would like to visit Israel. They agreed to pay half of my ticket if I would earn the other half myself. I tutored a younger yeshivah student to pay for my share. So I spent the summer of 1968 in Israel. Reb

Shmuel arranged for me to stay in the Breslov Yeshivah in Meah Shearim.[14]

The entire Breslov community was extremely friendly and warm toward me. As soon as I walked into the shul, Reb Shimon Shapiro, son of the Breslover *tzaddik*, Rabbi Shmuel Shapiro, invited me to meet his father to "see if you're related." I became very close with Rabbi Shmuel.[15]

Rabbi Eliyahu Chaim Rosen, the founder and dean of the Breslov Yeshivah, personally made sure that I had a mattress—a three-sectioned straw mattress, which was the norm then—to sleep on. During my entire stay in Israel, Reb Shmuel Chechik, a Breslover chassid, insisted that I join him for supper. It was a long walk from the shul to his home, and we talked about Breslov and about Israel. He was very learned, but also very emotional. He was very close to Rabbi Shmuel Shapiro, and he encouraged me to speak to him more. Reb Yochanan Galant, recently arrived from Russia, invited me for Shabbat to his one-room flat and wouldn't let me eat elsewhere the entire time.

On Erev Rosh Chodesh Av, Rabbi Levi Yitzchok Bender, Rabbi Eliyahu Chaim Rosen, Reb Yochanan Galant and others asked me to complete a *minyan* at the grave of Shimon HaTzaddik[16] to recite the Yom Kippur Katan prayers.[17] Rabbi Eliyahu Chaim Rosen was the *chazzan*. When he recited the words "*Ve-lirushalayim ircha be-rachamim tashuv*—May we return in

---

14 Although the yeshivah was not in session at the time, the dormitory rooms were available.

15 After Rabbi Shmuel passed away, we did become related through marriage, when his grandson married my daughter.

16 Shimon Hatzaddik was a *Kohen Gadol* (High Priest) in the Second Temple, and one of the last of the Men of the Great Assembly (*Anshei Knesset HaGedolah*). He is buried in East Jerusalem, behind Meah Shearim.

17 The special penitential prayers recited on Erev Rosh Chodesh are called Yom Kippur Katan (the "mini" Yom Kippur). When a person repents on Erev Rosh Chodesh, the past month's sins are forgiven.

Your mercy to Jerusalem, Your city," he started to sob. I had never seen prayer like that—totally from the heart and incredibly moving. It made a deep impression on me.

He was very learned, but also very emotional.

That summer, Reb Dovid asked the Breslov elders his question. Although he did not find an answer that satisfied him, he gained an insight into the source of his confusion.

When I first met Rabbi Levi Yitzchok Bender, he asked, "Are you new to Breslov?" I told him that I was.

"What do your parents think of you becoming a Breslover chassid?" he asked.

"It doesn't make too much of a difference to them. They have no idea what it is," I replied.

I was surprised when he said, "That's not good. If you have no *meni'os* (obstacles) from the outside, you will have *meni'os* from within."

I felt that even without my parents, I had enough *meni'os* from the yeshivah where I was learning. They were not pleased that I was drifting toward Chassidut, and especially toward Breslov.

At the end of the summer, Reb Dovid returned to the United States and to his yeshivah, even more determined to resolve his doubts and strengthen his bond with the Breslover chassidim. While spending a Shabbat with the Breslover chassidim in Boro Park, he discovered Rabbi Gedaliah Koenig's book, *Chayey Nefesh*. This book came close to touching on his questions.

Chayey Nefesh was originally a letter that Rabbi Koenig wrote in response to a student's question. It discusses the entire question of "binding oneself to the *tzaddikim*," and has several letters of approbation from prominent rabbis who are not Breslover chassidim. Reb Dovid was particularly impressed by this. It meant that the explanations were based on general Torah principles rather than solely on Breslov philosophy.

I asked my study partner, Reb Shmuel Breines, if he thought Rabbi Koenig would answer me if I wrote to him. He had no idea. He arranged that I spend a Shabbat in Boro Park with one of Rabbi Koenig's students, Reb Shlomo Fried. Beardless, without *peyot*, and wearing a sports jacket, Reb Shlomo looked like a typical, modern American yeshivah guy. Reb Shlomo showed me several letters that he had received from Rabbi Koenig. I was deeply impressed by both the content and clarity. Reb Shlomo was positive that Rabbi Koenig would respond to my letter.

I wrote Rabbi Koenig a very long letter—thirty-six pages!—asking all my questions. Three months later, just as I was giving up hope of hearing from him, I received an aerogram completely filled with Rabbi Koenig's beautiful script. When there was no more room to continue—even on the flaps—he stopped in mid-sentence and wrote, "To be continued."

I received a total of four aerograms, each one completely filled with Rabbi Koenig's tiny script. They addressed all my questions, mainly directing me to appropriate sources in *Likutey Halakhot*. I continued to correspond with Rabbi Koenig. But although I was going deeper into the study of Breslov, I did not yet consider myself a Breslover chassid.

Reb Dovid attempted his first trip to Uman in the summer of 1971.

I was already twenty-two at the time, and I had difficulty finding a *shiddukh*. Reb Shmuel Breines suggested that I travel to Uman to pray there. I spent the entire summer working as a driver for a yeshivah camp to pay for my trip. At the end of the summer, I traveled to Russia together with a Breslover *bachur* from my yeshivah.

In those days, there were no direct flights to Kiev. We traveled to Kiev via Moscow. When we entered the Soviet Union, the custom officials confiscated all my Jewish books except for my personal *siddur*, claiming that they were propaganda.

We flew to Kiev the next morning. As soon as we were settled in our room at the Dnieper Hotel, we went to the hotel's Intourist office to apply for a visa to Uman. In those days, it was impossible to get a visa to Uman from America. Anyone traveling to Uman first went to Kiev to apply for a visa. No one had yet been refused.

But we were! When we asked why, we were told that the road was in disrepair. I suggested that we hire a helicopter, but the Intourist woman said that was completely out of the question.

In those days, there were no direct flights to Kiev.

We didn't even consider traveling to the *tziyun* without a visa. We were afraid of ruining other people's chances of getting there.

I flew on to Jerusalem, disappointed that I had not been able to get to Uman. Upon arriving, I went directly to the Batei Wittenberg section of Jerusalem to introduce myself to Rabbi Gedaliah Koenig. His son, Rabbi Elazar Mordekhai Koenig, opened the door. He had heard about me and warmly welcomed me into his father's home. Once I met Rabbi Gedaliah Koenig, I knew that I had come to the right address. I had found my mentor.

Again that summer, I ate my evening meals at the home of Reb Shmuel Chechik. Once night, while walking with Reb Shmuel, we met Reb Shmuel's brother, Reb Velvel Chechik, a well-known disciple of the Brisker Rav. "This *bachur* tried to get to Uman," Reb Shmuel said to his brother, "but without success. What should he do?"

Reb Velvel responded, "Try again!"

THAT'S EXACTLY WHAT I DID several years later, in 1978. By then I was living in Israel and was fully integrated into the Breslov community. My friend, Chuna Bloom, asked, "Do you want to travel with me to Uman?"

I did not hesitate. "Let's go!"

Since there were no diplomatic ties between Israel and the Soviet Union then, the chassidim traveled to Vienna to apply for a Soviet visa. I went first and arranged the visas for both of us. That took over a week. Then I sent Chuna's passport back to Israel so he could join me. The Vienna Jewish community was famous for its hospitality. When I arrived there, a Jewish woman stopped me on the street and said, "Oh! You're traveling to Uman? We have someone staying with us who is also going there. You can join him."

The plan was to travel by train to Kiev through Czechoslovakia—a thirty-hour trip in a sleeping car—and from there take a taxi to Uman. This meant making the trip illegally, since we didn't have a visa to visit Uman. Moreover, the Soviets counted people's money when they entered and exited the country, and expected a receipt for every ruble that was spent. So we wouldn't be able to account for the money we spent on traveling to Uman.

We were informed that the taxi ride to Uman would cost 300 rubles. Since we couldn't pay for it legally, we had to smuggle rubles into the country. The official Soviet rate was $1.25 per ruble, but in the Vienna bank, they cost twenty cents each! We bought 400 rubles. I hid them in the split soles of my shoes, which I then glued together.

In Kiev, we stayed again at the Dnieper Hotel.

Before traveling to Uman, Chuna and I walked around the park until we were positive that we were not being followed. Then we went to the synagogue and immersed in the *mikveh*. In order not to stand out, I wore a straw hat with my *peyot* hidden inside and a sweater, while Chuna wore a short jacket and a Russian cap.

As soon as we arrived at the bus station, a taxi driver approached us and, using hand gestures, asked, "Are you going to Uman?" (So much for our disguise!) He wanted 300 rubles, as we expected. We told him (also with hand gestures) that we would give him 100 rubles up-front and the other 200 rubles upon our safe return to Kiev.

The driver drove us to a house where he met two friends. We understood that he said to them, "These guys will pay you 200 rubles to take them to Uman." (It was necessary to travel in a private car since the police regularly stopped taxis to check one's personal papers.)

Chuna and I got in the back seat of the car, put our hats over our faces, and pretended to be sleeping. When the policemen at the roadblocks saw us sleeping, they waved our car through.

We had to smuggle rubles into the country.

The car brought us to the house on Bilinsky Street where the Rebbe's *tziyun* is located. The woman who usually "greeted" visitors to the *tziyun* did not appear, but her husband was there. We gave him some presents that we had brought for his wife—perfumes and textiles—and then entered the yard to pray at the Rebbe's *tziyun*.

Before I had left Israel, Rabbi Gedaliah Koenig instructed me that the first thing I should do upon arriving at the Rebbe's *tziyun*—even before putting aside a *perutah*[18] for *tzedakah* and reciting *Tikkun HaKlali*—was to introduce myself to the Rebbe, telling him my name and how I was connected to him. He said I should say that my connection to the Rebbe was through spending Rosh HaShanah in Meron and going to Uman, as we "were taught by the grandson of his disciple [Reb Noson], Rabbi Avraham ben Naftali Hertz [Sternhartz]."[19]

This meant that my main connection with the Rebbe was not through learning the Rebbe's books or from spending time in *hitbodedut*, or even from praying in a Breslov shul, because those could never be done to perfection; something was always missing. But spending Rosh HaShanah in Meron (and later, in Uman) was different. Rabbi Koenig always said that the main work of Rosh HaShanah is to bring the *zekel beiner* (bag of bones)

18 Literally, "a coin"; a small amount of money.

19 After the Russian border was closed to pilgrims to Uman in 1917, the Breslover chassidim established a Rosh HaShanah *kibutz* in Lublin and in Jerusalem. When Rabbi Avraham Sternhartz arrived in Israel in the spring of 1936, he established the annual *kibutz* in Meron by the gravesite of Rabbi Shimon bar Yochai, author of the *Zohar*, citing a very deep connection between Rabbi Shimon and Rebbe Nachman. See Prologue to the *Likutey Moharan*.

to the *tzaddik*, and that was solely dependent on my physical presence.

Rabbi Koenig also told me not to forget to recite Reb Noson's prayer (to be said after the *Tikkun HaKlali*), even if it meant I would not have a chance to say the *Tikkun HaKlali* a second time. I was able to do both, since we were able to be there about an hour and a half.

We were elated that we had accomplished our mission. We felt like we were walking on air, but at the same time, we were apprehensive. We noticed the neighbors staring at us, and we were worried that the police would show up.

THE LADY WHO LIVED IN THE HOUSE had indeed called the police.[20] The moment they arrived, the Russian driver drove away. But not too far; after all, he still wanted his 200 rubles.

The police asked to see our documents. We didn't have our American passports with us because we had handed them over to the hotel clerk in Kiev, and they had been kept there "for our safekeeping." I showed the officers our Czechoslovakian transfer documents. "But where are your visas to enter Uman?" they asked us.

We played dumb. "Visas to enter Uman? Why do we need a visa? In America, we don't need a visa to travel from one city to the next."

They asked us how we got to Uman. We explained that we had come by taxi. They asked us how we were planning to return to Kiev. We said that we would find another taxi.

The police left us and went looking for the driver who had brought us to Uman. They found him a few streets away—his Kiev license plate gave him away. Meanwhile, Chuna and I stood

---

20 Chuna Bloom recalls, "It was like a well-rehearsed play that repeated itself every few weeks when Breslovers arrived at the *tziyun*. The woman had to call the police; otherwise, the neighbors would get her in trouble. She was actually very nice. She gave us some water to drink and allowed us to remain at the *tziyun* for over an hour before calling the authorities."

in the woman's yard, wondering what was going to happen next.

Half an hour later, a large police van pulled up with fifteen policemen and we were ordered inside. We assumed that we were being taken to

> We were worried that the police would show up.

the police station. Instead, they took us to the bus station.

Meanwhile, the driver was negotiating with the police for our (and his) release. The police were willing to let us go if we paid fifty rubles, which we gladly agreed to do.

Now that we had paid off the entire police force (with fifty rubles, which had cost us $10 in Vienna!), we had nothing to hide. We were treated like royalty and were waved through all the checkpoints. We even sang *chassidishe* songs, much to the driver's amusement.

The following morning, we asked at the Intourist office at the hotel if it were possible to get a visa to Uman. We were told that it was impossible.

In 1990, Reb Dovid made his first attempt to spend Rosh HaShanah in Uman. Since Israel still didn't have diplomatic relations with the Soviet Union, the visas were issued in Bulgaria. With Rosh HaShanah fast approaching, the travel agent sent Reb Dovid and eleven others to Bucharest, Romania, to pick up their visas there. Through a maddening chain of mishaps, the men were stranded on the Russian-Romanian border without visas. With the assistance of the Israeli embassy in Bucharest, they managed to return home to Israel the night before Rosh HaShanah, and Reb Dovid spent that Yom Tov in Meron.

After Rosh HaShanah, I told the story of my failed attempt to get to Uman to my *rosh kollel*. He said, "Well, I guess after that experience, you're not going to try again."

"Of course I'm going to go," I told him. "Now I'm even more determined than ever to get to Uman for Rosh HaShanah!"

The following year, I did succeed in getting to Uman for Rosh HaShanah. That was the year that the chassidim rented a teachers' college campus, and we prayed in a huge gymnasium.

The college was a distance from the *tziyun*, so we ended up doing a lot of walking.

Every year, I return with another story. The accommodations are far from luxurious—at least five or six men to a room—and I always meet interesting—and sometimes challenging—people.

One year, we waited seven hours in Ben Gurion Airport for our plane to arrive. The Ukrainian airline informed us that they were experiencing "technical difficulties." We later learned that the pilots were drunk.

Then there was the year that the Breslov committee decided to make things easier for us and arranged for small planes to fly us from Odessa to the military airfield in Uman, saving us the four-hour bus ride.

The plane was tiny. As a matter of fact, it was so small that we were instructed not to sit in the back, since that might cause it to tip over! Instead of seats, there were long benches. Since there was not enough room for everyone, the children sat on our laps. Once we were all seated, we waited and waited. Finally, someone from the Odessa Jewish community came aboard and explained in Yiddish that the airfield in Uman was a military airfield and that the commander refused to allow the plane to land before three o'clock in the morning. It would have been much quicker had we taken the bus.

The committee tried using the Uman airfield one more time and then gave up. It was well that they did. Later, I found a copy of *The Murderers Among Us: The Simon Wiesenthal Memoirs*, and I looked to see what he said about Uman. There was only one incident. Uman was under German occupation. The Allies had bombed the airfield. The Germans needed something to fill the holes in the field, so they brought local Jews and shot them there. They are probably still there.

It is amazing that today, we can easily board a plane or charter flight to Uman and arrive quickly and safely, ready to visit the *tziyun*. For so many years, we dreamed of the day. On Erev Rosh HaShanah in Meron, we would recite Rabbi Yitzchak Breiter's prayer to merit reaching Uman, but it never seemed real. It was like saying, "When the *Mashiach* comes..." And today, it is real. We struggled and dreamed and prayed, and then it happened! Although I have spent many Rosh HaShanahs in Uman, I still can't believe it. It's a modern-day miracle.

We later learned that the pilots were drunk.

No Regrets

Zvi Hager

Originally from Brooklyn, New York, Zvi Hager is presently studying in the Lakewood Kollel in Lakewood, New Jersey. His parents are Breslover chassidim.

My father brought me to Uman when I was a child, but I never went for Rosh HaShanah. This past year, I was learning in Israel and decided to go there for the Yom Tov.

I spent my entire Yom Tov in Uman sick with food poisoning. The first night, I was too ill to pray. The following day, I somehow dragged myself to shul to hear the shofar, but that was as much as I could do.

Rebbe Nachman says, "Whether you eat or don't eat, whether you sleep or don't sleep, whether you pray or don't pray—just make sure to be with me for Rosh HaShanah!" Those words fit my situation perfectly. I couldn't eat, I couldn't sleep and I couldn't pray. But I have no regrets. I was in Uman for Rosh HaShanah, and it was worth it! I don't feel bad about what happened, and I will go back again. The main thing is that I was there. I was at the *tziyun* for Rosh HaShanah.

The Real Thing

Rabbi Jonathan Rietti

Originally from London, England, Rabbi Jonathan Rietti presently resides in Monsey, New York, where he works as a senior lecturer for Gateways, a Jewish outreach organization.

My mother escaped from Iraq in 1951. Her mother was the granddaughter of the Ben Ish Chai,[21] and she was raised in a very strong, traditional home. But when she immigrated to England, there was no Sephardi community there. We basically observed just Rosh HaShanah and Yom Kippur. Still, though we were not observant, my mother instilled within me a strong belief in God. She told me that if a teacher ever tells me that God does not exist, I must never believe the teacher. This was said with such simple conviction that for me, belief in God was non-negotiable.

My parents sent me to the most progressive school in world history, the King Albert School. The school was already co-ed in 1898, at the end of the Victorian era. There was no school uniform and we called the teachers by their first names. I loved the school. I don't remember a day that I said, "I don't want to go to school today."

---

21 Rabbi Yosef Chaim of Baghdad (1832-1909), a leading authority on Jewish law and a master kabbalist. His major work, *Ben Ish Chai*, is a standard *halakhic* reference in Sephardi homes.

My first introduction to Breslov was when I was fourteen years old. I went with my father to pick up my younger brother from a birthday party. The father of the birthday boy came out of his house carrying a carton of books—some that he had obviously read. He explained that he had heard I wanted to be a rabbi, and he wanted to give me this box of books. Among the books were a few volumes on Chassidut. I was particularly enthralled by the descriptions of Rebbe Nachman of Breslov. What I read about Rebbe Nachman resonated within me because it touched on something about my own relationship with God.

When I was about ten years old, I had prayed to God for a younger brother. My twin sisters were younger than me, and I basically lost every battle with them. Not physically—because I could beat them up every time—but emotionally. My mother would always tell me that I was the oldest, that I should know better, that I must set a good example. My sisters drove me so nuts that I literally could not see an end to my dilemma. Every fight that I ever got into, I lost. It really wasn't fair—two sisters against one brother. I found myself crying to God, and it was this memory that evoked in me an immediate affinity with Rebbe Nachman.

I remember praying to God that if He would give me a brother, then in return, I would be a good Jew. I told God that if He were to give me a brother on my birthday, it would prove to me that He was the One giving me the brother and that it was not just my mother having another child.

A few months later, my mother announced that she was expecting. This was a bit of surprise, since my sisters were already nine years old. In addition, the doctors had warned my mother that it would be dangerous for her to have any more children.

I informed my parents that since I had put in a request for a baby brother, it would be a boy and the baby would be born on my birthday.

Years later, my mother told me that she had been afraid that if she did not give birth to a boy on my birthday, I would lose my belief in God.

My baby brother was born a few days before my birthday. It was very close, and the explanation I was given at the time was that my mother's doctor had to leave on a business trip and he had offered to either induce early or let one of the other staff members deliver her. She preferred her doctor to deliver the baby, and so my brother was not born on my birthday.

It really wasn't fair— two sisters against one brother.

A FEW YEARS LATER, just before my bar mitzvah, I felt that I had to keep my part of the bargain—to become a good Jew—but I had no idea what that meant. After all, no instructions came with the baby!

One of the boys in my class celebrated his bar mitzvah. The party was so lavish that I decided that this was one day of my life that I definitely had to be religious. I told my parents that I also wanted a bar mitzvah.

They brought me to the shul rabbi, and he said that in order to have a bar mitzvah, I'd have to pass a test. He gave me a list of books to read. Although I was not much of a reader then, I really wanted to pass the test and have a bar mitzvah, so I read all the books. (At the time, I didn't realize that the test was just a gimmick to get the boys to know something before their bar mitzvah. No one ever failed.)

I was surprised when I read how much Judaism had contributed to the world. After my bar mitzvah, I continued attending post-bar mitzvah classes. Out of a dozen or so kids, I was the only one who did.

When I was fourteen, the rabbi said to me, "Your father's a famous actor. You've worked with him on movies and commercials and you've met all these big-name personalities. The other kids are into movies and won't come to post-bar mitzvah classes. But although you are part of that world, you're not at all interested. What's your motivation for learning about Judaism?"

I explained to him that God had performed a miracle for me when He gave me a baby brother on my request. After I told him the whole story, the rabbi said, "Jonathan, if God wants to give you a brother on your birthday, do you think He'd give it to you on your Jewish birthday or on your Christian birthday?"

I had no idea that Jews had their own calendar.

The rabbi looked up my birthday—March 6, 1959—which was the twenty-sixth of Adar. Then he looked up my brother's birthday, and it was also the twenty-sixth of Adar! So God had actually come through with my request!

WHEN I WAS SEVENTEEN, I went to Israel to study at Yeshivat Dvar Yerushalayim.[22] Chaim Kramer was the teacher and counselor for the evening sessions and through him, I was introduced to Breslov.

The first thing that hit me about Breslov was that Breslov is all about forging a relationship with God, and that the most powerful way to create that relationship is by talking with Him. This is not dependent on knowledge or on intellectual capacity or on how much Torah a person has learned or on how well one can read Hebrew.

This affirmed something that I didn't even realize was so important to me, because speaking directly with God was how I used to deal with my problems. As a kid, I would use the time walking the block or so from the bus stop to my house to speak to God. I would get so emotional that sometimes I would even break down in tears. So without even realizing it, I had been following certain dictates of Breslov.

Breslov struck a deep chord within me. I realized that it was what I was looking for. As soon as I was able to read and translate Hebrew, one of the first books that I read was *Sefer HaMidot*, because it is written in an easy Hebrew. Then I read *Sichot HaRan*, using the English translation (*Rabbi Nachman's*

---

22 See note 8, p. 25.

Wisdom) to help me understand the original Hebrew, and *Hishtapkhut HaNefesh* (*Outpouring of the Soul*). I would also attend *Motza'ei Shabbat* (Saturday night) learning sessions with Chaim Kramer.

> I explained to him that God had performed a miracle for me.

After three years of studying in Dvar Yerushalayim, older friends who had graduated from *ba'al teshuvah yeshivot* and had gone on to mainstream *yeshivot* such as Netivot or Gateshead started pressuring my parents to persuade me to enter a mainstream yeshivah.

One night in 1979—I was eighteen years old at the time—I was walking Chaim home and told him that I wanted to go to Uman. He put me in contact with Yossi Amsel, another yeshivah student who wanted to go to Uman, and we arranged to travel together.

During the yeshivah's summer break, I biked through Europe with a *rosh yeshivah* who had never had a chance to see the world. The *rosh yeshivah* assumed that at the end of our tour, I would fly to England to attend Gateshead Yeshivah. Instead, Yossi and I flew to Kiev. Years later, when I told the *rosh yeshivah* that I had traveled to Uman instead of flying back home to England, he said that had he known, he would have joined me.

CHAIM GAVE US THE NAME of the head of Intourist, the official Soviet travel bureau, who had been friendly with his father-in-law, Rabbi Zvi Aryeh Rosenfeld. As soon as we arrived in Kiev, we applied at the Intourist office for visas to travel to Uman. I remember going up to the Intourist desk and saying, "Mmm, I'd like to go to Uman. I've heard there are some beautiful gardens there, the Sofiefka Park ..."

The lady at the desk immediately responded, "Oh, you want to go to the *tzaddik*!"

I was positive she was a Breslover chassid! But she was not even Jewish; she had just heard that people travel to Uman to pray at the *tzaddik*'s gravesite.

Our application was rejected. We applied a second time and were rejected again. So of course, we applied a third time. We weren't about to give up!

During our entire stay in Kiev, Intourist took us on ridiculous trips around the city. But we weren't interested; we just wanted to get to Uman. Finally, we asked the hotel manager to give a copy of Rabbi Aryeh Kaplan's *Gems of Rebbe Nachman* to Chaim Kramer's contact in Intourist and inform him that we wanted to speak with him.

A few hours after we gave the hotel manager the book, we were asked to come downstairs. We were petrified!

We found the head of Intourist waiting to speak with us. We informed him of Rabbi Rosenfeld's passing, and he told us that he was very sorry to hear of it. He also thanked us profusely for the book, and said he was doing his utmost to get us permission to travel to Uman.

Later on, when we went outside for a walk, someone came up to us to ask the time. But I noticed that he was wearing a watch. He expressed admiration for Yossi's watch (it cost $120 in 1978, so it was a very expensive watch). We asked him if he could help us travel to Uman, and he replied that he could—if we gave him the watch, plus a little extra money.

The man told us that he had a friend, a physics professor, who owned a car. Although the professor wasn't Jewish, his wife was. He contacted them and they agreed to take us to Uman. But we had met this man on a Thursday and we were supposed to be leaving Russia on Sunday morning, which meant that if we were to travel with the professor to Uman, it would have to be on Friday. It was a risk—what if Shabbat came and we were stranded somewhere?

Yossi and I didn't know what to do. We decided that on Friday morning, we'd wake up early and pray with the sunrise. After our *hitbodedut*, we'd open a *siddur* and ask God to guide us so that wherever our fingers would land, the words would give us a clear answer.

On Friday morning, we awoke before dawn, prayed with the sunrise, spent some time in *hitbodedut* and opened the *siddur* to ask for God's guidance. Yossi's finger landed on a verse that, when translated into

> We asked him if he could help us travel to Uman.

English, read, "The angels will be with you."[23] Eerily enough, it was a clear day, and then completely unexpectedly, it started thundering and there was lightning. We were spooked.

So we traveled to Uman with the professor and his wife. She knew nothing about *Yiddishkeit* except that she was Jewish. Between our broken Yiddish and her broken English, we managed to converse.

In Uman, the woman who lived in the house adjacent to the *tziyun* came out and spoke to the professor and his wife in Russian, while my friend and I recited *Tikkun HaKlali* and the afternoon prayers by the Rebbe's gravesite. I just wanted to do what I had to do and get out of there so that we'd make it back to Kiev before Shabbat. Before we left, we gave the woman who lived next to the *tziyun* a large sum of money.

When we got back in the car, the couple told us that the woman had asked them why they were not wearing their Intourist uniforms. They lied and told her that since we were VIPs, they weren't supposed to wear uniforms. The woman told them that when people came illegally, she was required to report it to the KGB. "I was positive that I would die and end up being buried next to the *tzaddik*!" the professor's wife told us.

On the return trip to Kiev, we had to stop for gasoline. I don't know how many miles long the line was, but it took us three hours to get the gas. And then we still had a long way to go. The roads were not what they are today; you couldn't travel more than forty miles an hour.

---

23 Cf. Psalms 91.

When we realized that it would be impossible to return to Kiev before Shabbat, we told the professor to let us out of his car just before sunset.

The professor refused. He explained that since we didn't speak a word of Russian, the peasants would probably kill us and take whatever we had. It was a matter of *pikuach nefesh* (danger to life)—we had no choice but to continue on to Kiev.

I couldn't believe that this was really happening to us! I had been so confident that we'd return to Kiev before Shabbat that I was expecting a miracle. It didn't make sense to me that I would fulfill the Rebbe's words through desecrating the Shabbat.

I fell asleep in the car and woke up when we arrived at the hotel. We left all our things in the car except our passports, which we carried under our caps so that we would be carrying with a *shinuy*.[24] In addition, we walked less than four steps at a time, stopped, and then continued.[25]

Upon returning to the hotel, we discovered that the Intourist desk was still open. "Where were you?" they asked us. "We've been looking for you all day. You have permission to go to Uman."

NOW THAT WE COULD TRAVEL to Uman legally, we canceled our flight and returned to Uman with Intourist. During the ride to Uman, we prayed that the woman who lived next to the *tziyun* would not tell the Intourist agents that we had been there two days before. We could just imagine her saying, "Oh, you're back again!" But she was very nice. She gave us wormy apples and didn't ask any questions.

---

24 When a Jew finds himself in a situation where he might accidentally desecrate the Shabbat, the *halakhah* permits him to use a *shinuy* ("difference" or "change") so that he does not transgress a Torah prohibition.

25 Rabbi Matisyahu Salomon later told me that we did the right thing once we were in that situation. And since our heads were higher than ten *tefachim* (about forty inches) above the ground, there was no real problem, and we weren't really desecrating the Shabbat.

Intourist dropped us off at the *tziyun* and told us that they would return in three hours to drive us back to Kiev. This time, when I said *Tikkun HaKlali,* I said it with the intent of doing *teshuvah* for our unintentional

> I took each of my boys to Uman before they turned seven.

and accidental desecration of Shabbat, which is too serious a mitzvah to be taken lightly.

I TRAVEL TO UMAN every year for Rosh HaShanah. I took each of my boys there before they turned seven.[26] When Rebbe Nachman died, it was as if he walked from one room to another, and he knows exactly what is happening.[27] When I go to Uman, to the Rebbe's grave, I know that Rebbe Nachman is still there. At such a place, God accepts our prayers on a different level. It's like going to a therapist who gives you an electric shock if you don't say the truth, and waives the fee if you do, so instead of needing to go to many sessions, you get to the point quickly and realize that what you really wanted to ask for was not what you thought you had come for.

Every time I go to Uman, I ask myself, *What do I want to do with my life?* I am forced to face the question of life's purpose, and this keeps me focused on the real, important things.

---

26 Many people bring their young sons to Uman because of a promise Rebbe Nachman made during his lifetime, that any boy coming to him before the age of seven would be protected from impurity until marriage (*Tzaddik* #517; see *Kokhavey Ohr,* p. 68).

27 *Rabbi Nachman's Wisdom* #156.

In The Merit Of Uman

Eliezer Kosoy

Originally from Toronto, Eliezer Kosoy presently lives in Jerusalem. He is a talented musician who devotes most of his day to his yeshivah studies, while playing for weddings and other events in the evenings.

I first encountered Breslov when I was twenty-five and living in Toronto. I found a Breslov book in shul and started leafing through it. It touched something deep inside me. Later on, when I was learning in Israel, I heard another Breslov *dvar Torah*[28] and, once again, I felt a tremendous sense of spiritual arousal.

While learning in a Jerusalem yeshivah, Rabbi Boruch Gartner, a Breslover chassid and *rosh yeshivah* of Derech HaMelech,[29] invited me to spend Shabbat with his family. Later, a friend of mine brought me to a *shiur* that Rabbi Ozer Bergman was giving on *Sichot HaRan*. The concept of *hitbodedut*—that I could talk to God in my own words—really spoke to me. I was moved to such an extent that I started setting aside two to three minutes a day for *hitbodedut*. Those few minutes had a tremendous impact on my life.

---

28 Literally, "word of Torah"; a Torah discourse.
29 See note 4, p. 18.

Although I didn't yet consider myself a Breslover, I felt very connected to it. A friend of mine urged me to travel to Uman. He argued that I must go before the *Mashiach* arrives! Since everything I had read or heard that Rebbe Nachman had written was so obviously true, it seemed that the next logical step would be to listen to Rebbe Nachman's advice and travel to Uman.

ALTHOUGH I TRIED TO PREPARE MYSELF, I had no idea what to expect. But God had compassion on me and made sure that on my first trip, everything would work out almost perfectly. Upon boarding the plane, the steward informed me that I had been upgraded to first class. I arrived in Uman cold and exhausted, but the moment I walked into my apartment, one of the men there offered me a bowl of steaming hot, fresh soup. On the plane home, I was once again upgraded to first class. In later years, there were plenty of major obstacles, but that year, everything went relatively smoothly.

Before traveling to Uman, I attended a *shiur* on what to expect there. We were told that we should concentrate on what we were trying to achieve by being there and make clear goals in our *davening*, and then all the other stuff—the craziness, the difficulties—would just fall to the side. Without that focus, it's very easy to be overwhelmed by the experience.

In Uman, much of my prayers were focused on finding my destined mate. One of the rabbis in Uman said something that totally changed my outlook on finding a marriage partner: "You guys need to stop worrying about all the silly things that don't matter, which are preventing you from finding the right girl. Instead of looking at a potential *shiddukh* with your limited vision, try to see it through God's eyes."

Shortly after I returned home from Uman, I met the woman who would become my wife. I'm sure it was a result of the prayers that I said in Uman, combined with that rabbi's sagacious advice.

EVERY YEAR, THERE ARE DIFFERENT OBSTACLES to overcome, some greater than others. Two years ago, for example, my wife was due to give birth around Rosh HaShanah. I assumed that I would stay home; after all, how could I leave her at such a time? But as Rosh HaShanah drew close, I found myself longing for Uman.

When my study partner asked, "*Nu?* So what's with Rosh HaShanah?" I answered, "I'm not going this year. My wife is due then."

My study partner was shocked. "That's impossible," he said. "Absolutely impossible. How could you not go?"

I tried to shrug him off, but he insisted that I talk it over with a Breslov elder. The Breslov elder told me to travel to Uman and not to worry. Everything would turn out fine.

I mentioned the idea to my wife. She wasn't thrilled, but I don't think she really took me seriously, because she didn't get upset.

By now it was just three weeks to Rosh HaShanah. I called a travel agent to see if there were any tickets available. He was able to arrange a flight to Uman that would arrive right before Rosh HaShanah and return just a few hours after the Shabbat that immediately followed the Yom Tov. Even the price was good!

My wife needed a support system for the five days I would be gone. A close friend of hers volunteered to stay with her during the holiday. Someone else offered to be on call to take care of our other children should she need to go to the hospital. As all the details fell into place, my wife became more and more supportive of my desire to travel.

Although I was very nervous about the trip, I went. In Uman, I told my worries to one of the Breslov elders. He told me that I can't go wrong if I'm with the Rebbe.

The moment Rosh HaShanah was over, I rushed to the bus that would take me to the airport. The man next to me was talking on a cell phone with his wife. I asked him if his wife would call my house to check that everything was okay. A few minutes later, his wife phoned him back. He turned to me and said very casually, "*Mazal tov!* Your wife gave birth to a boy." I was in shock!

This birth was the quickest and easiest of all my wife's births. She almost delivered the baby on the way to the hospital. I'm sure it was in the merit of her being so supportive of my trip to Uman.

After all, how could I leave her at such a time?

I landed in Israel early Sunday morning and took a taxi straight from the airport to the hospital. My wife had just been discharged and was waiting for me to take her home. The *brit* (circumcision) was held on Erev Yom Kippur. Yehuda Simcha is our first son after three daughters.

EACH TRIP TO UMAN IS DIFFERENT. A friend of mine once asked me if traveling to Uman is a spiritual experience. I told him that although I don't always feel so spiritual while I'm there, I know that when I am with the Rebbe for Rosh HaShanah, I am following the Rebbe's advice—and following the Rebbe's advice will benefit me both spiritually and materially.

Where There's A Will, There's A Way

Chaim Kramer

Chaim Kramer founded the Breslov Research Institute in Jerusalem in 1979. He grew up in a Modern Orthodox family in New York and came to Breslov through his rebi in grade school, Rabbi Zvi Aryeh Rosenfeld, who later became his father-in-law. "Rebi taught us, I liked what he taught, so I remained," he says.

I wanted to travel to Uman because I had learned about Rebbe Nachman's promise.[30] My first trip was in 1965, just a few months after my wedding.

My friend, Gedaliah Fleer, had succeeded in traveling to Uman in the summer of 1963. The following winter, my *rebi*, Rabbi Zvi Aryeh Rosenfeld, got permission from the Soviets to bring a group of Breslover chassidim there. But after that one trip, the Soviets refused to issue visas again. I didn't go on that trip since I was studying in yeshivah in Israel at that time. I was very jealous of all those who had made it, and resolved to go at the first opportunity.

In April 1965, I married Gita Rosenfeld, my *rebi's* daughter. I also began planning a trip to Uman in the summer. I hoped

---

30 See p. 4.

that just as he had done with my friend, Gedaliah, Reb Michel Dorfman would agree to meet me in Kiev and take me to Uman. Since Gedaliah was planning to go to Uman for Rosh HaShanah, the plan was for me to travel to Russia, contact Reb Michel, speak to him about Gedaliah's planned trip, and ask him if he would be willing to accompany me to Uman.

I was really asking Reb Michel for a tremendous favor. Although traveling to Uman without a visa was dangerous for me, it would be much, much more dangerous for Reb Michel to be caught helping a foreigner travel to Uman. He had a record with the KGB and had already spent time in a Siberian labor camp. If I were caught, I would be thrown out of the Soviet Union and told never to return. If Reb Michel were caught, he would be sent to Siberia, perhaps for life.

I MADE THE TRIP IN EARLY JULY 1965. I arrived in Moscow on a Monday afternoon. The following afternoon, I went to visit Reb Michel. He lived in Malachovka, a suburb of Moscow, about an hour's drive from my hotel.

Reb Michel was not expecting me. He assumed I was Gedaliah. He knew Gedaliah, but he didn't realize that there were others like him—young, observant people who lived in vibrant Jewish communities around the world, far removed from the oppressive life of Jews in Russia. I introduced myself and spoke with him about Gedaliah's Rosh HaShanah trip. Then I asked him if he would be willing to meet me in Kiev and take me to Uman. He began to tremble from fear; he knew the risks involved far better than I. Still, after just a few minutes of thought, he agreed. This was a tremendous act of self-sacrifice on his part.

The following day, Wednesday, Reb Michel came to my hotel to pick up a package that I had brought for him. He didn't come inside; he stood near the hotel and then I followed him. Once we were sure that no one was following us, I gave him the package, and then we walked around for an hour or so talking.

I asked him if it were possible for me to meet the other Breslover chassidim in Moscow. There were two others: Reb

Avraham Yehoshua Rosenvald (known as Reb Shika) and Reb Yisrael Korsonski. Reb Michel told me to come to his house the following day, Thursday.

I don't remember much about that meeting we had on Thursday. We were four Breslover chassidim: Reb Michel, Reb Shika, Reb Yisrael and myself. Toward the end of the meeting, the brother of Levi Eshkol, the former prime minister of Israel, knocked on the door. He was *shomer Shabbat*, and he had come to let us know about someone who had just received an exit visa to Israel. We started dancing and singing the Breslov song that is traditionally sung on Purim, "*Velo yikalmu la-netzach kol ha-chosim bakh*—They will never be ashamed, those who trust in You." The others sang the song slowly, with a tremendous sense of yearning combined with joy. It was something I cannot even describe, but I was awed, and I hope that I will never forget that dance of *simchah* tinged with deep longing.

On Friday morning, I flew to Kiev. Intourist, the Soviet travel bureau in charge of all tourists, had arranged for a private driver to pick me up at the airport together with my Intourist guide. On our way to Kiev, the car broke down. The Intourist guide kept pushing the driver to fix it. By then it was almost nightfall, and the guide told him that we *must* get to Kiev before nightfall.

We made it to the hotel just minutes before sunset. Although there were several people waiting in line at the reception desk, the Intourist guide shoved me to the head of the line, glanced at his watch and explained, "I'm in a rush. I have to leave now. It's late!" He asked me if it would be all right for him to leave even though he had not yet checked me in to the hotel. I agreed, and he disappeared. This was very unusual—the Intourist guide usually sticks with his client from the moment he arrives until the moment he leaves. I have often wondered if he was a Jew, and a *shomer Shabbat* one at that!

I spent Shabbat in my hotel room. That entire Shabbat, the Intourist office rang my phone every half-hour. Eventually, they sent someone up to my room with a note asking if I wanted to tour Kiev on Sunday. I agreed, and explained that I had stayed in my room that day because I wasn't feeling well and had to rest. They knew I hadn't left the room because Russian hotels kept a "floor lady" on duty twenty-four hours a day to keep track of all the guests' comings and goings.

> The informer started a conversation with me.

AFTER ARRANGING WITH REB MICHEL to meet him in the shul on Monday morning at eleven o'clock, I spent Sunday touring Kiev. On Monday, I told my Intourist guide that I wasn't feeling well and that I wanted to rest most of the day, but that I might go outside to get some fresh air.

Soon after, I left the hotel. After making sure that I wasn't being followed, I walked to the shul. I arrived there at a quarter to eleven to wait for Reb Michel. It was a known fact that the shul's custodian was a government informer, so I had to be careful.

I made sure to sit in an area of the shul where I had a clear view of the entrance to the courtyard. The informer started a conversation with me. I talked with him, but was careful not to give him any information. The moment I noticed Reb Michel poke his head in the door, I raced out. He had a car waiting for us around the corner. Together we jumped in the car and sped off.

Reb Michel told me that he had taken a taxi from the airport into Kiev. He had asked the taxi driver if he would take us to Uman. The driver wasn't interested, but he had a friend who owned a car and would be willing to take us. That was to our advantage, since a private car was much safer than a taxi.

We managed to reach Uman without incident. Reb Michel asked the driver to let us off in the marketplace and told him that we'd be back in about an hour and a half. We walked to the *tziyun*, about a ten-minute walk, but when we arrived there, we saw workers in the yard.

Reb Michel spoke with the woman who owned the house adjacent to the *tziyun*. She was afraid to let us in to her yard with the workers there. Meanwhile, I was able to catch a view of the *tziyun*. Since we were unable to get to it, we sat outside the gate and recited the *Tikkun HaKlali*. We looked like two laborers resting after a long day of work. After reciting the *Tikkun HaKlali,* we spent some time in *hitbodedut* and returned to the marketplace.

It was July 12, 1965 (12 Tammuz). I felt horrible that I didn't get in, yet grateful to have seen the *tziyun*. I realized that everything is in God's hands and I had done what I had to do.

On the return trip, the driver had to fill up on gas. A long line of cars waited their turn at the gas station, with a policeman directing traffic. The driver was nervous; he didn't want the policeman asking questions. So instead of waiting in line with all the other cars, he went directly to the pump and asked, "Is it okay if I fill my car with diesel rather than regular fuel?" Thank God, we made it back to Kiev without incident.

IN THE SUMMERS OF 1966 AND 1967, several groups traveled to Kiev and were granted visas to enter Uman. But because of financial restraints, I was not able to join them. Then in the summer of 1968, I traveled to the Soviet Union with a group headed by my father-in-law and merited to reach the *tziyun*!

Five years later, in February 1973, I traveled to the Soviet Union with a group of ten people: the travel agent, Sidney Reiner; Max Assoulin; Moshe Schorr; Simchah Druck; Berel Krieger and his son, Eliyahu; my wife, Gita; and several others, led by my father-in-law, Rabbi Zvi Aryeh Rosenfeld. We spent several days in Kiev, but Intourist refused to grant us a visa to enter Uman. We returned to the United States without getting to the *tziyun*.

I felt rejected and wondered, *Were my sins so numerous that I wasn't worthy to reach the tziyun?* I realized that there were many things about myself that I had to work on.

After that trip, I began planning different strategies for getting to Uman. I considered renting a car in Western Europe and driving it to Odessa via Uman. But that summer, my eldest son was born. That, together with financial

> I knew that I needed to be there for any spiritual growth.

difficulties, made it out of the question for me to consider such a trip.

From then on, I prayed and prayed and prayed some more that I would get to Uman as soon as possible. I knew that I needed to be there for any spiritual growth. In the winter of 1974, I started making plans again and hoped to merit to reach Uman by the spring.

REBBE NACHMAN ONCE SAID, "If only I were worthy of seeing the clear, radiant light of the road you travel to be with me."[31] Reb Noson writes that he was told that the Rebbe took issue with those who traveled to him by coach and did not come by foot. Reb Noson placed importance on this and wanted to fulfill this dictum, which he did several times.[32]

Because I felt such a burning desire to get to Rebbe Nachman's *tziyun*, I, too, wanted to fulfill this precept. Of course, it was impossible for me to physically walk from New York to the Ukraine, but I could take care of all the arrangements for my trip on foot. So I walked to the photographer for my visa pictures and I walked to the travel agent. From where I was working in Manhattan, I walked miles and miles as I made preparations for my trip to Uman.

What was amazing to me was that every effort I put into the trip only strengthened my resolve to get to Uman. But I told

---

31 *Tzaddik* #291.

32 Ibid., #328. Rebbe Nachman refers to the greater physical efforts one places in the mitzvah when walking, as opposed to traveling in a wagon (or vehicle). But see *Eikhah Rabbah* 1:30.

absolutely no one—including my wife—about these arrangements, or about how strongly I desired to travel there. Rebbe Nachman teaches that if you want to do something and you want your desire fulfilled, you shouldn't speak about it.[33] So I prayed and prayed and did more *hitbodedut*, asking God to help me to get to Uman.

Rabbi Yitzchak Breiter was one of the leading Breslover chassidim in prewar Poland—perhaps the leading Breslover chassid (he was murdered by the Nazis in Treblinka in 1943, may God avenge his blood). Rabbi Breiter traveled to Uman in the early 1900s, but was prevented from going there again after the Russian Revolution of 1917. Because of this, he composed a very moving prayer asking God to help him get to the Rebbe's gravesite in Uman. I memorized that prayer and recited it every day. In addition, I composed my own short prayer, which I also said daily.

I WAS AN ELECTRICIAN BY TRADE. Two months before Pesach 1974, I made a few contracts that would more than pay for the trip. At that time, the price of the trip was about $1,500 (in current dollars, about $6,000). I was able to put down half.

I was planning to leave on the Sunday night following Pesach (April 21, 1974), arrive in Moscow on Monday night, and then travel directly to Odessa. I would stay four nights there, travel to Kiev on Friday, and remain in Kiev until Tuesday (April 30). I had names of people in the Jewish underground in both Odessa and Kiev who might be able to assist me, and I assumed that between the four days in Odessa and the four days in Kiev, I would find some way to get to the *tziyun*.

I was happy. I was making enough money to support my family, I had enough money to travel to Uman, and I was even able to buy the *matzot* and wine for Pesach. But then, on Purim, the contracts were put on hold. The people who had ordered the

33 *The Aleph-Bet Book, Repentance* A:62.

work decided to wait a few months
before starting. Now not only did I lack
the funds to pay the remaining $750 for
my ticket, I also did not have money
to buy bread and milk for my family.
I didn't have any money to cover the
rent, let alone the upcoming Pesach
expenses.

> Reb Noson writes that
> the main obstacles are
> within our mind.

The truth is, although I was upset about the delay in the
contracts, this was really what I had been praying for. I didn't
want the trip to come easy, because we don't fully appreciate
something that comes easy. I was expecting obstacles, and even
asked God to send me obstacles. Now that my source of income
had dried up, I felt that my prayers were heard and being
answered!

Every day was another miracle. Somehow, we managed to
cover our basic expenses. But I was worried. I had a wife and
two children. Soon it would be Pesach, and I had no idea how we
would cover the extra holiday expenses. I would drive around in
Brooklyn from place to place crying, literally screaming, "God!
Help! Get me to Uman! Get me to the Rebbe's *tziyun!*" (I rolled
up the car windows so I wouldn't get arrested for disturbing the
peace.)

Reb Noson writes that the main obstacles are within our
mind. As is its wont, the *yetzer hara* invades a person's thoughts
with various ideas, and somehow—actually always—they are
conflicting ideas; many even appear as *mitzvot*.[34]

In 1970, my wife and I had purchased an apartment in
Jerusalem, and we decided that we would move there by June
1975 (we made it, thank God!). We were concerned about the
differences in the cost of living and decided to pay off the entire
apartment before moving to Israel. And so the *yetzer hara*'s
argument took the form of a mitzvah: *Why are you so concerned*

---

34 See *Likutey Moharan* I, 1.

about going to Uman? You were there already. You should be using every penny to pay off your apartment so that you will be able to move to Israel.

Other times, the *yetzer hara* enticed me to spend money on other "*mitzvot*" and also on things that were not *mitzvot*—anything, as long as it was not on Uman.

SOMEHOW, WE MADE IT TO PESACH. I was scheduled to travel just a week after Pesach. During *Chol HaMo'ed*, ten days before my scheduled trip, I spoke to Gedaliah Fleer about my plans and the financial problems I was facing. He suggested that I sell shares in my recital of the *Tikkun HaKlali* at the *tziyun* at $100 per share.[35]

That night, I discussed the trip with my father-in-law, Rabbi Rosenfeld. When I told him that I had made all the arrangements and was planning to leave the following week, he didn't know if he should believe me. After recovering from the initial shock, he told me that he firmly believed I would succeed in reaching the *tziyun*, even though at that point, the Soviets were refusing to grant visas to Uman. He offered to purchase a share in my recital of the *Tikkun HaKlali*. In shul the following morning, my father-in-law raised enough shares to cover the balance of my plane fare. My brother-in-law, Shelly Rosenfeld, lent me another $400 for expenses. All the people who helped me were struggling financially themselves, but they wanted the privilege of helping me reach the *tziyun*.

---

35 The idea of "buying" a share in a mitzvah hearkens back to the days of the Holy Temple. The responsibilities in the Temple were divided into three groups. The *kohanim* performed the required service (the *avodah*) as detailed in the Torah; the Levites acted as the guards and also played the musical instruments; and the Israelites stood and read the Torah passages during the offering of the sacrifices. As explained in the Talmud (*Ta'anit* 26a), the Israelites were the representatives of the entire nation, teaching us that in the performance of certain *mitzvot*, one Jew can represent another. Taking this further, when one "buys" a share in the mitzvah, he is certainly represented by the messenger. Purchasing shares in another person's trip to Uman entitled those buyers to share the merit of reciting the *Tikkun HaKlali* at the *tziyun*!

I left on Sunday night, April 21, which was Rosh Chodesh Iyar. By the time I boarded the Aeroflot flight to Moscow, I was emotionally exhausted. The wear and tear on my finances, combined with the emotionally-charged feelings about traveling to Uman and the brokenhearted prayers that just kept pouring forth from me, put me in a strange frame of mind. I was elated at traveling toward my goal; and I was concerned about the many obstacles and barriers I had yet to face.

> They pointed at me and ridiculed me.

The plane was packed with high-school-age kids from Vermont who were traveling to the Soviet Union on an intercultural exchange. I had a middle seat in the back row. Since I wanted to remain as inconspicuous as possible, I stayed up the entire night waiting for the first rays of dawn so I could begin praying while the other passengers were still asleep. But it was Rosh Chodesh, and the prayer service was longer than usual. Many of the youngsters woke up while I was still wearing my *talit* and *tefilin*. They pointed at me and ridiculed me, making crude comments about my being a Jew. Have you ever seen the famous photo of the elderly Jew crowned in his *talit* and *tefilin*, surrounded by sneering Nazis? I felt like that old man. It was a very humbling experience.

I had brought with me contact information for several members of the Jewish underground in Russia, and I didn't want the Soviets to discover it. Yet I did not want to hide the list, because if the Soviets were to find it, it would be obvious that I knew I was doing something illegal. I placed the list deep inside my wallet and hoped they wouldn't search there. I also placed an extra *talit* among my clothes, which was destined for an elderly Jew who lived in Berdichev. He was preparing for his death and wanted to be buried, as is the Jewish custom, in a *talit*.

In Moscow, the customs officers went through my suitcase with a fine-tooth comb, tapping every can and even sticking their fingers into my box of tissues. I was nervous that they would discover the list with the contact information. I had also brought with me several small-print *sefarim* (a volume of Talmud and a *Likutey Moharan*, among other books) to learn, plus a few novels to show that I was an avid reader of both Hebrew and English literature. It was my tiny *Tikkun HaKlali* that caused the officers to go berserk. They called over the head customs officer, a war hero with some twenty medals on his chest. He interrogated me for over forty-five minutes. When they asked me why I was traveling to the Ukraine, I explained that I was on vacation and that my ancestors had emigrated from there and I wanted to see where they came from.

As they made a thorough search of my belongings, I prayed and prayed and prayed some more. Suddenly, the customs officer stopped, looked up and ordered, "Go!" Miraculously, despite their search, the only things they did not discover were the list with the contact information and the extra *talit* which I had placed among my clothes.

By the time I was "safely" inside Russia, I was totally broken and humiliated. I had expected obstacles, but obstacles that *I* would be able to break. Instead, the obstacles were breaking me. Still, I was happy to be another step closer to Uman.

FROM MOSCOW, I FLEW TO ODESSA. On Tuesday, I behaved like the perfect tourist, going with my guide to all the interesting sights. At the end of the day, I took a taxi to the home of someone in the Jewish underground whom I had been told might accompany me to Uman. Since it was against the law for Soviet citizens to speak with foreigners, I was trying to be as inconspicuous as possible. But the moment I stepped foot in the common courtyard where he lived, a huge dog loudly announced my presence.

I went to my contact's house, knocked on the door and waited—and waited and waited. After twenty minutes of waiting with the dog's continuous barking, I didn't know what to do. I noticed window shades moving slightly to the side, and people peering out to see why the dog was making such a racket. I couldn't remain standing there with all the people watching me, so I left the courtyard and returned to the street.

> I had no idea where I was or how to return to the hotel.

Standing there on this huge street, I suddenly realized that I had no idea where I was or how to return to the hotel. Praying to God to help me, I felt like I was in one of those Eliyahu HaNavi stories[36] when I saw a car passing and stuck out my hand for it to stop. I told the driver, "*Gastinitza Metropol* (Metropol Hotel)." He answered, "*Da* (Yes)," and without another word between us, he drove me straight back to my hotel!

But I was in a quandary. How would I get to Uman? I didn't have any other contacts in Odessa. Who could help me? I prayed the entire night, crying to God and begging Him to help me get to the *tziyun*. After just an hour or so of sleep, I felt as if someone or something were dragging me out of bed. I got up, cried, recited *Tikkun Chatzot*, spent some time in *hitbodedut* and recited the *Shemot HaTzaddikim*. This occurred several times during the night; I would fall asleep for about an hour, then drag myself out of bed—or more accurately, feel myself being dragged from bed—to pray. Each time, I felt more humble and brokenhearted. I felt that I *must* get to the Rebbe's gravesite; otherwise, what would my wasted life be worth?

The following day, Wednesday, I behaved like a regular tourist and continued touring the city with my Intourist guide. I told her that my ancestors were from Uman and asked if there were any possibility of visiting the city. She told me that she'd put in a request. She'd have the answer the following day.

Again I spent that entire night in prayer, crying and pouring out my heart as I begged God to bring me to the *tziyun*. (Today, I still yearn for the power and sincerity of those prayers!)

---

36 Elijah the Prophet is known to appear in bodily form from time to time to help Jews in need, often accompanied by a miracle.

In the morning, the woman at the Intourist desk apologized that they had not yet received an answer and told me to return that afternoon. I noticed a Scottish man wearing a kilt sitting in the Intourist office. I found this very encouraging and thought, *If he's allowed to do what he wants and wear a skirt, I should be allowed to do what I want and travel to the tziyun.*

I spent that morning touring Odessa with my guide. I pretended to be interested in the sights, while inside I was praying, begging God that I be privileged to travel to the *tziyun.*

When I returned to the Intourist office around four-thirty in the afternoon, the clerks smiled at me and told me that I had a visa to travel to Uman! They asked me how I was planning to find my grandparents' grave. I explained to them that although my grandparents had left Russia in the early 1900s, they often spoke about Uman and told me that it was a beautiful city, with the Sofiefka, a world-renowned botanical garden.

THE FOLLOWING DAY WAS FRIDAY, April 26 (4 Iyar). An Intourist driver was scheduled to drive me to Kiev, and now that I had a visa to Uman, he was supposed to stop in Uman on the way. But it was a seven- or eight-hour drive from Odessa to Kiev. Intourist guides usually start work at nine o'clock in the morning, which would make it very difficult for us to stop in Uman and still get me to Kiev before Shabbat (which, of course, they had no idea was a problem).

I asked the woman at the Intourist office if we could get an early start and leave at eight in the morning instead of the usual nine. The woman replied, "It's a long ride. Why don't you leave at seven?"

That was more than I had hoped to hear, and inside, I was dancing for joy. I thought of the verse in Proverbs, "When God accepts a person's ways, He will cause even his enemies to make peace with him."[37]

---

37 Proverbs 16:7.

I awoke early Friday morning and left Odessa at seven o'clock. During the four-hour drive from Odessa to Uman, I prayed almost the entire time that I would make it to the *tziyun*. Despite Intourist guarantees and visas, there were cases where the

> One's prayers *are* answered. We just need patience.

trip was sanctioned yet the people never made it. I kept reciting Rabbi Yitzchak Breiter's prayer, as well as my own composition, for almost the entire four hours.

We arrived in Uman around eleven o'clock in the morning and drove straight to the *tziyun*. I arranged with the driver that he should go get something to eat and return at one o'clock to drive me to Kiev.

Reb Michel had given me a letter of introduction to give to the woman who lived in the house next to the *tziyun*. I had also brought her a present. She let me in to her yard and allowed me to spend time at the *tziyun*.

As I approached the *tziyun*, my knees were literally knocking together, and I began to cry. As I recited the *Tikkun HaKlali*, I cried and prayed over the past, and kept asking God for a brighter future. Our Sages teach that a person can buy his world in an hour.[38] I spent only one hour at the *tziyun* on that trip, but that one hour has kept me going ever since.

We left Uman at one o'clock in the afternoon and, thank God, I arrived in Kiev with plenty of time to spare before Shabbat. In Kiev, I asked for permission to return to Uman, but I was turned down.

And I learned a very important lesson: One's prayers *are* listened to. One's prayers *are* answered. We just need patience.

AS OF 2009, I HAVE BEEN to Uman nearly 100 times. But no trip has had an impact on me like that trip. God humbled me again and

---

38 *Avodah Zarah* 17a.

again until I was reduced to almost nothing, and yet at the same time, He strengthened me even more, again and again. At one and the same time, I felt God concealing Himself and revealing Himself to me, until all I could do was cry out to Him. This I did, and God answered my prayers—through the agent of His great Treasury of Unearned Gifts[39] with which He brought me to the *tziyun*. It was a beautiful lesson for all of life, one that I thank God for until this day.

---

39 See *The Treasury of Unearned Gifts: Rebbe Nachman's Path to Happiness and Contentment in Life* (Breslov Research Institute).

Journeys

"Eileh (These) are the journeys of the Israelites" (Numbers 33:1). *Because the Jews sinned with "Eileh (This) is your god, O Israel"* (Exodus 32:4), *the Israelites journeyed as a result. We see, then, that all of a person's journeys are because of a blemish in faith (i.e., an aspect of idolatry). Consequently, the journey indicates a blemish of faith.*

This is why it is written about idolatry, "You will tell it, 'Get out!'" (Isaiah 30:22). *It is an aspect of journeying and wandering.*

By virtue of his wandering, a person rectifies the wandering caused by blemished faith. His journey actually rectifies blemished faith and strengthens true faith! (see Likutey Moharan I, 40).

*

Rebbe Nachman once said, "If only I were worthy of seeing the clear, radiant light of the road you travel to be with me" (Tzaddik #291).

Getting To Know The Real Me

Huna Friedland

Huna Friedland lives in Jerusalem with his family. He is the director of the Kesher Institute, a yeshivah program designed for "at-risk" young men, and maintains a private practice offering therapy, counseling and consulting for individuals and institutions.

I was born in 1955 and grew up in a family that placed great emphasis on intellectual pursuits. My father, a Harvard graduate, was a university professor.

I was introduced to the laws of *kashrut* when I was about four years old. We were eating a meal at my grandmother's house—capon, brisket and kreplach—and she asked me what I would like to drink. I said, "Oh, I'll have a glass of milk." My mother kicked me under the table. That's when I became aware that some people consider drinking milk while eating meat unacceptable behavior.

In "religious" school, we were taught that the *kashrut* laws were instituted for health reasons, and that with contemporary hygiene and refrigeration, they were no longer applicable. The renovation of Judaism was not limited to eating kosher. The parting of the Red Sea was a combination of low tide coinciding with a simultaneous solar/lunar eclipse, which people later turned into a bigger-than-life story about the miraculous parting of the sea. What I was taught about Judaism could not even be considered a distortion—it was not even a faint shadow of true *Yiddishkeit*.

THE ONLY PERSON I EVER SAW with *tefilin* was my grandfather. When I asked my mother about it, she explained, "He's doing his Jewish homework." Although my grandparents were not religious and ate non-kosher food out of the house, they were traditional enough to keep a kosher home.

My grandfather passed away shortly before my bar mitzvah. For the bar mitzvah, he had bought me the requisite polyester "prayer shawl," and my grandmother gave me my grandfather's *tefilin*.

I had a little book about the *tefilin* with illustrations showing how to wear them. But I was putting them on three times a day, because I misconstrued putting on *tefilin* with reciting *Shema Yisrael*! I was doing this totally on my own, with no outside support, so it didn't last long.

One of the things I remember vividly about my Reform youth group was when they took us to a church for an interfaith experience. There was a massive cross on the wall, and in front of our seats were little stools for us to kneel on. In the middle of the service, all the non-Jews started to bow to this cross. The Jewish kids looked around uncomfortably, wondering what they were supposed to do.

I was sitting in the back, and something about this just didn't feel quite right. I just wasn't convinced that bowing to a cross in church was something that we, as Jews, should be doing. Unfortunately, the majority of the Jewish kids did bow. They didn't want to offend their hosts.

With sixty percent of Jews intermarrying, it was crazy for our "rabbinic" figures to take us to a church, and insanity not to give us any instructions.

WHEN I WAS EIGHTEEN, I started playing the drums. By the time I turned twenty-one, I was playing professionally. I traveled through a chunk of the world and had my fair taste of what is euphemistically called a "slice of life." I was taking music very, very seriously, playing and practicing between eight and twelve hours a day. I did not believe in God. Music was all the spirituality I needed.

> Music was all the spirituality I needed.

As a professional musician, I was exposed to all sorts of bizarre things. People were always trying to convert me to the spiritual flavor of the month. I shared a house with a group of musicians—several black men from Jamaica and Trinidad and a Japanese guitar player (racist I was not). We used to rehearse in the basement. One day, we heard a knock on the door and eight huge black men walked in. They started talking about Islam and Allah and managed to convert our percussionist on the spot, giving him a new Muslim name. Then they turned to me.

"What about you? Are you ready to take on the faith?"

I replied, "If I were to believe in God—which I don't—and if I were interested in a monotheistic religion—which I'm not—then since I was born a Jew, I would check out Judaism first." Those missionaries were not happy campers!

One day, my friends and I were performing a musical experiment in harmony, using a variety of unconventional sequence chords. As we were playing, I had a revelatory sort of experience. It felt as if I were the musical instrument being played. I came away with a few profound insights. One was that music and time already exists; the question is if we are able to free ourselves from an ego-based approach and plug into it.

I had always known that everything in the world is interrelated, but through this experience, I realized that within and behind all things, there is a greater consciousness: God. I also realized that I was a Jew, and unless I found out what that meant, I was missing out on who I was intrinsically as a person. And so I decided that I must investigate my Jewish heritage.

The following day, I began talking to God, asking Him to help me. God became a real presence in my life. I felt truly attached to my Creator.

I asked my mother if she still had my grandfather's *tefilin*. She did. She gave them to me, and I started wearing them again. Then one Shabbat morning, I woke up and had this random desire to go to shul. I was living in Toronto at the time. I went to Kensington Market, a section of downtown that had previously been a Jewish area (my black friends referred to it as "Jews' Market"). I recalled that I had seen an old shul there, found the place, and went inside.

I looked like a typical jazz musician—with a goatee, jeans, suede jacket and a beret. As I entered the shul, I saw a lot of older men walking downstairs. They told me that the services were finished and invited me to join them for a *kiddush* of *kichlach* (sugar cookies), herring and schnapps. They were warm and open. I would have been wary of someone who looked the way I did, but they weren't, and I started attending that shul every Shabbat.

ONE DAY, THE PHONE RANG. It was a rabbi that a friend of mine had become close to, a very straight, yeshivah-type guy with the plastic suit, the tie that's too wide and the big, plastic glasses. After speaking with me for a while, he said, "You've got to come to my house for Shabbat!"

I explained that it was impossible. I was working and couldn't afford to take the time off.

"Can't they find a replacement?" he asked.

"Yes," I said, "but I really need the money."

He offered to pay me whatever I would lose by not working.

"I can't accept your money," I told him. My friend had told me before that this rabbi was far from wealthy.

He offered to lend me the money, and I told him that I couldn't accept it because I had no idea when I'd be able to pay him back.

He was absolutely insistent. He said, "I'll lend you the money and you can pay me back whenever you want. But you must come to my house for Shabbat."

I would have been wary of someone who looked the way I did.

So I went. I wore what I thought were appropriate clothes: a pair of khaki pants, an olive-green corduroy jacket and a bright red shirt with yellow polka dots. I thought I looked pretty dapper.

When I entered the rabbi's house, he handed me a yarmulke and introduced me to his wife. I extended my hand. He intercepted me and said, "I'm sorry, but my wife doesn't shake hands with men." I liked that. After all, why should she? After all the fake intimacy and lack of boundaries, I found this refreshing.

Then the rabbi's four-year-old son came up to me and said, "You're going to sleep in my bed tonight!" I could never imagine myself giving up my bed to a stranger. I could see that the family was very special and the rabbi was so real, so sincere.

But it was the *cholent* that ultimately convinced me. It was soul food! Real Jewish soul food! The *cholent* made me do *teshuvah*. It was with great reluctance that I removed my yarmulke as I made my way downtown to play with the band on Saturday night.

MY MOTHER HAD ALWAYS BEEN CONCERNED about my alternative lifestyle, and now that I was interested in something Jewish, she seized upon the opportunity and offered to send me to Israel. Before I left for Israel, the rabbi spoke to me privately. He said, "You must start keeping Shabbat."

"I'll start as soon as I'm in Israel," I said.

He pointed out, "You don't keep Shabbat because of a geographical location. You keep Shabbat because you make a decision to keep Shabbat, because you know it's the truth!"

I was the drummer in a band. After a year and a half of working together, we were scheduled to play for a showcase gig that Shabbat for a variety of record executives and secure a record deal. I couldn't let my friends down.

But the rabbi was not about to accept no for an answer. In the end, I quit the band. My friends were furious with me and the bassist even threatened me physically. They felt betrayed and abandoned. But I had made my choice. I was committed to keeping Shabbat.

On the day I left for Israel, I put on a pair of *tzitzit* and a yarmulke. It was 1981. I arrived in Israel late at night and went straight to Yeshivat Dvar Yerushalayim,[40] which was in the middle of Geulah, a religious neighborhood in Jerusalem. Dinner was less than appealing, and I was given a mattress on the floor of a huge room that slept twelve men. The next morning, I was totally depressed. I had given up everything—my work, my friends, my life—to end up on the floor of a building in desperate need of renovation.

I had come to yeshivah with a friend. He had told me about this tremendous rabbi and kabbalist who lived far from Jerusalem. The following morning, as I lay on the dormitory floor, pleading with God to "please, give me a sign," I overheard my friend ask one of the other men in the room, "Have you heard of a Rabbi Yisrael Abuchatzeira?"

The man he spoke to, a yeshivah type of guy, answered, "I'm going there today. Would you like to come?" All I could say was, "Thank you, God!"

The three of us went to Netivot, a development town in the south of Israel, to see Rabbi Yisrael Abuchatzeira, the great Baba Sali. On our way back to Jerusalem, the typical yeshivah guy said to me, "I'd like to give you this book, but you must promise me that you'll read it from cover to cover."

The book was *Restore My Soul*.

---

40 See note 8, p. 25.

Rebbe Nachman's *Restore My Soul* really spoke to me. I cannot count how many copies of that book I've given away, but I still have that original copy, though it's yellowed and falling apart.

> The rabbi was not about to accept no for an answer.

The next day, I left Dvar Yerushalayim and moved into the Diaspora Yeshiva,[41] located on Mount Zion just outside the Old City. I loved Mount Zion. It was awesome, beautiful. But it wasn't what I was looking for. A few months later, I transferred to Ohr Somayach.[42]

Shortly after I started learning in Ohr Somayach, I received a job offer to play with a band. The drummer wanted to quit, but he wouldn't do it unless I agreed to replace him. The band's songwriter and percussionist was a Breslover chassid by the name of Yitzchak Attias. We started learning *Mesillat Yesharim*[43] and Breslov books together in the mornings. Breslov really spoke to me. It teaches how much God loves us, how precious every small thing we do in His service truly is, and that we should "never give up!"

I MET RABBI AVRAHAM GREENBAUM when a crew came to film our band for a show that was being produced for American television. The sound man and I kept making eye contact. Later, we spoke, and I discovered that he was Rabbi Greenbaum—the man who had translated Rebbe Nachman's *Restore My Soul*, the book that

---

41 See note 7, p. 24.

42 A *ba'al teshuvah* yeshivah founded in Jerusalem in 1970 which has since established branches in New York, Detroit and Miami; Toronto and Montreal; Johannesburg, Cape Town and Sandton, South Africa; London; and Sydney, Australia.

43 "Path of the Upright," a classic *mussar* text written by Rabbi Moshe Chaim Luzzato (1707-1746), known as the *RaMChaL*.

had been the impetus to bring me to Breslov. Rabbi Greenbaum invited me to come to his house for Shabbat. After that, we started learning together in the mornings.

In 1982, he invited me to Meron for Rosh HaShanah. That was it. From that time since, I've spent every year with the Rebbe.

But although I was learning Breslov Chassidut regularly and I was friends with many Breslover chassidim, I did not define myself as a Breslover chassid. I looked more like a stereotype of a yeshivah guy than I do now. I had a trimmed beard and kept my *peyot* tucked behind my ears. People would ask me, "Oh, you're a Breslover chassid?" and I would answer, "No. I'm God's chassid." It was really a matter of pride and ego. I just couldn't allow myself to be defined as a Breslover chassid.

People think of Breslover chassidim as a bunch of nuts whose idea of *avodat HaShem* is to take Ecstasy and dance on top of vans. But all the Breslover chassidim I knew, suffered. Sometimes, it was financial; other times, social. They seemed to encounter difficulties finding schools for their children.

I wasn't sure if I was ready to take what felt like such a monumental step. I tried to follow the Rebbe's teachings, I did *hitbodedut*, I learned Rebbe Nachman's Torah, I spent Rosh HaShanah with the Rebbe. But there was the problem of affiliation. When people would ask me, "Are you a Breslover chassid?" would I be comfortable answering, "Yes, I am," being aware of the baggage—that I might be classified as a weirdo or a freak?

I was really being asked *the* question: "What does God desire of me?" I realized that the more I let go of my "image" of myself, the more I would become who I truly am.

I accepted the challenge and began to call myself a Breslover chassid.

I TRAVELED TO UMAN for the first time in 1991, when Gorbachev was still in power. About three weeks before Rosh HaShanah, I went to Chaim Kramer's office to pick up my ticket. He laughed as he handed me the ticket and said, "They just had a military coup in the Soviet Union." I thought he was joking. But he was completely serious.

> It was an unimaginable dream that suddenly came true.

"Don't worry, everything will be all right," he assured me. "By the time we go to Uman, it'll be over."

It sounded crazy, but he was right. Glasnost was in full swing, and the coup folded.

In Russia, there were six-foot busts of Lenin everywhere— Lenin, not Marx, because Marx was Jewish. I never imagined that I'd actually be able to travel to Uman for Rosh HaShanah. I had just prayed that someday, somehow, I would be able to travel there. I had friends who couldn't get in. It was an unimaginable dream that suddenly came true.

That year, the Rosh HaShanah gathering was small, perhaps a few thousand people. There was a tremendous feeling of connection with the Rebbe. I thanked God for allowing me to have this special relationship with the *tzaddik*.

The Key To My Soul

Guillermo Beilinson

Guillermo Beilinson lives in La Plata, Argentina, where he heads the Breslov Research Institute's Spanish branch. In the past seventeen years, he has translated nearly thirty of BRI's books into Spanish.

I was raised in a non-religious Jewish home that placed a tremendous emphasis on secular education. My father was born in Russia and my mother's family came from Poland, but we were totally assimilated. Although we were culturally sophisticated, we were absolutely ignorant when it came to our Jewish heritage. Yes, of course I knew that I was Jewish, but I had no idea what that meant. I had never entered a synagogue, nor had I ever met a rabbi!

In my quest for meaning, I studied philosophy at university and was involved with the "hippie generation," including everything that comes with that way of life. I became involved in films and theater, and lived for six years in Venezuela where I tried to find some solid ground as an "artist." Years later, it all ended in absolute rock 'n' roll, nihilism and desperation.

When I was in my thirties and feeling that life was completely meaningless, I discovered Martin Buber's *Tales of the Hasidim*. It touched me in a very deep way. I had always been interested in philosophy, but Chassidut was much deeper and intellectually satisfying than any of the many philosophical works that I had read.

I went to a Jewish bookshop in Buenos Aires to look for more books about Chassidut. All I found was a book about the history of the Chassidic movement, and it was basically anti-Chassidic. But it included many quotes from the rebbes—and that was what I was looking for. Those words...their words...they sounded so intelligent...

The history book of the Chassidic movement included an appendix with a list of nearly twenty Chassidic books that the author had used as sources. I copied the list (of course, I didn't understand the meaning of the words being transliterated from the Hebrew). Months later, while on vacation in Paris, I brought that list to the only bookstore in the Jewish Quarter that sold religious books.

The proprietor told me that he only had books on Breslov Chassidut. I had read about Rebbe Nachman in the history book. There, Breslover chassidim were called the "dead chassidim,"[44] and I wasn't sure if that was what I was looking for. But I purchased the books anyway.

BACK IN BUENOS AIRES, I opened one of the books that I had bought in Paris. The first page was written completely in Hebrew, which was meaningless to me (later, I found out that it was the first page of the *Likutey Moharan*). At that time, I didn't even know how to read the *aleph-bet*. But just looking at those foreign forms stirred something very deep inside me, and I began to cry. I understood that if these letters had such a deep impact on me, then they must contain the key to my innermost soul.

Staring at those meaningless letters, I realized that I had wasted my life because this—my heritage—was mine, yet I did not even have the basic skills necessary to unlock that treasure.

---

44 A derogatory name coined by opponents of Breslov, since the movement, unlike other Chassidic dynasties, was flourishing without a "living" Rebbe.

I closed the book and stopped crying. Then I opened it, looked at the Hebrew letters, and started crying again. Every time I opened the book, I burst into tears. This continued for three days. Now I realize that those tears came from the same source as the tears one sheds (if one merits it) while standing at the *Kotel* or praying at the Rebbe's *tziyun*.

The book contained exactly what I had been searching for. Its title was *Hitbodedut, La Porte du Ciel* ("*Hitbodedut,* The Gate of Heaven"), and it was written by Itzchak Besançon. It spoke about *hitbodedut*, something that I immediately began to do. As I read the book, I realized that Rebbe Nachman was my Rebbe. But though I realized that Rebbe Nachman was my spiritual guide, I was not at all observant.

I read in one of those books something about how letters can save a life. I wrote a letter to Chaim Kramer (whose address I found at the end of one of the books), telling him a bit about myself and how I was drawn to Breslov. He answered me with very encouraging words (it's a pity I lost his letter, because it was an excellent example of how to encourage a *ba'al teshuvah*), together with another book and a cassette of Breslov music.

After that, I started becoming religious. I began studying Hebrew and delving deeper into Torah. Two years later, prior to Rosh HaShanah 1992, Chaim Kramer invited me to join him in Uman. That was something I was waiting for. I already knew about Uman, but it seemed so far away from me. Although I was "religious," I was still not doing everything properly.

On my way to Uman, I stopped in Israel to meet Chaim. He introduced me to his circle of friends. Sitting on the plane to Uman with all the religious people around me, I started to cry. I was overwhelmed that I was actually going to a place where I never dreamed I would ever go. I grasped that the journey to Uman was a journey of the soul rather than a journey of the intellect.

I returned home from Uman with such a strong desire to share what I had received that I started translating the Breslov books into Spanish, and I am still doing this work over seventeen years later. Since that first trip, I travel to Uman for Rosh HaShanah every year.

> Every time
> I opened the book,
> I burst into tears.

It's impossible for me to say what I get from being in Uman. Of course, it's the Rebbe. It's the fulfillment of a year's yearning. It's the friendship forged with people with a common goal. Traveling to Uman keeps me spiritually grounded. Whatever happens, I can say, "But I was in Uman!"

Full Circle

Yonatan Lipshutz

*Yonatan ("Yoni") Lipshutz lives in Tzefat. He is the violinist for
the Simply Tsfat Band.*

Yoni Lipshutz grew up in Tarrytown, New York. As a young child, he
dreamed of playing the violin.

For an entire year, seven days a week, fifty-two weeks of the
year, I begged my parents to send me for violin lessons. I
began studying violin when I was seven, and continued for the
next seventeen years.

In 1984, after Yoni graduated SUNY Purchase with a degree in performing
arts and got married, he and his wife, Talya, began exploring their Jewish
roots.

We decided to "do" the Shabbat and kosher thing. This was
very different from how I had grown up; I don't recall knowing
the difference between Pesach and Rosh HaShanah. Those were
just times that the family got together for a festive meal.

The Lipshutz family slowly grew in their commitment to Torah and *mitzvot*.
At first, they ate only vegetarian at their favorite, non-kosher restaurant
and drove to shul on Shabbat.

Eventually, we realized that Shabbat was an all-or-nothing
venture. I stopped answering the phone on Saturday, and declined

Friday-night gigs and Saturday matinees. But as soon as I stopped performing on Shabbat, I stopped receiving offers for the rest of the week. Left without a source of income, I enrolled in a vocational computer course.

> Yoni found a position as a computer programmer and network engineer in Minneapolis. He sold his expensive violin and used the proceeds to put a down payment on a house there.

I did not miss the Bach, Beethoven or Mozart. As I was reconnecting with my Jewish past, I actually started thinking— no, feeling—how all that musical culture stood by, as a supportive witness, while we walked into the gas chambers.

> But although the Lipshutzes were financially successful ("We had three daughters and three cars") and were religiously observant, they felt something lacking in their lives. It never occurred to them to look into Breslov.

I recall when my wife purchased a new book, *Rabbi Nachman's Tikkun*. It had a picture of a hand on the cover, and of course, being American, we *did* judge the book by its cover. When a member of the Orthodox community saw that book in our home, he shouted, "What are you doing with that? Don't read it! It will make you crazy!" I gave the book away before I even began looking at it.

> As the Lipshutz family grew religiously, they found themselves more and more drawn to Israel.

Every time I recited the blessing *"Boneh Yerushalayim,"*[45] the words stuck in my throat. How could I be so hypocritical as to pray for the rebuilding of Jerusalem when I wasn't doing anything about it? I felt I couldn't just give lip service to an idea.

> The Lipshutzes arrived in Israel on January 1, 1991, two weeks before the start of the Gulf War.

---

45 "Rebuild Jerusalem," the third blessing in the Grace after Meals.

We were Modern Orthodox, black hat with a Zionist tilt. The Jewish Agency sent us to an absorption center where we met people from all over the world. To add to our bewilderment, I went through about five jobs that first year. We were really lost!

It was in the absorption center that Talya started reading about Breslov, and she liked what she read.

She kept seeing Chaim Kramer's name on the books and contacted him. We didn't really know anyone else in Israel that we could contact. She was impressed with their initial conversation and insisted that I get in touch with him.

At that point, the family's main concern was schooling for their three daughters, ages six, three and one and a half.

In the United States, it had been very easy. There was one school; no choice. But in Israel, there are a multitude of choices, and the choice also becomes a political statement.

Yoni and Talya met with Chaim and his wife to discuss their children's schooling.

We met in the Breslov Research Institute's "worldwide headquarters"—really, just a large, walk-in closet. It was a breath of fresh air. We hit it off immediately. Chaim is a long-time Breslover, yet completely down-to-earth. Meeting him made me realize that Breslov is not "crazy" and that traveling to Uman is not a nutty thing to do. Suddenly, traveling to Uman was "on the plate."

Nine months after moving to Israel, Yoni traveled to Uman for Rosh HaShanah.

I've been there every year since. Rebbe Nachman gives people the freedom to be who they really are. A Breslover chassid doesn't have to wear the costume. He doesn't have to fit a particular mold—to wear his hat a certain way, or dress a certain way—to become part of the community. Breslover chassidim are encouraged to be who they are, but to be the *best* of who they are!

Rebbe Nachman's teachings reach out to everyone. When a *ba'al teshuvah* encounters a Rebbe figure, he sees him as a perfect *tzaddik*, completely faultless. Rebbe Nachman is the true *tzaddik*, yet he is very real. He openly

> A Breslover chassid doesn't have to wear the costume.

discusses being down and how to deal with that. It's refreshing to see that despite having dropped low, he attained such tremendous heights.

Traveling to Uman had a tremendous impact on my life. First of all, the fact that my wife and I are still married is thanks to my going to Uman. It made me a different person.

Traveling to Uman also taught me the definition of prayer. Uman gave me an experiential jump-start into the art of connecting to the Almighty. In Breslov, our learning is brought from the sphere of the intellect into the emotions through prayer.

The truth is, I would have never gone to Uman if Talya hadn't urged me to go, and it's only thanks to her that I am able to continue going. But that's because she understands the importance of Rosh HaShanah. She realizes that it's a day of judgment. If a woman's husband is being judged by the Supreme Court, who would she prefer sitting next to him—herself and their children, or the best lawyer in the world? Obviously, she would prefer the best lawyer. On Rosh HaShanah, we are being judged, and we want Rebbe Nachman's promise to act as our advocate! Rosh HaShanah is not a vacation. It's hard work. We're begging for our lives.

> Two years after moving to Israel, the Lipshutz family decided to move to Tzefat.

This was fifteen years after we started the *teshuvah* process. I had become a Breslover chassid, complete with long *peyot*. Suddenly, after all those years of not playing the violin and not even owning a violin, I yearned to make music again. The poignant Breslov *niggunim* (melodies) haunted me. I thought, *If only I had a violin, I would be able to play all those holy niggunim and bring a smile to someone's face.*

Rebbe Nachman often talks about the power of *hitbodedut*. I decided that after seven years of traveling to Uman for Rosh HaShanah, I would go after Pesach with a small group of people so that I could spend more time at the *tziyun* in *hitbodedut*.

There were only twenty-five of us. It was wonderful to be able to spend a week at the *tziyun* without the noise and confusion that so many people bring with them on Rosh HaShanah. The quiet solitude was deafening. Shabbat in Uman was the ultimate. The learning, the singing, the prayers, the *niggunim*—oh, the *niggunim!*—it was beautiful.

After Shabbat, I stood next to the Rebbe's grave and did *hitbodedut*. I prayed, *If only I had a violin, I could play all those beautiful niggunim. After all, what were those seventeen years of learning violin for, if not that?*

Every time I was in Uman for Rosh HaShanah, I saw chassidim purchasing clarinets, flutes and accordions at the local marketplace at ridiculously low prices. But when we arrived after Pesach, there was no market or peddlers trying to sell us things.

I stood by the Rebbe's grave in the pitch-black, freezing-cold night, talking to God. I wanted a sense of direction. What should I be doing with my life? Where was this spiritual journey taking me?

When I finished my *hitbodedut* and left the *tziyun*, I saw a Ukrainian standing outside selling a violin.

Now, after fifteen years of being religious, I was finally beginning my "real" *teshuvah*. Before that, I had devoted seventeen years of my life to playing music for music's sake, but now, with this violin, I would be able to rectify those years and play music for God! I would be able to make people happy with Jewish music.

Uman Is For Everyone

Moshe Hamburg

Moshe Hamburg lives in Ramat Beit Shemesh, Israel, where he studies part-time and works in high-tech sales. He is currently studying to become an Israeli tour guide.

Originally from Los Angeles, California, Moshe went to Southern Connecticut State University in New Haven on a baseball scholarship. At age twenty, he went through what he calls an "early midlife crisis." He had always dreamed of becoming a professional baseball player. Now he realized that he would never make the major leagues, and wondered what he would do for the rest of his life.

I was taking a class at the university called "Transitions," which discussed dealing with life's challenges. The teacher recommended that before entering the job market, we take some time off to travel and see the world. I thought that was a phenomenal idea.

In 1992, I set off. While touring Greece, it occurred to me that since I was so close to Israel, I might as well visit. I spent a week with my relatives in Tel Aviv, eating at the restaurants, touring the sights. It was amazing to see so many Jews in one place. I decided to visit Jerusalem. There, through a series of "coincidences," I ran into an old high-school friend of mine who was studying at a yeshivah for men with limited Jewish backgrounds. He convinced me to try it out.

After one month, I realized that it was time to leave. But although I did not stay at the yeshivah, I felt deeply connected to the Jewish people and wanted to learn more about my heritage. I ended up spending a few months studying at Isralight, a Jewish enrichment program in the Old City, before returning to the United States.

I left Isralight committed to Judaism, but not strictly religious. I was religious enough, however, to tell a girl I was dating that I wouldn't mix meat and milk.

I ended up on New York City's Upper West Side. One day, I went into a pizza place and saw the guy mixing milk and meat onto my pizza. I said to myself, "That's it. No more eating in non-kosher restaurants." After that, I ate only kosher.

My parents were extremely upset at my religious "radicalism." A few months later, when I told them that I was leaving my job to learn in a yeshivah, there were tremendous, *tremendous* fights. When I told my boss that I wanted to take off for a few months to learn in yeshivah, he fired me. That's how I ended up spending the last couple of months before leaving for Israel helping out at the Isralight New York office.

My boss was a Breslover chassid, but he never mentioned that fact to me. Before I left for Israel, he gave me a copy of Rebbe Nachman's *Advice*. I threw it in my backpack and basically forgot about it.

I studied in a large *ba'al teshuvah* yeshivah for two months, but I was looking for something more intimate. I transferred to Shapell's[46] and learned there for a year and a half. Afterward, I returned to the United States and got a summer job working for a doctor in the Catskills. I now identified myself as Orthodox, but I felt I was missing a sense of direction. I had not yet found myself in the religious world.

---

46 Yeshivat Darche Noam—David Shapell College of Jewish Studies, commonly known as Shapell's, was founded in 1978 by Rabbi Chaim Bravender for young men with limited Jewish backgrounds.

Then Rabbi David Aaron, the founder and dean of Isralight, phoned me from Israel. He was in desperate need of a counselor for one of his summer programs. It was starting in Jerusalem in just one week's time, and Rabbi Aaron was not about to accept no for an answer.

I felt deeply connected to the Jewish people.

I met my future wife at Isralight. She was also working in the summer program, as a counselor for the female students. After two months of working together, we started dating. A few months later, we were married.

After our wedding, I studied in a very *litvishe kollel* in Har Nof, a neighborhood in western Jerusalem. But I wasn't learning well, and financially, we weren't making it. We returned to the United States and settled in Passaic, New Jersey.

SINCE MY WIFE IS ALSO FROM LOS ANGELES, we traveled there often to visit our families. My wife's best friend, who had also become religious, insisted that we spend a Shabbat at her rabbi's house. That's how I met Rabbi Elchonon Tauber.

In Rabbi Tauber, I encountered a person who was dedicated and steeped in Torah, and so connected to Rebbe Nachman. He is so, so connected to him, and at the same time, totally solid— solid as a rock.

Rabbi Tauber and I started learning together on the telephone. It was just five minutes at a shot, very simple. We learned *Likutey Moharan* and then, later on, *Sichot HaRan*. I asked him questions; he answered. In addition, a few friends and I started studying Breslov books together. Every once in a while, we even brought a Breslov rabbi to Passaic for a special Breslov Shabbat.

I started learning the Breslov book translated by Rabbi Aryeh Kaplan, which was edited by Rabbi Zvi Aryeh Rosenfeld (*Rabbi Nachman's Wisdom*). I asked myself, "Who is this Rabbi Rosenfeld?" I was fascinated by him. And then I saw a picture of him, and he looked so incredibly normal. So I discovered an entire Breslov track of normalcy.

Passaic is a very *litvishe* town. One Shabbat, a guy walks into shul wearing a *shtreimel* and long *peyot*. I go over to him and say, "I don't know you, but we must learn together."

The man with the *peyot* was a Breslover chassid, Rabbi Elya Succot. He stayed in Passaic for a couple of months. During that time, we would eat the Third Meal of Shabbat together. He was so centered, so focused, so full of *simchah*, yet so, so normal. After meeting him, I wanted to be as deeply connected to Breslov as he was.

THAT SUMMER, MY FRIEND, Tanchum Burton, said to me, "Moshe, we gotta go to Uman for Rosh HaShanah!"

I phoned Rabbi Tauber to ask him what he thought of the idea. He said, "I go every year, and of course, you should go."

But I was worried about how my wife would take the idea of me being away from home for Yom Tov. Rabbi Tauber suggested that she and I phone him to discuss it together. He explained to her what a privilege it was for her to be able to let her husband travel to the Rebbe. I was very lucky that there was no argument.

Many of my friends were shocked that someone who appeared as normal as me would travel to Uman for Rosh HaShanah. When I told the *rav* of my shul in Passaic that I would be in Uman for Rosh HaShanah, he said, "You're going *WHERE*?" When he heard it had to do with Breslov, he explained that Breslov is fringe Judaism, not the real thing. "After all," he added "many great rabbis don't travel to Uman for Rosh HaShanah." I thought, *Yes, they are great rabbis, but they are not my Rebbe.*

The following day, the *rav* phoned and said, "May you go and strengthen yourself, and come back to strengthen me."

Just obtaining the tickets was a tremendous hassle. In the United States, most travel agents do not sell tickets to Ukraine. So I had to travel to Brooklyn to pick up my ticket, which was easier said than done because first I had to locate the guy. Then there was the problem of payment—only cash, no credit cards.

Even before traveling to Uman, I felt as if I were in the Soviet Union!

Then there was the question of food. I made arrangements to eat with Chaim Kramer, but I also bought a meal ticket for the communal dining hall "just in case."

He was so centered, so focused, so full of *simchah*.

By the time I arrived in Uman, I was exhausted from the traveling. But I didn't have time to rest: *Selichot* was in just a few hours. The *davening* was fantastic! Even the food was good. It was a great experience.

I never experienced a tremendous "spiritual high" while I was there. But that's not the reason I went. I went because I have faith in the people I trust, people like Rabbi Tauber, Chaim Kramer and Nosson Maimon, and they told me to come. Rebbe Nachman wrote that "I should come."

And there was the opportunity to meet amazing people. Reb Michel Dorfman, Rabbi Moshe Burstein and Rabbi Elazar Mordekhai Koenig were there. There were representatives from every walk of life, from the non-religious Sephardi to the Torah-observant Jew in Meah Shearim.

I had a good time. There were so many new experiences all at once. I discovered that Uman is a place for fixing things, for attaining true *emunah* and connecting to the *tzaddik*.

Opening My Heart To God

Shimon Elkaslai

Originally from Montreal, Shimon Elkaslai became religious after attending an Arachim seminar.[47] He teaches at Montreal's Breslov Centre.

After I realized that God exists and that I must grow in my Judaism, I saw that if I did it halfway, I'd fall right back. So I went straight to Israel to learn in a yeshivah for a month. Then I returned to Montreal to complete my studies at McGill University. During my last year at the university, I met my wife on a *shiddukh*. We were married in August. Immediately after *sheva berakhot*, we returned to Israel, where I attended yeshivah full-time.

I was very straight, *litvishe* with a Sephardi element—with the kabbalistic spice of the Ben Ish Chai[48]—but all the learning was intellectual, without an emotional element. I wanted to become a Torah scholar, and I was learning around the clock to attain that goal.

---

47 Over 500,000 people worldwide have attended the Arachim seminar, which was developed in Israel in 1979 by a group of scientists and educators. The three-to-five-day retreat includes lectures, workshops and discussion groups to examine basic questions of Jewish outlook.

48 See note 21, p. 51.

I felt akin to a computer—constantly learning, learning, learning. But I was lacking emotion in my relationship with human beings, with my wife, with my children. This was very difficult on me and on the people around me. I realized that I couldn't continue this way and understood that for my Judaism to be real, I needed to create a relationship with God as well as with people.

I advanced very rapidly in my yeshivah studies. After just four years of learning, I was teaching in the yeshivah. I had self-discipline and willpower, and lots of *siyatta diShmaya* (help from Above). But the main thing was missing—a connection with God.

I went to other *yeshivot* to seek what I was lacking. I spoke with great rabbis; I studied different approaches. But I did not find anything that satisfied me.

MY BROTHER-IN-LAW INVITED ME to go with him to Uman for Rosh HaShanah, and I decided to take him up on it for my son's sake. My son was six years old at the time. I knew that Rebbe Nachman made a promise that any child who comes to him before his seventh birthday will be clean from impurity until his marriage.[49] I wanted to protect my son. There are so many terrible things going on in this world.

Before I made that trip to Uman, I was anti-Breslov. I had logical arguments against the whole thing. But after experiencing Rosh HaShanah in Uman, I became a changed person.

It wasn't the *tzaddik* that got to me; it was Rosh HaShanah itself. The prayers, immersing in the *mikveh*, the passion—it's the place to be on Rosh HaShanah. Although in Jerusalem, I had prayed in a beautiful *minyan* where everyone sobbed from the intensity of their emotions, Uman was different. My heart was opened there.

In Uman, I realized that I had been brainwashed against Rebbe Nachman for the last four years. I began learning Breslov

---

49 See note 26, p. 59.

books. I had a study partner in *Likutey Halakhot* and *Likutey Moharan*. As I delved deeper into the Rebbe's words, I realized that these words contained the tools to reach perfection.

After learning in yeshivah for another two years, I returned to Montreal to become the rabbi of a shul. I was the rabbi there for two years, and during that time, there were lots of positive changes in the community. Although most of what I taught in the shul was based on Breslov, I never told anyone. My goal was to bring the people there close to Torah and *mitzvot*.

The first year that I was there, I did not go to Uman for Rosh HaShanah. I was afraid that if I went, I'd lose my job. The second year, I went together with several members of the congregation. The third year, the shul's board of directors told me that if I traveled to Uman for Rosh HaShanah, I would not have a job when I returned. So before Rosh HaShanah, I made a speech explaining the importance of traveling to Uman and informed the congregation that I would be going even if it meant that I would lose my job. Today, I teach working men at the Montreal Breslov Centre every morning from seven-thirty to nine o'clock.

How did going to Uman impact my life? I feel that my connection with Rebbe Nachman is bringing me close to God by giving me the challenges I need to be able to improve myself. When I first became involved with Breslov, I slowed down in my learning. I didn't work so hard at trying to complete the entire *Shas*[50] and *Shulchan Arukh*.[51] I was looking for connection with God, to be able to pray with a full heart and proper intent.

Now I am once again placing an emphasis on my studies; only now the studies are on a much deeper level than before. I'm more in touch with myself, and therefore, my learning has much greater depth.

---

50 An abbreviation for *Shisha Sidarim*, the sixty orders of the Mishnah and Talmud, known collectively as the Gemara.
51 Literally, "Set Table," the Code of Jewish Law compiled by Rabbi Yosef Caro (1488-1575), the benchmark of *halakhah* for all Jews.

The Excitement Is Back

Yossi Katz

*Originally from Toronto, Canada, Yossi Katz resides in Lakewood,
New Jersey, where he is studying to be a rabbi.*

My parents were not religious. It wasn't as if they had negative
feelings toward Judaism; they just didn't know much.

In 1995, when I was twelve years old, my mother suggested
that I attend the only shul in our area—which was really a *kiruv*
(Jewish outreach) shul—in preparation for my bar mitzvah. I
went on Simchat Torah night, and had such a great time that
I returned the following morning. One of the families there
invited me for the meal. I enjoyed it so much that I asked my
mother's permission to spend the following Shabbat with them.

The family was overjoyed to have me. For the next two
years, I spent every single Shabbat with this family. After my bar
mitzvah, I wanted to study in a yeshivah, but my parents insisted
that I remain in public school until ninth grade. For ninth grade,
I transferred to Yeshivas Ner Yisroel in Toronto. After graduation,
I traveled to Israel to learn in the Mir.[52]

---

52 The Mir Yeshiva, with branches in Jerusalem and Brooklyn, New York, is
one of the largest *yeshivot* in the world.

I LOVED MY STUDIES, but I felt that my learning was missing warmth. We learned *mussar*, which makes you aware of where you are lacking, and I wanted something more positive.

One day, I felt like relaxing with an English book. I borrowed Rabbi Yaakov Meir Schechter's *In All Your Ways* from my roommate, who was a Breslover chassid. I was completely taken aback by the book's totally different outlook on the world. I had a lot of questions about what I read; it was so different from what I was used to. I spent a lot of time talking with one of the Breslover chassidim who learned with me in the Mir. We would walk to the *Kotel* together and I would ask him all my questions.

That's when my real interest in Breslov began. The chassid introduced me to Chaim Kramer, and I began attending Chaim's weekly *Likutey Moharan* class.

CHAIM ASKED ME IF I was going to Uman for Rosh HaShanah. I really wanted to go, yet I was afraid of what my friends in yeshivah would think. In the end, I decided to go.

I called my parents, who in the meantime had also become observant. They gave their consent, but said that I'd have to come up with the money. Earlier that year, before leaving Toronto to study in Israel, I had injured my back in a serious car accident. I had only then received the insurance compensation. This covered the cost of my ticket to Uman.

The trip itself was amazing. In Israel, the flights to Uman left from a special terminal used only for charter flights. It was packed with singing and dancing chassidim. The energy was incredible. When the plane landed, everyone started dancing. In the taxi, the closer we got to Uman, the more our excitement grew. And then in Uman...There were so many different types of people, such a variety of ages!

It's difficult to find a Rebbe who fits one's personality, but Rebbe Nachman is for everyone. So many different types of Jews come to Uman. So many types of people join together for the same purpose in a city so old and decrepit. It was there, in Uman, that I realized I had found my Rebbe.

Rosh HaShanah and Yom Kippur in yeshivah are somewhat depressing. But in Uman, although the services were very serious and many of us were sobbing from emotion, there was an all-pervading feeling of *simchah*. I've never experienced such a combination of seriousness and joy before. It was unbelievable.

As a result of being in Uman, I search for meaning in my mitzvah observance. When I first became religious, I experienced tremendous excitement in doing *mitzvot*, but over time, it became almost mechanical. The excitement had faded away. Traveling to Uman brought that excitement back.

> There was an all-pervading feeling of *simchah*.

Search For Meaning

Ozer Bergman

Raised in a Modern Orthodox home, Ozer Bergman's search for truth brought him to Breslov. He has spent the past thirty years teaching Breslov Chassidut to Jews of every stream, in English, Hebrew and Yiddish, on three continents. He is also a writer and editor for the Breslov Research Institute.

I grew up in Woodmere, Long Island. My family is Modern Orthodox, and I attended yeshivah schools through high school. But although I was intelligent and did well in the secular studies, I didn't really pay much attention to the Torah learning.

By the time I finished high school, I had had enough of Judaism. But my Jewish soul was searching for meaning. I tried to find it in philosophy.

I attended Johns Hopkins University, majoring in philosophy. Although I discovered that philosophy was not the truth I was searching for, I was privileged to have Rabbi Dr. David Gottleib[53]

---

53 Dr. Gottlieb later became a senior faculty member at Yeshivat Ohr Somayach in Jerusalem, where he inspires students with his lectures on Jewish philosophy.

as one of my professors. He introduced me to the Bostoner Rebbe.[54]

At that time, I was far from observant. It didn't take much work to get good grades at university, so I had plenty of time to search for meaning. I experimented with drugs, and they confirmed two things: there is a meaning to life, and drugs aren't the way to get to it.

The Bostoner Rebbe understood where I was holding spiritually, and tried to convince me to study in Boston so that I could be close to him. I transferred to Harvard and started attending his shul, the New England Chassidic Center. But although I was basically *shomer Shabbat* and had stopped taking drugs, my Weltanschauung was far from Orthodox, let alone Chassidic, in any sense of the word. Intellectually, I was not learned enough to really understand the Bostoner Rebbe's teachings, but I was getting personal guidance and a sense of community from living in a close, supportive environment.

IN 1976, JUST A COUPLE OF MONTHS after I started attending the Chassidic Center, a *chassidishe* young man came to the shul to sell books. Among the books he was selling was a paperback edition of *Rabbi Nachman's Wisdom*. It said $2.95 on the cover, but he only wanted a dollar for it. A bargain! I bought it.

The book spoke to me. I read it from cover to cover and couldn't put it down. I still carry the original Hebrew edition with me wherever I go. I couldn't believe that Judaism had all this to offer. I was particularly intrigued by Rebbe Nachman's teachings on *hitbodedut*—the idea that I could talk to God directly,

---

54 Grand Rabbi Levi Yitzchok Horowitz (b. 1921) carries the distinction of being the first American-born Chassidic rebbe. Son and successor of Grand Rabbi Pinchos Dovid Horowitz, who founded the Chassidut in Boston, Massachusetts, Rabbi Levi Yitzchak established the New England Chassidic Center to attract the many Jewish students who attended local universities like Harvard and Massachusetts Institute of Technology (MIT). He also founded an American-style Chassidic community in the Har Nof neighborhood of Jerusalem.

in my own words, and in this way, build a relationship with my Creator.

For the first time, I was reading something I could understand that spoke directly about *emunah*. I was moved by the simple truth of the Rebbe's words.[55]

The following year, I returned to Johns Hopkins for one final semester to complete my B.A. After graduating in the winter of 1978, I traveled to Israel to study in Yeshivat Dvar Yerushalayim.[56]

I ATTENDED DVAR YERUSHALAYIM through the summer and then transferred to Ohr Somayach's[57] Zichron Yaakov branch. It was there, in Zichron Yaakov, that I realized I needed to be Breslov.

I noticed that as long as I studied *Rabbi Nachman's Wisdom* regularly, my Judaism—and my life—went smoothly. But whenever I stopped, everything fell apart. I would feel that my life was meaningless, and although I continued to do everything that I was supposed to do, my actions were less than mechanical and I felt deflated. I understood that I needed to continue learning the Rebbe's books and build a connection with Breslov.

While studying in Ohr Somayach, I met my wife, Udel. We were married in the United States in April 1979 and returned to Israel the following summer. For the first half a year, we lived in Jerusalem. I learned in a yeshivah and attended the local Breslov shul. That's where I met Chaim Kramer, head of the Breslov Research Institute, and many other Breslover chassidim that I am still close to today.

---

55 Interestingly, a couple of years earlier, when Ozer Bergman had worked as a waiter at a Modern Orthodox resort, a *chassidishe* man came to the resort to sell religious books. Ozer wanted to buy a present for his brother, Symcha, who was already religious and learning in a yeshivah at the time. He picked out a book that he could afford, having no idea what he was buying. It turned out to be Rebbe Nachman's *Sefer HaMidot*. His brother eventually became a Breslover chassid.

56 See note 8, p. 25.

57 See note 42, p. 87.

But Jerusalem is an expensive city, and we were unable to make ends meet. We moved back to Zichron Yaakov, where I continued my studies at Ohr Somayach.

> I was moved by the simple truth of the Rebbe's words.

We remained in Zichron for close to four years. The community there was extremely *litvishe*, yet I was "into" Chassidut. I was wearing Chassidic garb, praying the Chassidic *nusach* (order of prayers), and trying to immerse in the *mikveh* daily. I encountered a lot of opposition, some of it well-meaning, all of it based on ignorance. People made fun of what they termed my Chassidic "*shtick*" and told me stupid jokes about chassidim.

I bought more Breslov books, *Sippurey Ma'asiyot* and *Likutey Moharan*, and learned them daily. For two months, I even studied *Likutey Moharan* with a study partner, but I suspect that the yeshivah was using my study partner as a way to monitor me, to make sure I didn't go "overboard." I wanted to learn the Rebbe's Torah because I saw the results, and the more I learned, the more I understood and the deeper I got into Breslov.

I was searching for guidance in Chassidut. Someone told me about a Chassidic rebbe in Bnei Brak. I spent hours waiting for a private meeting with him. When I told him that I wanted to learn about Breslov, he basically pushed me off and told me to come back after Yom Tov. I was extremely disappointed.

By the time I finished speaking with that rebbe, it was very late and I had missed the last bus to Zichron Yaakov. So I spent the night in Bnei Brak in the home of an acquaintance. He suggested that I speak with Rabbi Nosson Liebermench, a Breslov elder who lived there.

Rabbi Liebermench literally breathed new life into me with his encouragement and words of support. I continued turning to him for guidance, and that relationship continues to this day. I was particularly impressed with his humility. He is a tremendous Torah scholar, yet he views himself as being nothing out of the ordinary.

At one point, I spoke to Rabbi Nachman Bulman[58]—who was then forming a community in Migdal HaEmek, a small town near Afula in northern Israel—about my connection with Breslov. Since I was a fairly recent *ba'al teshuvah* and new to everything, I was very insecure about what I was doing. Instead of telling me to stay away from Breslov, Rabbi Bulman told me that if I wanted to be a Breslover chassid, I should do it within the structure of a community, not alone.

So after living in Zichron for close to four years, we moved back to Jerusalem. My brothers, Symcha and Yehoshua (who passed away twenty years ago), were both studying in Jerusalem. I prayed in the Breslov shul and resumed my friendships with the Breslover chassidim there. Eventually, I started studying in the Bostoner *kollel* and remained there for four years. During the half-hour *mussar seder* (learning session), I studied *Likutey Halakhot* and later, *Meshivat Nefesh*. This learning session literally kept me going.

Life is challenging and overwhelming, and there were times I wanted to admit defeat. But learning the Rebbe's Torah as brought down by his disciple, Reb Noson, replenished my *emunah* and gave me the strength to hang on and continue.

THE FIRST TIME I WENT TO UMAN was just before Pesach 1985, when the Ukraine was still under Communist rule. I went with my brother, Symcha, and three other American Breslover chassidim.

We flew to Bucharest, Romania. The plan was to take a train from Bucharest to Kiev, and then, in Kiev, to request a visa to travel to Uman.

The plane to Bucharest was almost completely empty. One of the other passengers was a Jewish fellow from Queens, New York, who worked at the U.S. embassy in Bucharest as the personal

---

58 Rabbi Nachman Bulman (1925-2002) was an influential, American-born rabbi, teacher, writer and translator. He established several English-speaking Jewish communities in America and Israel.

secretary for the ambassador's deputy. We spoke together for most of the flight.

In Bucharest, the clerks at passport control refused to allow us into the country. They kept saying, "We know you guys already. We know what you're up to. Your passports are all counterfeits."

> The plan was to take a train from Bucharest to Kiev.

The accusation was false. Although other Breslover chassidim had traveled to Uman on counterfeit American passports, ours were completely legitimate.

We were in a real bind. The plane that had brought us to Bucharest had already returned to Israel. The next flight would be leaving in several days' time, and the officials at the airport expected us to remain in the airport waiting room until then. We had visas to enter the Soviet Union, but in order to use the visas, we had to be in Kiev by the following night; otherwise, the visas would become invalid. To get to Kiev, we had to catch our train. With such a huge delay, it would take a miracle for us to get to the train station in time. We wanted to call the U.S. embassy and ask someone to advocate on our behalf, but to get to a telephone, we first had to pass through customs.

We started reciting Psalms and *Shemot HaTzaddikim*. Meanwhile, a diplomat from the British embassy entered our section of the airport to wait for his wife, who was arriving on a different flight. One of the people in our group approached him, explained our situation, and asked him to contact the fellow from Queens whom I had met on the plane.

About an hour and a half after the British chap left, our contact at the U.S. embassy arrived with his superior, the deputy ambassador. With them to vouch for us, we were waved through passport control. But now that we were out of the airport, we still needed a miracle to get to the train station in time to catch our train to Kiev.

Because of a gas shortage, there was only one taxi waiting at the airport, and there were too many of us to fit into it. The

American diplomat offered to drive some of us to the train station.

The station was enormous. When we arrived, we realized what a real miracle it was that the diplomats had accompanied us—we didn't know a word of Romanian, and the station was confusing. Without them there to help us, we would have never found the right track. One of the diplomats brought us to the train while the other raced to the ticket counter to buy our tickets, and we succeeded in boarding our train.

THE RUSSIAN-ROMANIAN BORDER STATION was in a small town called Yeush (which, when translated into Hebrew, means "Despair"). In addition to checking our passports, the train wheels were changed there.[59] While everyone else remained on the train, our little group was taken to an enormous waiting room—a huge room with no windows and only a broken clock to tell the time—for a baggage inspection.

The inspection, which turned into an interrogation, lasted several hours. We told Bill, the soldier in charge, that we lived in Brooklyn. Then he discovered my Israeli identification card. After that, he was positive that we were not American citizens and that we were trying to enter the country on false passports. At one point, he walked away from me and then quickly turned around and said, "Symcha!" (my brother's name) to throw me off track. But I kept my cool and immediately replied, "Ozer."

We arrived at our hotel in Kiev on Tuesday night. On Wednesday morning, we applied for a visa to Uman. In the Intourist office, we saw a car-rental advertisement and put in a request to rent a car, but the clerk responded, "Nyet (No)." On Thursday morning, we received our visa to Uman. On Thursday afternoon, we traveled to Uman with our Intourist guide.

59 To prevent foreign armies from invading, the Soviets set the train rails in their empire to a nonstandard width. When friendly trains came and went, they had to stop to change their wheels.

116

It was extremely cold, and we were fasting because we didn't want to eat until after going to the gravesite. The Intourist guide left us at the *tziyun*, and we presented the woman who lived in the adjacent house with a bottle of vodka and a few yards of material.

> I was too numb from the cold to really feel anything.

I was too numb from the cold to really feel anything, except the cold. I certainly didn't feel ecstasy. But when I prostrated myself on the *tziyun*, I sensed that I was coming home, *mamash* coming home. It was an inner, warm feeling, and definitely supernatural. The word that comes closest to describing that experience would be "ethereal."

Today, too, whenever I prostrate myself on the *tziyun*, I have that same feeling, a sense of coming home, of being alone with the Rebbe. Just me and the Rebbe.

THE NEXT TIME I TRAVELED TO UMAN was for the first official Rosh HaShanah gathering in 1989. It was relatively small, only around 1,000 people. But we considered it huge! One of the chassidim there told me, "There will come a time when we'll say, 'I remember when there were only 2,000 people in Uman for Rosh HaShanah.'" We laughed.

There are many facets to traveling to Uman. One is being present at the *tziyun* and saying *viduy devarim* (verbal confession) in front of the Rebbe.[60] Another facet is that as a chassid, I obey

---

60 It is a positive commandment to confess one's sins (*Rambam, Yad HaChazakah, Hilkhot Teshuvah* 1:1). It was customary for several of the Chassidic masters, including the Baal Shem Tov himself, to have the chassid confess before him. The *tzaddik* would then direct the follower to perform certain devotions according to the needs of that chassid's rectification. As explained in *Likutey Moharan* I, 4, confession is a recognition of the sin, but the person who is repenting still needs new direction in his life. This was one of the reasons why the Chassidic masters asked their followers for confession. Admitting the sin to them was akin to asking for direction.

my Rebbe. My Rebbe, Rebbe Nachman, told his chassidim to travel to Uman to be with him for Rosh HaShanah. So even if I am not interested in going, I go because my Rebbe told me to go. We have no idea what is really going on there, in Uman, below the surface. I trust my Rebbe's judgment; he was much smarter than I am! Of course, I come out cleaner—at least until I blow it the next time. Then there are the extras: renewing old friendships, getting to see my brother (who lives in Flatbush).

My connection to the Rebbe and to Uman has grown deeper over the years. I come to appreciate it more with each passing year, and I can't wait to go again.

There Are No Coincidences

Yaron Jackson

*Yaron Jackson lives with his family in Tzefat, Israel. He works
in real estate and studies part-time in a yeshivah.*

When I was growing up, I never realized that I was a Jew. It
wasn't that it was kept a secret. My mother told me that she
had some Jewish blood, but then again, I had some Indian blood
on my father's side, and just like having Indian blood didn't
make me an Indian, it never occurred to me that having Jewish
blood would make me Jewish. I grew up without any religion
and viewed myself as a regular, red-blooded American.

When I was in my early twenties, someone mentioned to me
that my mother was Jewish because her mother was Jewish—
which meant that I was Jewish. I accepted it as a fact, and when
people asked me about my religion, I'd tell them that I was
Jewish (after all, I didn't have any other religious affiliation). But
I didn't really know anything about it, and couldn't care less.

When I was around thirty, I met Laya, a wonderful woman
who happened to be Jewish and who would eventually become
my wife. The person who introduced us said, "Laya, you should
go out with Tyrone—he's Jewish!" At that point, Laya was already
lighting Shabbat candles and knew that she wanted to raise
children with a strong Jewish identity. It didn't matter to her if
she married a Jew, though, since she knew her children would

be Jewish no matter what. But her parents had become religious, and for them, it was very important that their daughter marry a Jew. They were happy that I was in on a (very important) technicality!

We had no idea where the journey would take us. Laya was teaching at a Hebrew school, listening to tapes of *shiurim* her mother sent her and reading books about Judaism. I went "drumming" in the woods (like the Native Americans). We were each trying to grow spiritually, only Laya started becoming religious on me, and I wasn't at all interested.

I tried to go along with her. She didn't force anything on me, but when she threw *mikveh*[61] at me, I was, well, to say the least, *shocked*! I remember at least one tearful discussion that I had with a rabbi, explaining that I wasn't willing to conform to the way she wanted me to live.

Thank God, I followed in my wife's footsteps, although I was always a few steps behind her. I had to take things at my own pace. That worked for us. She honored my process and I honored hers. Together we grew spiritually as we slowly kept more and more *mitzvot*.

WHEN OUR OLDEST SON WAS FOUR YEARS OLD, we took a family trip to Disney World in Orlando, Florida. My wife was already keeping Shabbat, but I wasn't yet there. With his *peyot* and yarmulke, our son definitely looked Jewish.

In Disney World, we noticed a religious couple heading into the Jungle Show. We were excited to see someone so obviously Jewish. My wife ran up to them, saying, "Hey, we'd love to sit with you," so we sat near each other. At the end of the show, we spent some time introducing ourselves and talking. The husband asked my wife, "Did you ever hear of Rebbe Nachman?"

My wife responded, "Oh, I *love* Rebbe Nachman!" When he asked her how she knew of Rebbe Nachman, she told him the

---

61 This refers to the laws of family purity.

titles of the Breslov books that she had read. He took out his card and presented it to her. She looked at it and exclaimed, "You're the publisher?" She was speaking to Chaim Kramer of the Breslov Research Institute.

> My wife was already keeping Shabbat, but I wasn't yet there.

Back home, my wife kept in contact with Chaim. He even came to visit us in Denver on two different occasions and both times, he stayed in our house. That's when I really got to know him. We became very close friends. He taught me about the mitzvah of *tefilin* and bought me my first pair.

WHEN OUR SON WAS EIGHT YEARS OLD, my wife heard that Rebbe Nachman had promised that if you take your young son to Uman, he will get that child into *Olam Haba* (the World to Come) "even if he has to pull him out of Gehinnom by his *peyot!*" The next time she spoke with Chaim, she said, "Had we known what the Rebbe said about bringing a boy to Uman before the age of seven,[62] I would have made sure that my son went last year."

Chaim responded, "Although you missed the age by a year, I guarantee that if you send your son to Uman, the Rebbe's promise will still be valid."

When my wife heard that, she was adamant that I take our son to Uman. She rarely insists on anything, but she viewed this as something positive that we could do to help our son grow strong on a Torah path. I really had no desire to travel to Uman. As a matter of fact, I wouldn't have gone even if the trip were free. But I took my son to make my wife happy.

We went for Rosh HaShanah. I really had no idea what I was getting myself into. It reminded me a little of a Grateful Dead concert. I felt very different from the people around me. Spiritually, nothing major happened, and I didn't feel any connection to the Rebbe. But it was a real adventure, traveling

---

62 See note 26, p. 59.

halfway across the world to jump up and down with 20,000 other Jews!

The entire time I was there, Chaim took care of me as if I were his own child. He did everything possible to make me and my son comfortable. We stuck with him the entire Yom Tov.

That was my one and only trip to Uman. Five years ago, in 2003, we moved to Tzefat, and in the last few years, I've become much closer to Rebbe Nachman's teachings and Breslov in general. So although I don't consider myself a Breslover chassid, I definitely have a strong affinity to Breslov.

My son has wonderful memories of that trip to Uman. Although he, too, does not define himself as a Breslover chassid, he feels a close attachment to the Rebbe's teachings. We are a simple family, and my wife and I are so grateful for our connection to Chaim and the teachings of Rebbe Nachman.

Breaking Through The Barriers

Simcha Moskowitz

Simcha Moskowitz (a pseudonym) is married with four children. He lives in Jerusalem, where he studies full-time in a litvishe kollel.

I was born in the early 1970s and grew up in a very religious, *litvishe* home, one that placed great emphasis on the intellectual aspect of Torah study. Both my parents stem from what can only be described as royal lineage. My paternal grandfather, a well-known *litvishe rav*, studied under the saintly Chofetz Chaim[63]; my father studied in prominent *litvishe yeshivot*. My maternal great-grandfather was one of the founders of a prestigious *litvishe* yeshivah.

I was very, very close to my paternal grandfather. He was a great rabbi, a true genius. He passed away when I was seventeen. I was in the room with him when he died. Although he was far from young and had a heart condition, for me, his death was completely sudden and unexpected.

---

63 Rabbi Yisrael Meir Kagan (1838-1933), called "the Chofetz Chaim" after the title of his first work on the laws of guarding one's tongue, was a *rosh yeshivah* in Radin, Poland, and a widely influential rabbi in the late nineteenth and early twentieth centuries.

After my grandfather passed away, I felt a tremendous void in my life. I completely immersed myself in my studies and had almost nothing to do with the social life at the yeshivah. I tried to cram as much Torah as possible into my head, hoping that that would fill the emotional void.

After graduating yeshivah high school, I left New York to study in an out-of-town yeshivah. There, as in the previous yeshivah, I was successful in my Torah study, studying long hours and really advancing. Yet despite all my learning, I continued to feel empty. Something was missing.

I WAS FOCUSING ALMOST EXCLUSIVELY on the intellectual side of Torah study, while paying little attention to developing my relationship with God. I thought that I could become close to God solely through learning Torah, while playing down the importance of praying and creating a viable connection to God. I was so ignorant of Chassidut that I viewed the Baal Shem Tov as no more than someone who loved to eat kugel and dance and work in *kiruv* (Jewish outreach).

A number of *chassidishe bachurim* were studying in the yeshivah. For the first time in my life, I had friends who were chassidim. I also started reading books by Rabbi Eliyahu Dessler,[64] and on Shabbat afternoons, I attended a *mussar shmooze* (talk) delivered by one of Rabbi Dessler's close students. I was amazed that *mussar*—something that I had always thought of as simplistic—could be so intellectually stimulating.

I was literally studying around the clock. In the predawn darkness, I had a regular study session with another student. He

---

64 Rabbi Eliyahu Eliezer Dessler (1892-1953) was a *rav* in London and later *mashgiach ruchani* (spiritual supervisor) in the Gateshead Yeshivah in England. In 1947, he traveled to Bnei Brak and assumed a leading position in the Ponevezh Yeshivah. He was a student of Rabbi Simcha of Kelm, a master of the *Mussar* Movement which stressed the study of ethical texts for personal and spiritual growth. His students collected his teachings and published them in *Michtav Me'Eliyahu* ("Letters from Eliyahu").

was amazing, constantly delving into his studies. Today, he is a tremendous Torah scholar living in Jerusalem. The yeshivah's administration, however, was wary of him. They suspected that he was becoming close to Breslov, and even questioned me about it. The administration also tried to discourage me from my interest in Chassidut. I was told that since I was born *litvishe*, it meant that God wanted me to remain *litvishe*. If I left my *litvishe* upbringing to become a chassid, and then failed in fulfilling my *tafkid* (mission) in life, I would have to make an accounting to Heaven on why I changed my religious orientation.

> The *litvishe* way of serving God was not working for me.

After a year and a half at this yeshivah, I decided to travel to Israel to learn in the Mir.[65] There, the feeling that something was lacking in my life became even more pronounced.

I understood that the *litvishe* way of serving God was not working for me and started asking the *chassidishe bachurim* about Chassidut. I wanted to understand the theory behind it, the structure, the system. The boys spoke to me about the warmth of Chassidut, but although that was very attractive, it was not a compelling reason to change my *mesorah*, my family tradition.

One of my friends directed me to a Chassidic rabbi who was connected with Breslov. I asked this rabbi many questions, especially about the differences between the various systems of Torah-true Judaism. He responded with a question of his own: "You seem to know a lot about systems for serving God, but how far have you, personally, progressed in any of these systems?"

When I explained that I hadn't succeeded in getting very far, he replied, "The Baal Shem Tov[66] and others like him also had a

---

65 See note 52, p. 107.

66 Rabbi Yisrael ben Eliezer (1698-1760), known as the Baal Shem Tov or "Master of the Good Name," was the founder of the Chassidic movement. He was Rebbe Nachman's great-grandfather.

problem. The system did not work for them, so they created a new system, a new path in serving God. They were successful with that path. Maybe you should abandon your need to understand everything. Rather than insist on an explanation, accept that they found a path that works, and try it out."

I thought about this rabbi's answer during the next week and realized he was right. I began to study Chassidic books, including those written by Rebbe Nachman of Breslov.

It wasn't long before I was extremely enthusiastic about Chassidut and went into it full steam ahead. I had found the path that was right for me, and I was determined to teach the world about it. But when a top-notch yeshivah student "goes bonkers" and starts doing all sorts of strange things, people get upset. A good friend of mine warned me, "The question is not what you do, it's *how* you do it. Don't make a lot of noise." But I did not heed his warning.

WHEN I CAME HOME FOR PESACH that spring, my father was furious. I had never seen him like that before. Screaming at the top of his lungs, he asked me, "What's wrong with Rabbi Aharon Kotler?[67] What's wrong with the Brisker Rav?"[68] He felt that by getting involved with Chassidut, I was turning my back on everything I had been taught. I later found out that one of his main worries was that I was becoming extreme, and that I might even get involved with Breslov.

---

67 Rabbi Aharon Kotler (1891-1962) was a prominent Lithuanian rabbi who helped lead *yeshivot* in Slutzk and Kletzk before World War II; he subsequently introduced the concept of full-time Torah study to American students with his establishment of Beth Medrash Govoha in Lakewood, N.J. in 1943. That yeshivah is still thriving today under the leadership of Rabbi Kotler's grandson, Rabbi Aryeh Malkiel Kotler, and three of his grandsons-in-law.

68 Rabbi Yitzchak Zev Soloveitchik (1886-1959), who succeeded his father, Reb Chaim Brisker, as *Rav* of the Lithuanian town of Brisk (Brest) and subsequently re-established the Brisker Yeshivah in Jerusalem after World War II. He perpetuated the "Brisker method" of Gemara study, also called *lamdos* (analytical study), developed by his father.

My father was close friends with the *rosh yeshivah* of a certain *litvishe* yeshivah, and sent me there to be "re-educated." Although I was determined not to give in, I wasn't openly rebellious. The *rosh yeshivah*, a very wise person whom I highly admired, helped me to understand my father's point of view and how to be careful not to antagonize him.

> When I came home for Pesach, my father was furious.

Many of the things that I had gotten used to doing—such as immersing in the *mikveh* each morning prior to morning prayers—were unavailable to me at this new yeshivah. I tried to bring some *chassidishe* spirit into my Shabbat and organized a group of boys to get together Friday night to sing and talk about Chassidut. I received tremendous *chizuk* (strength and encouragement) from these weekly get-togethers.

One day, one of the other *bachurim* mentioned to me that he had discovered a book that I might find interesting, hidden in the back of a dorm closet. It was Rebbe Nachman's *Likutey Etzot*. It meant a lot for me to have that book during that bleak period. When I left the yeshivah, I put it back where the boy had found it so that if another person would need it, God would lead him to discover it, just as He had led me to discover it.

At the end of the semester, the *rosh yeshivah* told my father that he, the *rosh yeshivah*, would not be able to make me into a Litvak, but it was more likely that I'd turn the *rosh yeshivah* into a chassid!

I was seriously considering going against my father's wishes and returning to Israel to learn for the next semester. My roommate was very close with a *chassidishe* rebbe—let's call him Rebbe X—and spoke to him about the conflict between my father and me. Rebbe X wrote me a beautiful letter, saying that it would be a mistake for me to go against my father's wishes so blatantly. It was obvious from the quotes he used to make his point that he learned Breslov books and was a great admirer of Rebbe Nachman.

The letter convinced me to remain in America. Since my father and I were unable to agree on a yeshivah for the coming semester, I spent the month of Elul with my grandmother in Monsey and learned in a yeshivah there. Unbeknownst to my father, I also spent a lot of time in the local Breslov shul.

After the holidays, I attended the Stolin Yeshivah in Boro Park. While I was there, I often sneaked out to *chassidishe tischen* and had some amazing conversations with Rebbe X. He showed me that in my youthful enthusiasm, I was in danger of becoming an extremist. I was willing to accept what he said because he was, so to speak, in my camp. Rebbe X also explained to my father that my becoming a chassid was not the worst thing in the world, and that since my father wouldn't be able to change me, he should stop trying.

That year, the Stolin Yeshivah sent the yeshivah boys to Russia to be counselors in a camp run by the Stoliner chassidim. Rebbe X urged me to go, adding that while I was in Russia, I could also travel to Rebbe Nachman's *tziyun* in Uman.

THAT WAS THE SUMMER OF 1996. Upon arriving in Uman, I felt as if I were breaking through tremendous barriers. The *tziyun* was still in the Ukrainian woman's yard, and I was worried that she would come out to bother us while we were praying. As I found out later, she did come out and even screamed at our group, but I was so immersed in my prayers that I didn't even realize she was there!

A few years later, I traveled to Uman with Rebbe X. Rebbe X encouraged me to learn Breslov books and spend time in *hitbodedut*. Although he did not encourage me to become a Breslover chassid, he urged me to follow Rebbe Nachman's directives. I basically became a Rebbe X chassid.

I married in 1998 and joined Rebbe X's *kollel* in Boro Park. I continued learning there for six years until 2004, when something happened that made me realize that my guide and mentor, Rebbe X, was also a human being with human frailties. It's not that he did anything wrong, but he was not the superhuman figure that I had imagined him to be.

Around this time, I ended up sitting next to a Breslover chassid at a *sheva berakhot*, and the two of us began speaking about Breslov. He urged me to come to a Torah class that had just started in the Breslov shul in Boro Park.

> Spending time in *hitbodedut* opened new frontiers for me.

The first time I came to the class was on Chanukah. Although I didn't realize it, that evening they were making a *yahrtzeit seudah* (memorial meal) in memory of Reb Avraham b'Reb Nachman. I was very impressed with the learning, which was replete with many stories about Rebbe Nachman and Reb Noson and showed me the flavor of Breslov. It taught me how to *live* Breslov.

I became close with the people in the Breslov shul. They organized groups of men to go out to Marine Park before dawn for *hitbodedut*, and I joined them. I discovered that spending time in *hitbodedut* opened new frontiers for me, as it does for many others. As a result of the time spent in *hitbodedut*, I realized that many of my preconceived notions about Judaism and Chassidut were incorrect.

I realized that Breslov is a way of life, that it's much deeper than just intellectual concepts. Until I had real contact with the chassidim, I viewed Breslov as important teachings that were written over a hundred years ago. Now I realized that it was a practical and vibrant lifestyle.

I never imagined that I'd ever consider myself a Breslover chassid and travel to Uman for Rosh HaShanah. In many circles, Breslov has a bad reputation, and there are lots of people who would be embarrassed to consider themselves part of it. But the more time I spent in *hitbodedut*, the more I realized that I didn't have to live inside the box.

Around that time, a very special Breslover chassid came from Israel to America to raise money to cover medical expenses.

Since he was not very successful at fundraising, he spent hours each day learning in my *kollel*, and we ended up having many conversations about Breslov. I invited the chassid to spend Shabbat with us. My wife was very impressed with him, which gave her a positive outlook toward Breslov.

Before Rosh HaShanah, my wife said to me, "You're probably going to Uman for Rosh HaShanah." She gave me her total support, which made my decision to travel to Uman much easier.

While in Uman, I spent a lot of time *davening* and doing *hitbodedut*. Although I had been in Uman twice before, this was the first time that I was there as a Breslover chassid. I felt that I was taken up another step on the path that Rebbe Nachman has set out for us to become better, more refined Jews.

THE WHOLE CONCEPT OF TRAVELING to Uman for Rosh HaShanah is beyond our understanding, but I know that it's part of my path in becoming close to God. In becoming a Breslover chassid and traveling to Uman, I accomplished something that I never dreamed I would accomplish. I was able to do it through *hitbodedut* and trust in God. None of the imagined catastrophes occurred. To this day, this experience gives me great encouragement to forge ahead in my *avodat HaShem* and not be discouraged by seeming difficulties.

Today, I live in Jerusalem and study full-time in a mainstream *litvishe kollel*. I view myself as a full-fledged Breslover chassid. I hope that my children will continue in this path. Over the years, Rebbe Nachman's teachings have encouraged me to continue. I hope to be able to spread these teachings to others, to give others the encouragement that I found when I so sorely needed it.

My Name Is Gavriel Aryeh
ben Avraham Avinu

Gavriel Sanders

A former Christian missionary, Gavriel Sanders now lectures internationally as a "missionary" for Judaism. He lives in Far Rockaway, New York.

My journey from evangelical Christianity to observant Judaism was anything but smooth. Having embraced a total belief in the Christian gospel at the age of sixteen, I spent twenty years convinced that there was only one valid path to God. It was exclusively through faith in J.C.

My early religious exposure was to my mother's Catholic heritage. While I entered public school in the third grade, I well remember the fear-driven, punishment-laced indoctrination I received in my early school years from the nuns and priests. The notion of God I envisioned in those years was more akin to Godzilla: angry, fire-breathing, destructive and unappeasable.

My parents had divorced when I was quite young. Raised nomadically by my mother, I rarely saw my father. I went to a different school each year, sometimes twice in a year. I was the perennial new kid with no old friends. My mother remarried, more than once, and a half-sister and half-brother were added to our fractured family.

We moved from Georgia to Florida and then on to Texas. The year was 1968. I had dropped out of tenth grade. Martin Luther King, Jr. had just been assassinated. Bobby Kennedy would be next. While working at Central Supply at Baylor Medical Center in Dallas, I connected with the free-thinking street people branded as "hippies."

It was a very different America in those days. I had discovered the power of my thumb to get rides from strangers. So I set out with a small group of like-minded hitchhikers to reach the mecca of the hippie movement: Big Sur on the central California coast.

I spent about two weeks in California, mostly in the surf town of Huntington Beach. Some locals offered me space on the floor of their tiny, narrow, railroad apartment suitable for one or two at most, but we shoehorned in six of us. No job, no money, no goals, no worries. We philosophized, pontificated, speculated, squabbled and reveled in the moment.

There was a need to eat, of course. And right there on Main Street, close to the Huntington Beach Pier, a local missionary group had set up a nightly outreach to the burgeoning youth culture. Their method was an adaptation of the skid-row missions to drunks up in L.A.: invite street kids in for free food on the condition that they listen to a gospel message before the sandwiches, chips and beverages were served.

The place was called the Teen Challenge Gospel Light Club. I was there every night. Arnie, one of the volunteer counselors, befriended me. My street friends cautioned me about Arnie: "Be careful, dude. Don't let him get you in that back room, or it's over." The "back room" was a prayer room where the group led penitent seekers in a prayer to be "saved and born again." But I didn't listen, and they did get me.

One Saturday morning, I arose early, gathered my meager belongings, "borrowed" a better pair of shoes from someone sleeping nearby, and wandered down to the Pacific Coast Highway. I was heading back to Texas. Don't ask why. I felt I had to go back.

I hitched a ride down to Oceanside where a meter cop asked me for ID. I told him I was seventeen and returning to Dallas because in Texas, I could legally live on my own. But I was really fifteen, and looked it.

Next stop: San Diego Juvenile Detention Center. Three days and nights, all expenses paid. To my surprise, they told me that my father, who'd been living overseas for years, was waiting for me in Atlanta. It was an odd reunion as I stepped off the plane. Neither of us really knew the other—and culturally, we were worlds apart.

We lasted barely three months. He sent me back to my mother, who hadn't a clue I was coming till I appeared on her porch back in Dallas one August midnight. After three months in a tropical paradise, it was surreal to be back in the Wonderbread culture of Texas. I returned to my hippie friends.

SITTING IN A PARK NEAR MY HOME one Sunday afternoon, a nicely-dressed couple approached me and asked, "Young man, do you know the Lord?" I thought of Arnie. I knew they were talking about God—more specifically, J.C. They gave me a butterscotch-colored booklet called "The Four Spiritual Laws," took my address, and said the youth minister from their church would come to visit me.

Within a couple of days, Reverend Dave Anderson knocked on my door. While pleased to have a rare visitor, I was embarrassed to let him in. We were poor. Very poor. My mother and sister slept on a mattress in the living room. My brother and I shared the nearby couch.

Dave invited me to dinner. This was an exceptional event in my life: a wholesome, home-cooked meal, a substantive conversation that included the meaning of life, and a gracious couple that took a personal interest in me.

They invited me to their youth group. One Sunday, when a visiting missionary gave a stirring call for new recruits to dedicate their lives to spreading the faith, I was one of the first on my feet.

A year after I'd been in the San Diego Juvenile Detention Center, our family migrated to Riverside, California. Soon after, I connected with a Christian commune that specialized in outreach to street kids. A converted Jew by the name of Les Springer introduced me to their New Testament lifestyle (it was very similar to the kibbutz ideology). I was hooked. Within a month, my mother, sister, brother and I all moved into the communal house.

I lived for outreach. Those were the early days of the J.C. movement. The world was ripe for revival. Just two years before, in 1967, Jerusalem had returned to Jewish rule for the first time in 2,000 years. Bible-believing Christians, like my communal group, interpreted this as a fulfillment of prophecy. Surely, the Second Coming was near.

We moved again—this time to Eugene, Oregon. One of my commune friends told me of a little church on 18th Avenue pastured by a twenty-six-year-old preacher who played the guitar and welcomed hippie Christians like us. So one day in November 1969, I walked into the little church for a midweek prayer service. I introduced myself to the pastor and said, "I write gospel songs." The pastor gave me a place in the church band and offered me the janitor position in the church. I took it.

Within three years, the congregation had mushroomed from about sixty on a Sunday morning to over 3,000. Pastor Hicks called me into his office one winter day in 1973 and quizzed me about my life's direction. Known for his directness, he looked at me intensely and said, "Contact the Bible college I went to in Los Angeles. Get the application package. I'll sign it. You leave for the fall term." He gave me the name of two L.A. congregations, both growing rapidly, where I could affiliate.

In July, I loaded up my '65 Ford Ranch Wagon and relocated to Southern California. With Bible classes in the morning, I took a swing-shift job at an electroplating factory in El Segundo. It was awful. Despite elbow-length rubber gloves, the chemicals I worked with burned my forearms. I looked leprous.

Arriving home one night, I saw a note of salvation on the bulletin board: "Call Pastor Hayson."

> The pastor gave me a place in the church band.

My pulse quickened. He was the minister of one of the fastest-growing churches in the San Fernando Valley. I'd been attending there and had become friendly with the media director who ran the audio division. He wanted to turn over the job to someone else. Having done the same work for the church in Eugene, I was well-skilled in audio operations.

As my Bible college education progressed, I took on more responsibilities at school and at church. I was elected sophomore class president. I began teaching high-school students at church. Pastor Hayson's brother had become the youth director and asked me to join his staff to expand the outreach to students. I was already in charge of the Friday youth concerts that brought in hundreds of kids. My excitement was high as I anticipated helping more and more youth "get saved."

Juggling the often competing priorities of church work and college, I also married one of the church secretaries. I was twenty-two. Patricia was twenty-eight.

Early in my graduating year, two friends of mine told me about a fascinating program they had done in Israel. They said I could enlist through the Jewish Agency and go to learn Hebrew for six months in something called *ulpan*.

I remember coming home from school and telling my wife, "We're going to study Hebrew in Israel for six months."

THE STORY OF OUR SEVEN MONTHS of *ulpan* would fill a couple of chapters. We'd been accepted to the program at Kibbutz Ein Dor, a population mix of *HaShomer HaTza'ir* Americans, Hungarians and Argentineans. After five weeks, we were out. The head of the *ulpan*, a former *shaliach* (emissary) for the Jewish Agency, had uncovered evidence of missionary activity. He had heard that Patricia and I converted a young Jewish girl in the program from California. He discovered that there was a young couple in *ulpan*, also from California, that were messianic Jews.

He was right on both counts. I had spent many hours with a searching "Jew for nothing" who was looking for spirituality. She liked my hybrid brand of Jewish and Christian theology. And she liked the other young, Jewish couple that, ironically, happened to be from my congregation in Los Angeles.

The five of us were abruptly ejected from the kibbutz. It caused a small furor, as Patricia and I were rather liked by many of the kibbutz members. While they were largely atheists, they didn't see us in the same threatening light as did the director of the *ulpan*.

Patricia and I were allowed to relocate to the *ulpan* of Kibbutz Ein HaMifratz, just south of Acco on the coast above Haifa. There were conditions. We could not talk about our faith. I could say I was a theology student who came to Israel to better my understanding of Hebrew, but I couldn't discuss any aspect of my theology. Since they didn't ask us to deny our faith, I agreed to the terms.

The half-year at Ein HaMifratz gave me a lot of time to think. Getting kicked out of Ein Dor for exercising my faith had been traumatic. My certitude that "J.C. is the only way to God" had a few hairline fractures. Within ten years, these would widen into a great gulf. But in 1978, the niggling question was "Do I believe in Christianity because it's true, or is Christianity true because I believe it?"

Upon returning to America, I threw myself into intense outreach, working for a major missionary organization in Los Angeles for two years. But the Middle Eastern bug had bitten me. I had strong, compelling thoughts to return to Israel—but to do what?

In June 1980, I flew to Israel for a three-week exploratory trip. I planned to revive a number of previous contacts and cultivate new ones, hoping to find some venue for us to teach English. I was stunned by what happened when I arrived at Lod Airport.

The five of us were abruptly ejected from the kibbutz.

THOSE WERE THE OLD DAYS when the buses ferried you from the airplane to the terminal. As I stood at the immigration desk, the agent checked the computer, looked at me, and asked me to go sit in a chair by the police office to my left. *"Le-shem mah?"* I asked, using a more sophisticated form of "Why?"

"Because I said so," she said flatly.

After a long wait, a portly officer asked me to come into his office. He was staring at a white card.

"Is there a problem?" I asked in English.

"Yes," he replied.

"A big problem?" I pushed.

He nodded. "Oh, yes."

"What is it?" I asked wearily.

"Mr. Sanders, I am ordered by the Ministry of Interior that you may not enter Israel."

"But why?" I implored.

"It doesn't say why, only what. And what happens now is you are on the next plane back to New York."

Besides being exhausted from the flight, I was numbed from the shock of what was unfolding here. It came crashing in on me as I realized what had taken place behind the scenes, after my previous stay as an *ulpan* student. The Ein Dor *ulpan* director had used his government connections to have us blacklisted.

After nine hours of sitting, with little food and no sleep, an officer named Menachem escorted me to a row of seats all my own in the nose of a 747.

It would take another long chapter to describe the next nine dizzying months, as some very high-profile contacts took place involving the Israeli Ministry of Interior, the U.S. State

Department, the White House, a popular American entertainer I knew with strong ties to Israel, and an Israel Air Force general. In March 1981, I was granted a three-month tourist visa to Israel.

AFTER A SHAKY START, Kibbutz Dafna, far in the north of Israel, hired us to teach English in the kibbutz schools. Our tourist visas were changed to bona fide work visas.

While I wasn't directly involved with the Christian outreach teams in the local kibbutzim, I did affiliate with them and frequently taught Hebrew classes for them, along with classes on Israeli and Arab culture, cross-cultural communication, and how to sensitively share one's Christian faith with kibbutzniks when they asked questions. It was this latter subject that eventually widened the hairline fractures I developed in my first trip to Israel.

By this time, well into my second year of teaching at Kibbutz Dafna, I was becoming very fluent in Modern Hebrew. I began comparing the Hebrew texts of some of the 300 messianic proof texts I had learned as a missionary with the English texts. Among the few I examined, I noticed some uncomfortable differences. There are many websites and other resources today that explain these passages in detail. It is not my place to elucidate them here. It is enough to say that the troubling passages were frequently mistranslated, taken out of context, and sometimes made up.

I was in trouble. My whole life was founded on J.C. being the messiah of the Jewish people and the only true way to God. The basis of that faith was the Bible. I fully believed that I was saved and that I had helped many others, including some Jews, to obtain salvation through faith in J.C. I used the Scriptures to support my convictions.

Attempts to speak to my coreligionists would be futile. Based on how I'd seen them deal with other doubters, I knew I'd be a candidate for an exorcism. After all, the devil was a regular character in our discussions, always lurking about to sow seeds of unbelief. In at least one effort to "share my thoughts" with another, I was told to stop this study and to just believe, to stop asking so many intellectual questions.

Depressed, I was sinking into further uncertainty. I didn't even voice my deepest concerns to Patricia. It didn't feel safe talking openly about something that would, in effect, be regarded as bordering on heresy. As much as I loved living in Israel, I thought it might be eroding my very foundation.

> It was really Christianity in a Jewish wrapper.

When Pastor Hayson unexpectedly called us just prior to Passover 1984, I jumped at the chance to consider a return to the big church in Los Angeles. And so we returned to America in July, just as the famous Summer Olympics commenced in the City of Angels.

WITH THE ONSET OF THE OLYMPICS, the church was involved in a number of high-profile outreaches, and as a senior member of the ministerial staff, I had a front-row seat. But on the afternoon before the Olympics opening ceremony, I got a call from another pastoral staff member reporting that "the Jews are all upset." Inquiring further, he told me about an anti-missionary rally scheduled that evening at the Westwood Chabad House down by UCLA. I was to go and report back what the issues were.

I knew some of the issues. Missionary teams were scheduled for door-to-door literature distribution in densely-Jewish areas of Los Angeles. Much of the literature had been deceptively crafted to pass as Jewish content. But it was really Christianity in a Jewish wrapper.

That was the dominant theme at the superheated anti-missionary rally in Westwood. I recall the speakers well: Rabbi Dr. Immanuel Schochet from Toronto and Rabbi Bentzion Kravitz, founder and West Coast director of Jews for Judaism. I sat in the front row wearing a knitted *kippah* that I'd bought in Tzefat (I still have it). I took copious notes and recorded the lectures on a small cassette deck (I still have a copy of it).

Rabbi Schochet and Rabbi Kravitz didn't know me. But they spoke to me. They presented a side of Christianity I'd been unwilling to look at. They described how missionaries, while denying the veracity of rabbinic Judaism, were employing rabbinically-mandated artifacts of Judaism to adhere a Jewish veneer over an essentially Christian message. This included the use of *tzitzit*, *mezuzot*, *talitot*, yarmulkes, Shabbat candles, menorahs, and even the printing and distribution of Jewish calendars complete with names of the *parshiyot*, the holidays and local candlelighting times.

I bought some literature and books, including Gerald Sigal's classic *The Jew and the Christian Missionary: A Jewish Response to Missionary Christianity*. Back in my study at the church, surrounded by my many commentaries, biographies and over thirty versions of the Christian Bible, I began to look at the counterpoints to my missionary proof texts. It was painful. If the Jews were right—if Judaism was a legitimate path to the Creator—where did this leave me?

I remember sitting on the platform, looking out over the congregation during Sunday services, with over 2,000 people packed into the sanctuary. Could all these people—and hundreds of millions of sincere, born-again Christians across the world—be wrong about what happened to them? Was their faith experience merely true because they believed it? Was the church providing a communal placebo for personal dysfunction?

Anyone who's been infatuated understands the shallow limitations of "I feel it in my heart." Left to itself, the human heart can become comfortably polygamous, spiritually or interpersonally. The wisdom of our Torah specifically cautions against turning aside to follow the dictates of one's own heart. We all need an objective set of standards, guidelines, principles and even commandments to help us live above our conflicting, animal urges.

RESUMING MY FERVENT ROUTINE back at the church after the anti-missionary rally was a bit like walking around with a small pebble in my shoe. I could choose to ignore it, but it was always there, exacerbating and deepening the irritation. I remember thinking in a moment of rare personal honesty, *If I let anyone really get inside me, they'll see I'm broken and not OK. Who will want to have such a person as a pastor, as a minister?*

I was told to stop this study and to just believe.

One day in May 1986, I decided to go see Pastor Hayson. I needed an honest exchange with the man I believed had a personal pipeline to God. I sat in his office and poured out my soul. I was facing crushing inner pressures (something he was later to minimize as "a spirit of melodrama"). He listened, smiled and then said, "I see the hand of the Lord pulling a small tree out of your heart which has tried to take root there. But because you have come and told me of your struggles, you are now free from it. Now I'm doing some long-range strategizing for staffing. Where do you see yourself over the next five years?"

Within sixty days of that meeting, I was no longer part of that church or that lifestyle. (Perhaps Pastor Hayson got the vision wrong. Maybe I was the uprooted tree?) I had pulled the ripcord and bailed out of the plane of my pretentious life.

When I left the church, I also left my home. It was a complete break with everything and everyone, including Patricia and my beloved daughter, Michelle. It was an ugly time. I was in great pain, and I caused great pain.[69]

Over the next two years, I played spiritual peek-a-boo with various churches. Nothing fit me. I drifted from job to job; my ability to focus for any length of time was limited. I'd had a core meltdown. The God I thought I knew was long gone. I had severed nearly all my previous connections. I moved—several times. At one point, in 1988, I was nearly homeless.

---

69 Gavriel and Michelle have an extraordinary relationship today. She's twenty-three and has served her country in Iraq. They share a love of languages, aphorisms and wisdom, and deep thoughts about why we are here.

One day, on a lark, I called my father. I told him I didn't know what to do with my life now. Speaking in his heavy, mid-Georgian drawl, he advised, "Son, you just go some place nobody wanna go and you do somethin' nobody wanna do, and you'll find yourself a job."

Where could I go that no one wanted to go? And what could I do when I got there? I put those questions "out there," and an inspired thought came back. I called the graduate school I'd attended for my linguistics work. I asked if they knew of any English-teaching jobs.

"Funny you should call now," the clerk said. "We just got a call from a recruiter in Florida. They are looking for English teachers in Saudi Arabia."

I'd found where to go.

OF COURSE, THE OLD ADAGE IS that when you move, you take yourself with you. But I had hope. I had a chance to turn things around. I was in a place where no one knew or cared what I'd been before. And I already had a head start on the Arabic language. While I'd lived on Kibbutz Dafna, I'd spent six months on the weekends working for an American gospel and country music radio station located just inside the security zone in southern Lebanon. But when I spoke in Saudi Arabia, the students and naval staff would look at me quizzically and say, "Maybe you or your father comes from Lebanon?"

It gets worse. There are many similarities between Arabic and Hebrew, sort of like Spanish and Portuguese. Sometimes, I would let slip a Hebrew word instead of the correct Arabic one. We had a few Palestinians on the technical institute faculty. More than once, I got a raised eyebrow. And more than once, they wondered how I knew so much about the villages they were from, near Bethlehem and Ramallah.

In the end, I was asked to leave Saudi Arabia. Looking back, I was very fortunate. It was another in a sequence of bad things that was really a good thing. In a quirky way, the Saudis helped me find my Jewish soul.

I WENT BACK TO SOUTHERN CALIFORNIA, ultimately settling in Orange County. A college-professor friend of mine asked me about my spiritual journey, and when I described how much I loved Israel, Israeli music, Hebrew literature and poetry, and—still—the Bible, she said, "What do you know about Judaism?"

In a quirky way, the Saudis helped me find my Jewish soul.

Hmm. No one had ever asked me such a direct question. By this time, in the early 1990s, I had disentangled myself from Christianity. But something was drawing me back to a connection with Israel that transcended the modern Zionist era.

I asked my professor friend, "Where should I go to learn about Judaism?"

With a slightly frustrated edge, the professor said, "I don't know, look in the Yellow Pages."

I did. And there in Irvine, near where I lived, was Shir Ha-Ma'alot, a Reform congregation known for its spiritual demeanor. I called and spoke to the educational director, whose name was Barry. "Do you have a conversion course?" I asked Barry.

I loved his answer: "Oh, better than that. We have a bar-mitzvah class for adults, and the rabbi accepts it as a conversion curriculum. You can have a conversion and a bar mitzvah at the same time." A two-for-one special. These Jews really knew how to market a spiritual product!

I enjoyed the rabbi's blend of traditional and modern ideas. When I first met him and shared my journey with him, he looked at me with warm, twinkling eyes and said, "You surely have a Jewish soul."

Of course, that's exactly what I wanted to hear, and philosophically, it wasn't too distant from "but I feel it in my heart"—but that's another discussion.

I first heard of Rebbe Nachman of Breslov through this Reform rabbi. There was one Breslover chassid in all of Orange County. He's still there. His name is Lee Weissman and he (an

Orthodox Jew) used to study *Likutey Moharan* with the Reform rabbi. Those lessons found their way into the rabbi's Friday-night and Shabbat-morning talks. I thrilled to hear the stories and thoughts of this young, Ukrainian, spiritual giant who'd spent so short a time on earth, yet left such a rich legacy.

Echoed almost in passing through the lips of the rabbi, Rebbe Nachman's wisdom was pure waters to slake my inner thirst. "All the world is a very narrow bridge and the main thing is not to fear."[70] "To be wise, a person must find the wisdom that is embedded in every single thing."[71] "In life, one can start over anytime, even several times a day."[72] "By engaging the body in happy actions, like dance, one can achieve new heights of genuine joy."[73] This was the celebration side of Judaism that I thought must still exist.

On the twenty-fourth of Kislev 5757, the eve of Chanukah 1997, I had my Reform conversion. Two days later, on Shabbat *parashat Miketz*, I shared in a group bar mitzvah. There were sixteen *aliyot laTorah*[74] that day, three men and thirteen women. A few friends attended the services to celebrate with me, including my Israeli Hebrew teacher who had shadowed my several iterations through the years. I took them out afterward to a nice Lebanese restaurant for a festive Middle Eastern lunch.

The Torah-observant reader is wincing at this point in the story. I wince in writing it. But that was what it was then, not now. It gets better.

HERE I WAS, A NEWBORN REFORM JEW in this very spiritual, though many things optional, congregation in Irvine, California. Within six

---

70 *Likutey Moharan* II, 48.

71 Ibid., I, 1.

72 Ibid., II, 48.

73 Ibid., II, 81.

74 On a regular Shabbat, seven men traditionally receive *aliyot*, the honor of being called up to the Torah.

months, I was appointed as the teacher of the Shabbat-morning *parashah* class. Through learning Torah to teach Torah, I was gaining a widening view of the world of Torah. Through early Jewish websites like Torah from Dixie, Ohr Somayach and Chabad, I learned about

> "If Judaism is a house, I'm just living on the porch."

Rashi, Rambam, Ramban, the Maharal of Prague, the Vilna Gaon and many others. Occasionally I would weave Chassidic stories into our class. Some loved it: "Oh, I haven't heard this since Bubbe and Zeide." Others disliked it: "I haven't heard this since Bubbe and Zeide, and that's why I moved out here—to get away from such ideas."

I was perplexed by the responses. I was beginning to perceive such beauty, such wisdom and such heights in the classic sources. They towered above the pop-psychology, watered-down Jewish thoughts I was hearing in services. I thought I could summarize the value system there in a few short phrases: "Remember the Holocaust. Be ethical. Give charity often. Celebrate the parts of Judaism you like. Support Israel. Give in to the Palestinians so they'll like us." This is the chapter in my life that I call "If Judaism is a house, I'm just living on the porch."

Curiously, one of my Israeli friends, a counselor at a women's center who often attended our *parashah* class, introduced me to the local Chabad House. "They have a *minyan* every day," she told me. This fascinated me. Jews meeting to pray daily? I was only accustomed to Friday-night *Ma'ariv* and Shabbat-morning *Shacharit*, both of which were rather abbreviated in the Reform *siddur*.

I found Rabbi Alter Tannenbaum warm and engaging. He let me know that since I hadn't been through an Orthodox conversion, I wouldn't count for an Orthodox *minyan*. Nevertheless, I was invited to come and pray anytime. I wasn't offended. By this time, I realized that my form of Judaism was a bit like having a Macy's credit card—while it was great for shopping on Broadway and Thirty-Fourth, I couldn't use it to buy gas or dinner at a restaurant. I needed a more universal card for that. And I'd already come to embrace the idea of an Orthodox conversion, though I didn't know what that would mean. But by now it was a question of how and where, not if.

Rabbi Tannenbaum offered some recommendations. Others also provided helpful guidance. In the end, though there were easier options, I knocked on the door of the Rabbinical Council of California. This is a very serious *bet din* (rabbinical court). Most candidates who inquire for conversion are turned down. At the time I came to inquire about *geirut* (Orthodox conversion), I was told they took maybe one out of three.

I remember my first meeting with Rabbi Avrohom Union. He was friendly but unbending. He affirmed what I had come to feel: I wasn't really Jewish. In spite of the fact that I'd lived four years in Israel, spoke fairly fluent Hebrew, had had a conversion and a bar mitzvah, and was the Torah-study teacher in a congregation, I had not taken on what the Sages call *ol malkhut Shamayim* (the yoke of the Kingdom of Heaven), meaning the commandments of the Torah.

Rabbi Union cautioned, "You've already been part of one major religion, and left that after many years of firm belief and devoted service. God forbid that we should convert you and after ten years or so, you decide this path doesn't fit you. Judaism is a path we follow for ourselves, but not by ourselves. You convert to become part of a people, not just a single Jew doing your own thing. We bear grave responsibility in this, and if it's not a sure, one-hundred-percent fit, we don't take a chance."

The rabbi referred me to a very thick book on the Thirteen Principles of Faith as articulated by the Rambam, and suggested I come back after the holidays. I worried for a minute. There are so many holidays in the Jewish calendar. To which was he referring? He smiled and said, "After Sukkos." I mentally translated—he meant Sukkot. I noted I would have to learn another dialect of Hebrew in order to comprehend the Ashkenazi pronunciation.

I called after the holidays and the *bet din* agreed to meet me. Rabbi Shlomo Holland and Rabbi Yitzchok Summers joined Rabbi Union on his side of the large table. Comfortable but mildly concerned, I spoke with them for an hour. They had tough

> I could only pledge to be an earnest student.

questions. What about the Noahide[75] option? To me, it wasn't an option. First of all, over twelve years ago, there was hardly any place to go in all of America to find a viable Noahide community. And besides, what did they eat or not eat? What did they study? What holidays did they celebrate? What rites of passage did they observe? What songs did they sing? How did they pray? Today, there's been progress on these questions, but a dozen years back, the choices were thin and sparse.

The RCC *bet din* wanted to know if I was prepared to move into an observant community, if I understood the severity of choosing the Jewish path, if I was prepared for the costs associated with kosher living, and if I understood the rigors of Jewish family life. I could only pledge to be an earnest student, giving each phase of learning my full effort.

Near the end of the hour, they asked me to step out of the room while they discussed their decision. After a few minutes, they summoned me back and said they were conditionally accepting me as a candidate for *geirut*. They gave me several pages of a curriculum and assigned me a rabbi, Rabbi Asher Biron, to learn with at least once a month.

MY APARTMENT WAS WITHIN easy walking distance of both the Chabad House and Beth Jacob of Irvine. I spent most of my time

---

75 According to *halakhah*, non-Jews are not required to convert to Judaism, but they are required to observe the Seven Laws of Noah. These are: 1) Do not blaspheme God; 2) Do not engage in idol-worship; 3) Do not commit adultery or other acts of sexual immorality; 4) Do not murder; 5) Do not steal; 6) Do not eat the limb of a living animal; 7) Set up courts to adjudicate the above laws (*Sanhedrin* 56a-b). Several Noahide groups have been established worldwide.

at the Chabad House. On Shabbat afternoons, Rabbi Tannenbaum held a class at his home on practical aspects of Judaism. I discovered he had initiated this for my benefit. Others attended, but he had graciously started this to help me deepen my understanding and observance.

By this time, I had also started learning *halakhah le-ma'aseh* (practical Judaism) with Orange County's only Breslover chassid, Lee Weissman. We began to study the *Kitzur Shulchan Arukh*,[76] which many warned me was too intense for a novice like me. With respect to observance, this is when I discovered the difference between the adjectives *machmir* (strict) and *meikel* (lenient). Lee helped temper my concerns by teaching me stories and concepts from Rebbe Nachman of Breslov.

I learned that the *bet din* that was guiding my conversion process was from the *machmir* school. I was both nervous and grateful to know that. Why nervous? I worried whether I could master the depth they knew so instinctively. I worried whether I could adapt my life to the rigors of fully-committed Torah observance. I saw many Jews, even in observant congregations, who seemed to be taking the more *meikel* approach. They had told me, "Don't judge Judaism by other Jews." So if I were going to judge anything, it would have to be myself today, in comparison to myself yesterday.

And why grateful? Because I knew they wouldn't let me settle for mediocrity in my learning.

I'd learned in a quote from the Rambam in the "Laws of Torah Study" that if one has a choice between living Torah and learning Torah, one should learn—because learning leads to living. So while attending what classes I could in Irvine, I regularly trekked up to L.A. on Sundays in search of further learning. I attached

---

76 "The Abbreviated *Shulchan Arukh*," a popular summary of the original *Shulchan Arukh* with references to later *halakhic* authorities, composed by Rabbi Solomon Ganzfried (1804-1886), a *dayan* (rabbinical judge) in Ungvar, Hungary.

myself for several months to a *shiur* on the laws of *bishul* (cooking on Shabbat) conducted by the great local *posek*, Rabbi Nachum Sauer.

> The *geirut* process took longer than I'd expected.

Rabbi Summers was on my *bet din*, but he also had a local congregation in the Pico-Robertson district. I began to attend *minyanim* there, as well as a number of Shabbat services. Wonderful, caring families from the shul hosted me for Shabbat. I occasionally attended classes with Rabbi Holland. Despite my lead advantage in Hebrew, I struggled to master the concepts as well as the *yeshivishe sprach*, the Ashkenazi verbiage.

Walking down Cashio Street with Rabbi Summers one Friday night, we encountered Rabbi Bentzion Kravitz of Jews for Judaism. I reminded Rabbi Kravitz about that anti-missionary rally he'd held at Chabad of Westwood back in 1984. He remembered it well. I shared a few highlights of my journey and he said, "We've got to talk." Over ten years later, we still talk. I've done a number of lectures on behalf of his organization and have helped provide some counsel or guidance on a few cases in which Jews have been caught up in missionary movements.

The *geirut* process took longer than I'd expected. Along the way, every four to five months, I'd have a check-in appointment with the *bet din*. They would ask questions about my learning and would encourage me to keep going. When I asked, "When will I graduate?" they replied, "Come back in another four to five months. Let's see how you are doing."

CHANUKAH 1998 WAS COMING. I so wanted to light the candles as a Jew, to make a *berakhah* on a latke as a Jew, to sing *"Ma'oz Tzur"*[77] as a Jew. I had nearly completed my studies with Rabbi Biron. A

---

77 "O Mighty Rock," a liturgical poem composed in the thirteenth century, traditionally sung after the nightly lighting of the Chanukah candles. It describes the four exiles of the Jewish nation and expresses hope for the Final Redemption.

scant bit remained. Rabbi Shmuel and Sherri Feld, both gifted educators, had brought me into their orbit. Rabbi Feld, then teaching at Irvine's Hebrew school, Tarbut V'Torah, is a master teacher. He spent many hours honing my understanding of *berakhot, kashrut*, holidays, the structure of the Jewish calendar and practical *halakhah*.

Finally, Rabbi Union announced the words I longed to hear: "We'll meet you at the Los Angeles *mikveh* on Thursday morning, the twenty-third of Kislev"—two days before Chanukah! I'd been well-coached on preparations for the *mikveh*. I was ready. Rabbi Feld came with me from Irvine. Since one of the rabbis on the *bet din* was delayed, Rabbi Feld became one of my three *dayanim* (rabbinical judges), and his was one of the signatures on my certificate of *geirut*.

With all the protocols completed, the rabbis greeted me with affirming hugs of welcome to the Jewish people. Then they urged me to go put on *tefilin* and say the *Shema* before the time for the *Shacharit* prayer passed.

That Thursday evening, returning from my first fully Jewish day in L.A., I stopped into Beth Jacob of Irvine for the *Ma'ariv* service. Rabbi Joel Landau looked at me and asked, "Did you do it?"

I nodded.

He pointed to the *bimah* and said, "Come, lead us in *davening*."

Here I stood, perhaps two years and 200 yards down Michelson Drive from the Reform congregation where all this started, leading an Orthodox *minyan* in the evening prayer. I've *davened Ma'ariv* over 3,000 times since then, but that's the *Ma'ariv* I'll most remember, nervously stammering my way through *Kaddish* with Rabbi Landau calmly prompting me by my side.

THE FIRST HALF-YEAR OF MY JEWISH LIFE, I worked with Rabbi Kravitz of Jews for Judaism. I moved up from Irvine, taking a tiny studio apartment in Beverly Hills. For several months, I was one of the migratory singles who moved fluidly from the Happy

Minyan at Beth Jacob of Beverly Hills to Aish HaTorah to Anshe Emes to Young Israel of Century City. I met amazing people, many of whom are treasured friends today.

Finally, Rabbi Union announced the words I longed to hear.

As the summer waned, I got an unexpected job offer from a friend and business mentor of mine. He wanted me to move to New York and assume field operations in marketing a technology platform he'd helped develop for the commercial insurance industry. I was thrilled. New York—the options for Jewish learning and living were endless, not to mention the choices in restaurants, supermarkets and neighborhoods.

I considered Brooklyn (too crowded), Kew Gardens Hills (way too crowded), Riverdale (nice but remote) and Far Rockaway. I knew some people in Far Rockaway. I'd visited them during my *geirut* process. In the language of Goldilocks, it was "just right."

I was warmly welcomed in Far Rockaway. Eventually, through the matchmaking efforts of Rabbi Yechezkel Kaminsky, I found a suitable, second-floor apartment on Reads Lane, a favored address in the area.

In the summer of 2002, on Tu B'Av,[78] I married a local Far Rockaway woman, Yehudit Tziporah Lapa. A descendant of the Tosafot Yom Tov and other rabbinic luminaries of the Gerrer Chassidic tradition, Yehudit grew up in a family steeped in the ways of Torah. She had three teenagers when we married.

I have several very close friends who have contributed to my spiritual development here. One is Rabbi Baruch Klein, a quiet, learned scholar who reacquainted me with the thoughts of Rebbe

78 The fifteenth of Av, a joyous day during the period of the Holy Temple when young girls would don white clothing and dance in the vineyards, and young men would select them as marriage partners (*Ta'anit* 30b-31a). Today, Tu B'Av has no special observance aside from the omission of *Tachanun*, a penitential prayer, but it is considered an auspicious day for weddings.

Nachman of Breslov. Rabbi Klein introduced me to some of the core Breslov texts, as well. From time to time, he would ask me about going to Uman. I knew about this town in the Ukraine where Rebbe Nachman is buried. I remembered that my Breslov study partner from Orange County had regularly gone to Uman each Rosh HaShanah.

One year, I'm guessing it was early in 2002, I was at LAX preparing to take a night flight back to JFK. I noticed another Jew sitting alone among the gathering crowd. I walked over, said, "*Shalom Aleichem*," and introduced myself. He gave me his name, Chaim Kramer of the Breslov Research Institute. A quick round of Jewish geography yielded up our common connections through Baruch and Lee. We had a memorable conversation. I felt my life would have a continuing linkage with his, though I wasn't sure how.

From New York, Chaim went back to his home in Jerusalem, and within a few days, he sent me several primary Breslov texts. Through these rich books, I renewed my earlier affinity with Rebbe Nachman.

In the summer of 2005, having spent a couple of heartbreaking days in Gush Katif, I made my first Rosh HaShanah trip to Uman. I've been back twice since. Each time, I sat around the table prepared by Chaim and his energetic sons and dedicated friends. There I heard amazing stories of palpable Divine guidance that produced substantive changes for the better in dozens of lives.

The Breslov movement taught me the power of a *tzaddik* to reach beyond the grave—indeed, to be greater than when he was confined to his body in this life—to effect a difference for people who seek to know God in truth. Rebbe Nachman's wisdom is, in my humble estimation, an appropriate prescription for our orphaned generation. His teachings are as relevant and as needed today as when he spoke them to his disciples 200 years ago. It is possible to access these teachings in a very visceral manner through a systematic process of learning, coupled with reflective meditation. Like waters that rise above fences, washing out distinctions that separate, the teachings of great Chassidic and *mussar* masters can stretch our capacity to love, nurture and connect with one another in significant, durable ways.

> Each of us is here to make a significant difference.

MY NAME IS Gavriel Aryeh *ben* Avraham Avinu. As a Jewish reader, you and I share a common ancestor. Unlike you, I chose the name I bear. I chose it reflectively. I wanted a name that was emblematic of the Jewish journey. Gavriel[79] represents the spiritual, angelic component of a person. Aryeh[80] represents the natural, animal instincts of a person. Our challenge is to learn and apply Torah principles in such a way that the spiritual has ascendancy over the animal soul. Rebbe Nachman's teachings are one source of transformational technology to achieve this goal of inner homeostasis.

Now you've read the thread of my story, but you have your own to weave. Each of us is here to make a significant difference. So I pray that the Almighty grant you health, wealth, wisdom and happiness to achieve your maximum capacity for greatness. I look forward to meeting you further up the road, perhaps around Chaim's table in Uman, and to hearing what great things our great King has done for you.

---

79 The name of an angelic messenger of God.
80 Hebrew for "lion."

The Power Of Song, The Joy Of Prayer

Rebbe Nachman said, "It is good to make a habit of inspiring yourself with a melody. There are great concepts in each holy melody, and they can arouse your heart and draw it toward God" (Rabbi Nachman's Wisdom #273).

*

The tale of "The Seven Beggars" (Rabbi Nachman's Stories #13) *also alludes to the importance of melody. The unconscious princess is cured mainly through melody, through the Ten Types of Song. Understand the depth of this.*

The Divine soul in every Jew is a princess—a king's daughter. She is weary and faint because of her sins. She is held captive by an evil king and is shot with ten poisonous arrows. Only a great tzaddik has the power to enter every place where the soul has fallen and remove all ten arrows from her. In order to heal her, he must be able to discern all ten types of pulse beat. He must know all Ten Types of Song, for her main cure is through melody and joy (Rabbi Nachman's Wisdom #273).

*

Melody brings to joy and prophecy, which subdue the forces of evil (cf. Likutey Moharan I, 54:8). *"Then one's words emerge in song, praise and acclaim for God"*
(Likutey Moharan I, 38:4).

The Courage To Grow
Danny Goldschmidt

Danny Goldschmidt is an active member and Trustee of Manhattan's Carlebach Shul. An attorney by training, he presently works as a financial advisor at a major brokerage house.

The first time I heard of Rebbe Nachman was when I read a book about Bob Dylan by Jonathan Cott. I think that Bob Dylan was in Israel for a concert. The author, who was somewhat knowledgeable about Jewish philosophy and Torah, began the story with a quote from Rebbe Nachman:

> The world is like a revolving die, and everything turns over, and man changes to angel and angel to man, and the head to the foot and the foot to the head. So all things turn over and revolve and are changed, this into that and that into this, what is above to what is beneath and what is beneath to what is above. For in the root all is one, and in the transformation and return of things, redemption is enclosed (cf. *Rabbi Nachman's Wisdom* #40).

I have been, and still am, very connected to the Carlebach Shul on the West Side.[81] Reb Shlomo Carlebach often spoke about Rebbe Nachman and quoted Rebbe Nachman's teachings.

---

81 Congregation Kehilath Jacob, commonly known as the Carlebach Shul, is located on West 79th Street in Manhattan. Its founder was Rabbi Naftali Carlebach (1889-1967). Later, it also became the shul of his son, Rabbi Shlomo Carlebach (1925-1994).

Gedaliah Fleer's book, *Rebbe Nachman's Fire*, made a tremendous impression on me. I had borrowed it from someone, and after diligent efforts to locate a copy for myself only to find that it was out of print, I personally made photocopies of much of it.

Around the same time, I heard that a friend of mine, Nachman Futterman, who was president of the Carlebach Shul at the time, had been making the trip to Uman each year for Rosh HaShanah since 1990 (which was only the second year that it was possible for foreign travelers to go there). So that opened up the idea for me.

But although I was intrigued at the idea of traveling to Uman for Rosh HaShanah, I was also apprehensive. My memories of Rosh HaShanah were of being confined to my place in synagogue for most of the day, or standing for long hours at a time, wishing I were somewhere else.

In 1992, I took the plunge and traveled to Uman with Nachman Futterman and two other friends. We stayed in the home of the local chief of police. I remember that he had a large collection of semi-full vodka bottles on prominent display. We *davened* and ate our meals in the auditorium and hallways of the local medical school, which was still under construction. After that, I've traveled to Uman for Rosh HaShanah every year.

TRAVELING TO UMAN IS LIKE traveling back in time. The buildings there are all either a hundred years old or the blank-looking, concrete towers that the Soviets built to provide its citizens with cheap housing. It definitely has a distinctive atmosphere of the third world—or of the fourth world. It is very different from any of the other places I've been to, and I've traveled to plenty of other developing countries, such as India. The entire country stinks of stale tobacco fumes, and many of the people there are difficult to deal with.

My parents had instilled within me an understanding and appreciation of the seriousness of Rosh HaShanah. But it was in Uman, inspired by the people around me, that I experienced for the first time the ability to really, almost effortlessly, pray with *kavanah* (concentration and feeling). While you are there, you have nothing to do except the things that you are supposed to be doing on Rosh HaShanah—to pray, to think, to be

In 1992, I took the plunge and traveled to Uman.

meditative, to look back and reflect on what you've done the past year and consider how you want to change. During those few days of uninterrupted time with friends and fellow pilgrims, we enjoyed the opportunity for extended conversations on these life issues, something that I would never have had the time, let alone the mental space, to do elsewhere.

The adventure aspect of the trip also appealed to me. We had to bring our own food; the trip back and forth was not exactly what you'd find on a luxury liner. All in all, it was conducive to the type of Rosh HaShanah I always thought I should have, but would never have been able to find elsewhere.

I also found that because there were no filters or distractions, I was able to open myself to experiencing emotion during the *davening*. In my regular shul, because of the presence of all my friends from the community that is part of my daily life and all of its concerns, it's easy to get distracted from the central purpose of Rosh HaShanah. But in Uman, it's easy to stay focused. It's an awesome opportunity that we have but once a year to really talk to God and examine ourselves. And if you do that honestly, and if you're like most human beings who have a year of spiritual, financial and personal ups and downs, that can be a very heavy thing.

The people around you are praying, too. It's obvious that they are really communicating with God and making their feelings and desires known to Him. People sing, shout out loud, scream, cry! It's not artificial; it's real. I dislike *davening* with people who think that they have to put on a show or act in a particular way to simulate emotions that they are not really experiencing. But in Uman, people *are* experiencing and in sync with their feelings.

That had a great impact on me. It's something that I still aspire to in my daily life.

TRAVELING TO UMAN HELPED ME bring out the best in myself and experience ridding myself of things that aren't important. It helped me to clarify my priorities and strengthen my positive and constructive tendencies, which had until then been obscured by unnecessarily focusing on details rather than looking at the broad view of things.

Rebbe Nachman teaches that both sin and despair are an inextricable part of the character and experience of every human being.[82] It is something to be worked with and overcome, rather than something to be ashamed of or to pretend doesn't exist. Rebbe Nachman taught me that when I fall, as all human beings do from time to time, I have the choice and the ability to elevate myself rather than remain where I have fallen. That gives us the courage and ability to continue to grow, despite the obstacles in our path.

---

82 Cf. *Likutey Moharan* II, 10; ibid., II, 12.

My Soul Yearns For God

Eliyahu Cohen

*Eliyahu Cohen is a businessman and a member of Montreal's
Breslov Centre.*

I grew up in Montreal in a traditional, but not observant, family.
All my friends were becoming religious. We lived in the same
neighborhood and were about the same age. I used to tell them
that they were crazy, that they were being brainwashed. I had
no idea what they saw in religion.

The change began one Rosh HaShanah. I was standing outside
shul, smoking a cigarette, feeling very cool. Then I went inside
to pray the *Amidah*[83] prayer with the rest of the congregation.
That prayer changed my life.

It was a small, Sephardi shul and totally packed—maybe 200
or 300 men cramped into a small area—yet suddenly I felt that I
was completely alone, that I was totally with God. It was a gift, a
true gift from the Almighty. I felt as if God were asking me, "Is
this what you want from your life? Is this how you're going to
continue?"

I realized that I wanted more. The next day, I started my
journey toward full Torah observance.

---

83 Literally, "Standing"; another name for the *Shemoneh Esrei* prayer which is
the centerpiece of the morning, afternoon and evening prayer services.

ALTHOUGH I KNEW THAT MY FRIENDS were becoming religious, I didn't realize that they were into Breslov. I just knew that they were becoming close to God. One day, someone brought me a French translation of the Breslov book, *Likutey Etzot*. I began to read it, and it really spoke to me.

I decided to check out the Breslov Centre in Montreal. When I got there, Rabbi Saadia Elhadad, head of the center, was giving a class on *Likutey Moharan*. I saw the truth in his words and started attending Rabbi Saadia's class regularly. That was five years ago.

Soon after I started attending the class, God sent me my soul mate. I had noticed her on Rosh HaShanah, but at the time, she was much more religious than I. I took her out for coffee. The following day, I had to travel to China on business. When I came back, I proposed. That was in the winter. We were married in the summer. As soon as the *sheva berakhot* were over, we traveled to Israel. It was wonderful. We went to all the holy places and visited all the holy rabbis.

Back in Montreal, I asked my wife if I could travel with all my friends to Uman for Rosh HaShanah. It was our first year of marriage, and I knew that during that year, I wasn't supposed to leave her. I thanked the One who brought me close to Him when she agreed.

Traveling to Uman was an unimaginable experience. I felt as if an emptiness within my soul disappeared. So many different types of people were there, some connected to God, others totally not religious, yet I sensed that everyone—not just me— felt something inside them changing, that they were becoming whole again. In going to Uman, I felt that my *teshuvah* had become complete.

Going to Uman allowed me to feel. Before that, my Judaism was intellectual. In connecting to Rebbe Nachman, my soul started yearning for God. My soul has emotions, and being in Uman gave me permission to express those emotions. I felt secure there, like a babe in his mother's arms.

"These Guys Know How To Pray"

Eliyahu Reiter

Originally from Manhattan, New York, Eliyahu Reiter presently resides in Tzefat, Israel, where he is a member of the Simply Tsfat Band, teaches in a women's yeshivah and studies Torah.

In terms of religion, I grew up with nothing. All I knew about Rosh HaShanah and Yom Kippur was that they were great days for playing tennis, because that was when the courts were empty.

My parents were German war refugees. They were go-getters, self-starters who came to the United States with nothing, worked hard, and succeeded in fulfilling the American dream.

Eliyahu was accepted into California's prestigious Stanford University. While studying engineering, he turned to Eastern meditation to find spirituality.

But I started to get suspicious. Everyone was into Xmas, and that didn't make much sense to me.

One summer, he spent a lot of time showing his Israeli relatives the sights. They begged him to come to Israel. He did.

Except for one aunt, all my relatives lived in Haifa and were not religious. It never occurred to me to look into Judaism. I

163

thought it would be the last place to find spirituality, and my bar mitzvah had only served to confirm that assumption.

Eliyahu saw some interesting Jewish books at his aunt's house.

I was enchanted by what I read. Judaism made sense intellectually. As I read these books, I realized there is a mystical side to being Jewish. There is more to it than bagel and lox.

When Eliyahu visited Jerusalem, he met a cousin who was learning in a yeshivah. He invited Eliyahu to spend Shabbat with him, and dragged him from one *chassidishe tisch* to another.

I observed the chassidim dancing to an amazing tune, and I loved it.

Eliyahu returned to the West Coast with contact information for Reb Michel, an Orthodox rabbi who was "Carlebach-Breslov."

There was guitar-playing by candlelight, stories...It was not mainstream, but it was beautiful. At the time, it was the only thing that could draw me to Judaism.

In the summer of 1984, Eliyahu returned to Israel to study in Ohr Somayach's[84] summer program.

While I was there, someone gave me the book *Azamra!* and a tape on Breslov. I visited the Breslov shul in Meah Shearim and loved it.

By the end of the summer, Eliyahu was completely committed to an observant lifestyle. After a year in California working, learning, and spending time with the Breslov community, he returned to Israel to study full-time in a yeshivah.

I told the head of the yeshivah that on Rosh HaShanah, I would be traveling to Meron to pray with the Breslover chassidim there (this was in 1986, before travel to Uman was possible). He tried to stop me. He even sent me to his *rav*, so that he could

---

84 See note 42, p. 87.

persuade me not to go. Instead, they succeeded in convincing me that that was where I really should be.

> I visited the Breslov shul in Meah Shearim and loved it.

Eliyahu was impressed by what he saw in Meron that Rosh HaShanah.

These guys know how to pray because they have an ongoing relationship with God. They speak to God. I had never seen prayer like that. It was beautiful. That was in 1986. Since then, every year, I have gone either to Meron or to Uman for Rosh HaShanah.

That same year, some of Eliyahu's friends traveled to Uman.

They returned full of enthusiasm about the trip. That was the impetus that pushed me to go to the Breslov shul and sign up for the next trip to Uman.

Eliyahu planned to travel to Uman in January 1987. But he didn't get there until the following summer.

After signing up for Uman, I left the Breslov shul and got on my bike to return to yeshivah. My pedal struck the curb and I fell over. I almost got flattened by an Egged bus. The trip was pushed off from January to February and then to March. But March was too close to Pesach, so I pushed it off until right before Pesach, and then until Lag Ba'Omer. In the end, I left the day after Shavuot, arriving in Kiev after Yom Tov, just two and a half weeks before my wedding.

Since it was illegal for tourists to spend the night in Uman, we slept at the hotel in Kiev and traveled by bus to Uman every day—a four-hour journey each way.

Two and a half years later, in 1989, Eliyahu was able to fulfill a dream and spend Rosh HaShanah in Uman.

There were 1,000 people; it was the first time the chassidim overtly gathered together in Uman to pray on Rosh HaShanah. Many of the Russian Jews came to the shul for the privilege of kissing the Torah scroll and dancing with us. The services were incredible! The building was made of glass blocks, and I was afraid the glass would crack from the power of our prayers.

We performed the *Tashlich* ceremony next to a factory that overlooked the river. The Russian Jews told us that this was the exact spot where the Nazis massacred the Jewish residents of Uman during the Holocaust. (Later, we found out that the spot was on a different part of the river.)

The living conditions were primitive. We slept in a leaky factory, there were no proper sanitary facilities, and the food was horrible. But the main thing was that we were with the Rebbe for Rosh HaShanah.

> For the last several years, Eliyahu has been taking his sons with him when he travels to Uman for Rosh HaShanah.

It's difficult to have a spiritual experience while supervising children. But the spiritual experience is just a perk. I have *emunah* in the Rebbe's promise; that's the reason I go.

Indefinable Joy

Moshe Emergy

Born in Israel, Moshe grew up in both Spain and the United States. Today, he lives in Montreal, Canada and is one of the co-founders of the Breslov Centre.

In 1989, after his junior year of college, Moshe took a year off to study in an Israeli yeshivah. His roommate took him to a *melaveh malkah* at a Breslov yeshivah[85] in the Muslim Quarter of Jerusalem's Old City.

I was freaking out to be going to a place like that, and wondered what the other guys from yeshivah would think of me. But I loved it—and returned again the following week. I loved the *simchah*, the all-pervading joy. I loved the feeling of brotherhood.

This was my first introduction to people who were not from a religious background and who had succeeded in doing *teshuvah*. I came from a traditional home, but many of them had come from terrible, horrible backgrounds. The first time I went to the *melaveh malkah*, I sat next to a chassid who showed me a paper stating that he had spent fifteen years in prison. I was frightened—who knew what that guy had done? He realized that I was afraid and said, "If I don't leave the Rebbe, I'll be all right. I won't make another mistake."

85 Yeshivat Shuvu Bonim, which opened in Jerusalem in 1980, "specializes" in returning wayward young men to their Jewish roots.

I met other people who came from backgrounds completely devoid of *Yiddishkeit*. I asked the people there where they found such power; after all, how could a person who is so far from truth come so close?

A while later, my roommate invited me to his parents' home for Shabbat. That's where I was introduced to *Likutey Moharan*. Although I didn't understand a word of it, I realized that there was something there for me. I purchased the *Likutey Moharan* and started learning.

After I received my rabbinical ordination, I was drafted into the Israeli army. That's where I really got hooked on Rebbe Nachman. Without the Rebbe's advice, I wouldn't have made it in such an environment. I was the only Orthodox soldier in my unit. I never shaved my beard or cut my *peyot* the entire time I served in the Israel Defense Forces.

After completing his army service, Moshe married and moved to Montreal via Venezuela and Florida. He was active in organizing the now-flourishing Montreal Breslov community.

I will never forget my first trip to Uman because that was the time I cried the most. I finally understood what Rebbe Nachman was telling me. I saw the place where Rebbe Nachman is buried. I met the people who are his followers.

During *Kabbalat Shabbat*, one of the men in our group was bawling like a baby from joy. I, too, began to cry from joy. In all my years of learning in yeshivah, praying at the *Kotel*, dancing at weddings, I never felt such joy as I felt that Rosh HaShanah while praying in Uman.

After the meal, I returned to the *tziyun* to recite *Shemot HaTzaddikim*. I wanted to get as much as I could from the *tziyun*. That's when I began to understand the essence of Breslov.

Moshe returned from his first trip to Uman on fire with Breslov. He spoke with Rabbi Saadia Elhadad about opening a Breslov center in Montreal. Today, Montreal's Breslov Centre is the core of a thriving Breslov community.

The Necessity Of Prayer

Bob Fleischman

*Bob Fleischman is a successful businessman in Miami Beach,
Florida.*

It's not simple to say how I got to Uman, because I'm a *ba'al
teshuvah*. I became religious when I was around twenty-five,
and today, I'm sixty-one. But Uman is certainly the root of all
journeys; it just depends in which direction you're traveling.

After I became religious, I worked as a fundraiser for different
Lithuanian *yeshivot*. That gave me an opportunity to learn Torah.
But I wasn't exposed to Chassidut. I must have it in my blood,
though, as my mother's family stems from the Ukraine.

Each person has a story as to how he came to Breslov. Our child
was very sick. The first discourse in *Likutey Moharan* discusses
the power of prayer. I found tremendous encouragement
through learning that Torah. I came to understand that although
my prayer might not be answered, the act of prayer itself is
necessary.

One afternoon, I was sitting on the sofa learning *Likutey
Halakhot* and praying to God. My sick son was lying on the
sofa next to me. I prayed to God to please give me a son who
would live, a *ben shel kayama*. Shortly afterward, I discovered
that, although we were far from being youngsters at the time,
my wife was expecting another child. A few months later, our

son passed away. Four months after that, my wife gave birth to a healthy baby boy.

During the entire time that my son was sick, I felt that God was very, very close to me. Rebbe Nachman's advice saved my marriage, my family and me, and brought me to where I am today. But no one else in my family is interested in Breslov. They have a completely different way of thinking.

I'm an orphan. My father passed away when I was a child. When a person is an orphan, there's nothing stopping him from following his heart's desire. A person who has a father is usually led on a certain path; there are guidelines to follow. But a person without a father can follow his heart—and my heart led me to Breslov.

I finally had the opportunity to travel to Uman in 2001, when my daughter graduated college. My wife promised to take her to visit Australia. I told her that if she could take our daughter to Australia, I could take our son to Uman. My son and I went to Uman for Rosh HaShanah.

I never saw such *simchah* as I saw in Uman. The prayers, the joy, the whole thing, just spilled over into everything else. Everything in my life, all the choices I had made, all led me to that experience, to that very special time in Uman.

Totally Me

Gil Zagury

Gil Zagury owns a clothing manufacturing company in Montreal, Canada. He is married with two children, and is a member of Montreal's Breslov Centre.

I began my spiritual journey at age twenty-five when I attended an Arachim seminar.[86] At the time, I was spiritually empty and searching for meaning in my life. The seminar blew my mind. After that, I started learning; I would go straight from work to learn. But although I was learning Torah, I had yet to encounter Chassidut.

One night, I attended a concert where the singer, a Breslover chassid, spoke about the power of prayer. *Ba'alei teshuvah* have tremendous help from Above. A *ba'al teshuvah* doesn't know anything, so every time he asks a question, he asks it with tremendous humility. For a *ba'al teshuvah*, prayer is such a new experience, so incredibly fantastic. After hearing the singer speak about the power of prayer, I found myself spending a lot of time just talking to God, asking Him to help me and guide me.

It wasn't long before I started going to classes at the Breslov Centre. If I heard of a class, I would run to hear it. Then I started

---

86 See note 47, p. 104.

reading the books put out by the Breslov Research Institute. By the time I had learned a few lessons of *Likutey Moharan*, I was a totally different person.

I was especially moved by the concept of prayer and the deep connection between prayer, miracles and the Land of Israel. It completely changed my perspective of life. I realized I that could pray to God all the time.

BUT ALTHOUGH I LOVED THE REBBE'S TORAH, I couldn't understand how a person could leave his family for Rosh HaShanah. I had been taught that *Yiddishkeit* has nothing to do with separation, that it's all about community and working together as a family, and I thought that this didn't fit in with traveling to Uman for Rosh HaShanah.[87] But when my friends returned from Uman, I saw that they had attained a different type of strength. They were stronger—much, much stronger. Rabbi Saadia Elhadad, head of the Breslov Centre, spoke a lot about belief in the *tzaddikim* and belief in what the *tzaddikim* say. That is what really convinced me to travel to Uman. By then I had been religious for about two years.

In Uman, I prayed with the Sephardi *minyan* at the *tziyun*. I can't describe the surge of emotions I felt when I heard such a large group of people shout, "*Shema Yisrael!*" as if in one voice. It was beyond anything I had ever experienced. I felt something within me come back to life. I felt so spiritually connected that I was almost surprised that I was still in my body!

Then there were the classes given by prominent Breslovers like Rabbi Elazar Mordekhai Koenig. Just being in the proximity of so many *tzaddikim* was unreal. I saw myself reflected in the faces of the Breslover chassidim I encountered there. I felt so connected with them, with their *shtreimel*s and *peyot* and *chassidishe* dress. I felt as if I were seeing a side of myself I never knew existed. Their cry was me, their yell was me, their

---

87 In truth, a wife is a full partner in her husband's journey to Uman.

"*Oy!*" was me. Standing at the *tziyun*, I realized that I had found myself.

> Just being in the proximity of so many *tzaddikim* was unreal.

A FEW YEARS LATER, I started teaching Breslov Chassidut at the university's Hillel Centre. At the end of the class, one of the girls came over to me and said, "By the way, I want you to know that I met your wife in Tzefat."

I was a bit taken aback. "What do you mean by that?" I asked.

"I met the woman you are destined to marry in Tzefat. She walks like you, she talks like you, and she laughs like you. Go there to meet her."

I hopped on a plane and traveled to Tzefat to meet my future wife (who came from Moshav Me'or Modi'im). We were engaged within two weeks.

ONE ROSH HASHANAH IN UMAN, I woke up in the middle of the night and started studying Torah. When I finished, I went outside to get some fresh air and met two men who were having difficulty understanding the exact same Torah that I had just finished studying. I realized that the reason I woke up in the middle of the night was so I could learn this Torah and explain it to these two men.

After that, I walked over to the main shul and asked an elderly rabbi a question on what I had studied that evening. He spent the next two hours teaching me, giving me a final dimension on the Rebbe's Torah that completed the puzzle. I felt as if he had been there, waiting for me to come and ask him my questions. These types of experiences are unique to Uman.

Traveling to Uman made me much more connected to the Rebbe, much more "into" his teachings. There are no words to convey the experience I had there.

New Directions

Nachman Futterman

*Nachman Futterman is in the textile import-export business.
Today, he lives in Jerusalem with his wife and children.*

How am I connected to Breslov? My first connection is that although I didn't grow up in a religious home, my name is Nachman!

I first began to seek spirituality when I was in my forties. My spiritual seeking took me to Eastern yoga. But although I was involved in yoga, culturally, I was still very Jewish.

One afternoon in the early 1970s, I told some of my friends at the tennis club that I wanted to meet a rabbi who looked at the world in a more accepting manner. One of my friends said, "My son is studying with a swami, and the swami is good friends with a rabbi named Rabbi Gelberman. The swami and the rabbi do evenings together."

I contacted the rabbi and we arranged to meet. We hit it off and eventually became very close friends. Rabbi Gelberman headed an interfaith organization. Among its members were prominent swamis, Sufis and other clergy. I became very involved with the organization and was even president for eight years.

But it bothered me that I was president of an interfaith organization and yet I knew so little about my Jewish roots.

God gave me a nudge: Rabbi Shlomo Carlebach[88] came to sing for our interfaith community. That one encounter impelled me to investigate my heritage. Eventually, Reb Shlomo started coming to my home in the East Side of Manhattan every week for a learning session. Every month that Reb Shlomo was in New York, he would bless the New Moon at my home.

There was a whole group of us, a *chevrah*; I had a large apartment, and we had beautiful learning and singing sessions there.

I started attending Reb Shlomo's shul in the Upper West Side. Eventually, I moved to the Upper West Side to be close to the shul. Later, I became its president.

Although I was president of the shul, I was not religiously observant. My becoming religious was very gradual, and today—well, I'm doing the best I can. One of the people I learned with was very involved in the historical aspect of Judaism. He showed me that all the things we read about in the Torah—Abraham, Isaac, the Temple—are true historical events. They actually happened. He showed me that there was a Sinai experience. Once I understood that, I realized that I had to take a new look at how I was living my life.

I TRAVELED TO ISRAEL FOR THE FIRST TIME in 1984. Of course, I was planning to go to the *Kotel* for Shabbat. After all, the *Kotel* is the holiest place in Israel, which is the holiest country in the world. I was really looking forward to the experience.

I remember going to the *Kotel*, walking up to a *minyan*, and then feeling as if I were being pushed away. I walked up to another *minyan*, and again I felt as if I were being pushed away. This kept happening again and again. I got to a point where I turned to God and said, "Maybe I don't belong here."

---

88 Known as the "singing rabbi," Rabbi Shlomo Carlebach (1925-1994) left a promising career as a yeshivah student to create his own movement combining Chassidic-style warmth and personal interaction, public concerts and song-filled synagogue services. Reb Shlomo, as he was called by his followers, influenced many non-religious Jewish youth to embrace their heritage.

I walked away from the *Kotel* to the plaza and started crying. I had traveled so far to come to the holiest of places and I was not comfortable praying there! It occurred to me that perhaps this whole religious thing was not for me.

When I was really at the end of the end, I noticed the section of the *Kotel* that is inside a tunnel. I felt as if there were a ray of light emanating from there. Something was drawing me, beckoning me to enter.

I went inside and saw two old men with white beards and *shtreimels* singing the Breslov song "*Sab'einu* (Sate us)." Their faces were shining! I'll never forget it. I was mesmerized.

As I was standing there and watching the two chassidim sing, a stranger (who later became a good friend of mine) patted me on the shoulder and asked, "Do you know who these guys are?"

"No, who are they?" I asked.

"They're Breslover chassidim. Would you like to meet them?"

I did. I told him that I was staying at the King David Hotel. We made up for him to meet me and my friends on Shabbat morning to take us to the Breslov shul in Meah Shearim.

That Shabbat, we prayed *Shacharit* in the Breslov shul and ate lunch with Rabbi Moshe Bienenstock. That was my first Shabbat in Israel. God had brought me straight to Breslov. It was most amazing.

FROM THAT EXPERIENCE, I came to the conclusion that I must travel to Uman. But as president of the Carlebach shul and the shul's main fundraiser, I was not sure that I could abandon the shul on such an important Yom Tov. I asked Reb Shlomo what to do. Not only did he say that it was all right, he even gave me a *kvittel*[89] and urged me to go.

The first year I went to Uman was the second year that the *tziyun* was open for Rosh HaShanah. There were only about 1,500 people there.

---

89 A *kvittel* (Yiddish for "note") is a piece of paper inscribed with the names and/or needs of the petitioner; it is usually given to a *tzaddik* together with a small sum of money as a request for the *tzaddik's* blessing.

Rosh HaShanah in Uman, it's not simple. The *avodat HaShem* is more sincere, truthful and intense than anything I've ever experienced in any practice in any shul.

> "They're Breslover chassidim. Would you like to meet them?"

I was privileged to bring both my boys to Uman before they turned seven.[90] It took me two hours to say *Tikkun HaKlali* with them. They will never forget that trip—ever. It's imprinted in their DNA.

Reb Shlomo used to say that everyone needs two rebbes: their rebbe and Rebbe Nachman. Rebbe Nachman gives a person the strength he needs to make it through life—the strength and the advice.

As we finished this interview, Nachman's wife entered the room. I asked her how she felt about her husband leaving her every year for Rosh HaShanah.

People sometimes ask me, "How could he go away for Yom Tov?" But I feel that his traveling to Uman really blesses us. My children have a different understanding of *Am Yisrael* (the Jewish nation), the power of the *tzaddik* and the power of our prayers.

90 See note 26, p. 59.

The Ultimate Cure

Yaakov Ben-Yishai

Yaakov Ben-Yishai lives in Montreal, Canada. He divides his time between running his jewelry business and studying Torah.

I became interested in Judaism in 1990 when I spent a few months in the New York Diamond District studying for my gemologist diploma. One of the Orthodox Jewish men I met there suggested that I accompany him to shul to put on *tefilin*. I enjoyed it enough to start attending shul every day.

Back in Montreal, I looked for a shul that had the "fire" that I saw in New York. I didn't find it until I met Rabbi Saadia Elhadad of the Breslov Centre.

Before becoming religious, I was a Jew looking for myself and, like everybody else, I was influenced by the non-Jewish world. Rebbe Nachman tells us to believe that through becoming attached to him—and with plenty of work on our part!—we can destroy those negative influences and purify ourselves. That's the reason I traveled to Uman—to destroy the negative influences and purify myself.

SINCE MY FIRST TRIP TEN YEARS AGO, I travel to Uman every year. One year, however, it was particularly difficult because my son, Shalom Moshe Nachman, was born about two months before Rosh HaShanah with a major heart defect.

When he was born, the doctors told us that without open-heart surgery, he would die within the week. But they weren't even sure he was a candidate for surgery. On top of that, the surgery itself was extremely risky. Over fifty percent of the cases didn't survive, and of those fifty percent, all were boys. According to the statistics, our son's chance of recovery was dismal at best.

When Shalom Moshe Nachman was two days old, the doctor informed us that it was possible to do surgery on him, which in itself was a miracle. The surgery was a success—another miracle—but the recovery was extremely difficult. And this was just the first in a series of three open-heart surgeries.

As Rosh HaShanah approached, our son was still in the pediatric intensive care unit. The doctors told us that they were doing their best, but the situation was extremely unstable.

I questioned if I should travel to Uman that year. But when I discussed it with my wife, she said, "The best thing you could do is pray for our son in Uman." So I went.

On the first day of Rosh HaShanah, the *Minchah* prayer was so powerful that I was positive something must have happened in Montreal. Somehow, I sensed that my son would survive.

When I returned to Montreal, my wife met me at the airport with a picture of Shalom Moshe Nachman and told me of the big miracle that had taken place on Rosh HaShanah.

During the two days of Rosh HaShanah, my wife had been unable to travel to the hospital to see the baby. When she left him before Yom Tov, he had been in the intensive care unit attached to innumerable machines, with several doctors constantly hovering over him. The moment Yom Tov was over, she raced to the hospital—and found his bed empty. She panicked and started screaming, "Where's my son? What happened to my son?"

The doctors quickly calmed her, "It's a miracle! Your son was well enough to be transferred to the regular ward."

His turnabout occurred on the first day of Rosh HaShanah, around *Minchah* time.

Today, Shalom Moshe Nachman is almost seven years old. He's completely healthy, and I am planning to take him with me to Uman this coming Rosh HaShanah.

The Difference That Personal Prayer Makes

Gershom Stubbs

Gershom Stubbs resides in Scranton, Pennsylvania, where he works with children with behavioral disabilities.

I was raised as a Catholic. In college, I began asking deep, philosophical questions about my beliefs. I was particularly disturbed by the concept of the trinity. How could God be comprised of three separate entities? In addition, I could not believe that God could take the form of a human being.

Although my parents are Catholic, they were supportive of my search for the truth. At first, I read about the many different Eastern religions, but I couldn't relate to any of them. Then one day, I noticed the Star of David on the roof of a synagogue. It dawned on me that Judaism was the only religion that I hadn't yet explored. I drove to Barnes & Noble and purchased an introductory book on Judaism. What it said made a lot of sense—a lot more than anything I had read about any of the other religions that I had researched.

The book piqued my interest to such an extent that I made an appointment to speak with a rabbi—a Reform rabbi. I began attending services at the Reform temple. But as I read more about Judaism, I noticed discrepancies between what I was learning and what was going on in the temple. I asked the rabbi questions such as "Why do you drive to shul on Shabbat?" Before long, I was more religious than the other people in the congregation, and the Reform rabbi suggested that I take my questions to a Conservative rabbi.

I graduated from Reform to Conservative, and then from Conservative to Orthodox. Within six months, I was completely religious, but I still wasn't Jewish. At the time, I was living in a very small community outside Scranton. Getting a *minyan* together was a real hassle. Very often, I would come to pray and then have to explain to the other men there that they couldn't count me in for the *minyan*.

I converted to Judaism in December 2004. Today, I am so completely Jewish that people are surprised to learn that I am a convert. I study Gemara regularly in Scranton's community *kollel* and feel very comfortable there.

SO WHAT BROUGHT ME TO BRESLOV? I was disturbed that while many people in the community took their Torah learning very seriously, some of them slept or talked through the prayers. It seemed that the emphasis on Torah study was, to a certain extent, at the expense of an emphasis on prayer. I had heard that Chassidut emphasizes prayer, and contacted some friends who were into Chabad to learn more. But I soon realized that Chabad was not what I was looking for.

So I did what any other young American does when searching for information: I did a Google search on Chassidut. The Internet has lots of material on Breslov. I started reading the material and noticed that the theme of prayer was constantly repeated.

I bought a copy of *Outpouring of the Soul* and was extremely moved by what I read. The concept of *hitbodedut* was not new to me; I had been doing it for as long as I could remember. But Rebbe Nachman validated what I had sensed all along: that in addition to formal prayer, a Jew should speak to God in his own words.

I noticed on Rabbi Dovid Sears' website, The Breslov Center for Spirituality and Inner Growth, that there were classes in Breslov Chassidut taking place in Lakewood, New Jersey, a three-hour drive from Scranton.

Rebbe Nachman validated what I had sensed all along.

A friend and I drove to Lakewood to attend a class. Rabbi Ephraim Portnoy, a Torah scholar who studies in the Breslov Kollel, was giving the lecture. After the class was over, I spoke with Rabbi Portnoy. He arranged for us to spend the night at the house of another Breslover chassid, Rabbi Shlomo Mier.

I was impressed with Rabbi Mier's dedication to and knowledge of Breslov. Rabbi Mier suggested I call a certain Rabbi Sol Goldman, who arranged for me to study with Reb Avraham Bloch, a member of Lakewood's Breslov Kollel. It wasn't long before I considered myself a Breslover chassid.

IN THE SUMMER OF 2008, I traveled to Israel for the first time. From Israel, I traveled to Uman, where Chaim Kramer took care of me.

I was in Uman for a week. The whole experience was amazing, the energy there unbelievable. While praying at the *tziyun*, I observed people crying, which made me feel comfortable enough to express my own emotions and break into tears.

On Erev Rosh HaShanah, I went to the Sofiefka Park to do *hitbodedut*. There I was attacked by a couple of Ukrainian anti-Semites. I succeeded in outrunning them, but I fell and dislocated my shoulder. Hatzolah[91] took care of me. The doctor on duty told me that if the shoulder was broken, I'd have to travel to Kiev to have it set. Since this occurred five hours before Yom Tov, that meant that I would end up spending Rosh HaShanah in Kiev.

The ambulance took me to the Uman hospital for x-rays. On the way, I did *hitbodedut*, begging God that my shoulder should

---

91 A Jewish volunteer emergency medical service which operates a clinic in Uman during Rosh HaShanah (may God spare us).

be only displaced and not broken so I would be able to stay in Uman for Rosh HaShanah. I was extremely grateful to discover that it was not broken. I wasn't even bothered by the fact that I had to spend Yom Tov in my weekday clothing with my arm immobilized in a sling. Actually, I was so grateful to have made it that I cried throughout *Minchah* and *Ma'ariv*.

Rosh HaShanah was incredible. It was unbelievable to pray in the *kloyz* together with thousands of other Jews. As everyone shouted, "*Shema Yisrael!*" I could envision the scale being tipped in our favor. I never experienced anything as intense as the Rosh HaShanah prayers in Uman.

The Yom Tov meals were also amazing. At the table that Chaim organized, everyone would tell their story of how they came to Breslov and what impelled them to come to Uman. I was inspired by the many different stories and was especially moved to hear people speak about their experiences with *hitbodedut*. Seeing the entire rainbow of Jews connected to Rebbe Nachman reinforced my desire to grow within Breslov and to continue studying Breslov.

Back in my apartment, I discovered that my camera and cell phone were missing. Someone had gone through my suitcase and stolen them. All the beautiful pictures that I had taken were lost, and now I am left only with my memories. Traveling has its bumps and bruises, both literally and figuratively, but that's all part of it. After all, the *tzaddik* told us that we should anticipate these challenges, since Rosh HaShanah in Uman is such a holy experience.

Still Going Strong

Rabbi Chaim Spring

Rabbi Chaim Spring does fine bookbinding and restoration
of old books. He lives in Ginot Shomron, a settlement in the
West Bank.

I grew up in a religious family in Brighton Beach, New York. Rabbi Zvi Aryeh Rosenfeld, a well-known Breslover chassid, was my first Gemara teacher. It wasn't until years later that I discovered his connection to Breslov.

At age nineteen, I got a job teaching at Congregation Shaarei Tefillah's afternoon Hebrew school, where Rabbi Rosenfeld also taught. Every afternoon before school began, Rabbi Rosenfeld and I would learn together for a couple of hours. He prepared me for my exam to receive rabbinical ordination.

One time, I mentioned to a friend that I was learning with someone named Rabbi Rosenfeld. He responded, "Oh, so you're learning with the Breslover chassid of America."

I was a bit taken aback. Rabbi Rosenfeld had never mentioned to me that he was a chassid. "What's Breslov?" I asked.

His explanation left me even more confused. "They're the 'dead chassidim,'"[92] he said.

---

92 See note 44, p. 91.

When I asked Rabbi Rosenfeld to tell me about Breslov, he began studying Breslov books with me. The more Rabbi Rosenfeld taught me about Breslov, the more I grew to appreciate it and to consider Rebbe Nachman my Rebbe.

BUT ALTHOUGH I CONSIDERED MYSELF a Breslover chassid, I did not travel to Uman for Rosh HaShanah until 1994. That was the year that I was diagnosed with a serious illness and underwent surgery. I was really shaken up from the ordeal and decided that I had better travel to Uman before it was too late. I had a lot to pray for. I also pledged that within the next few years, I would publish the book that I was working on, which talks about our Patriarchs and presents an in-depth explanation of Rashi.

Uman was amazing! I never prayed the way I prayed that Rosh HaShanah. When the *chazzan* intoned "*HaMelekh* (The King)" and everyone began clapping in unison, the joy was indescribable. I was totally immersed in my prayers; it was a taste of *Gan Eden*.[93]

I went to Uman again the following year. The second Rosh HaShanah in Uman, I begged God to grant me another ten years of life. Ten years later, I was very much alive! I wondered what I could do to assure additional years. Chaim Kramer suggested that I travel to Uman a third time, which I did.

This time, I traveled to Uman right after Sukkot. I stayed at the Uman hotel and ate my meals with Chaim. This time, I was able to get right up to Rebbe Nachman's *tziyun* to pray. Today, thank God, fourteen years later, I am still going strong!

My connection to Breslov now is mainly through supporting Breslov institutions and studying Breslov books. I was privileged to meet many Breslov elders of the previous generation, and try to convey their message to my children and grandchildren.

---

93 "The Garden of Eden"—i.e., Paradise.

Making The Connection Every Day
Dr. D.

Married with ten children, Dr. D. has a thriving dental practice in the center of Jerusalem. He devotes his mornings to Torah study and his afternoons to taking care of patients.

I grew up in a Modern Orthodox home in Brooklyn. After graduating yeshivah high school, I went to Israel to learn for two years in Yeshivat Kerem B'Yavneh.[94] Back in America, I attended Yeshiva University and had the privilege of studying under Rabbi Aharon Soloveitchik. I married soon after graduation and started dental school. In 1981, I finished school and my wife and I, together with our three children, moved to Israel. Living in Israel was important to us, and we wanted to make the move before I became too settled in New York.

I was *frum* (religious). I had received my foundations in *emunah* and Torah from the many years that I had studied in yeshivah. After I opened my dental practice, I devoted my mornings to learning with a study partner in a yeshivah study hall and my afternoons to taking care of my patients.

---

94 Founded in 1954, this yeshivah emphasizes both a love for Torah and for the Land of Israel..

But although I was going through the motions, I questioned why God wants us to study only Gemara and *halakhah*. Does He really want us all to become a bunch of lawyers and judges? The learning was not bringing me to feel a closeness to the Almighty.

I was raised with the understanding that learning Torah is the most important thing that I could possibly do, that when I learn another page of Gemara, I am saving the world. But it didn't make sense to me. Although I was learning, I was not fulfilling my obligation to *love* God. I sensed that my connection to the Almighty was shallow, that my *davening* was weak. It felt wooden and dead rather than alive and full of vitality. I knew others who had gone through the same system and were able to be vibrantly religious. But I wasn't. I knew that this couldn't be all that God wanted of me.

I BEGAN RESEARCHING CHASSIDUT. In my younger years, I had heard about Chassidut from Rabbi Shlomo Carlebach,[95] who had been a great influence in my life. I was a musician and loved both his music and his *chassidishe* Torah ideas. But when Reb Shlomo had talked about Chassidut, he talked about it in the context of the shtetl (Eastern European village life). It sounded exotic and spiritual, but it wasn't part of my world.

The first step in my research was to ask one of my patients, a Chabadnik who delivered classes in *Tanya*,[96] to learn *Tanya* with me. I also attended a weekly class in *Sefat Emet*[97] in my neighborhood shul. It was all interesting, but not moving. I decided to look into Breslov.

---

95 See note 88, p. 175.

96 *Likutey Amarim* ("Collected Statements"), popularly called *Tanya* ("It was taught") after its opening word, is a seminal work of Chassidic Judaism written by Rabbi Shneur Zalman of Liadi (1745-1812), founder of the Chabad-Lubavitch movement.

97 Torah insights arranged according to the weekly *parshiyot* and festivals by Rabbi Yehudah Aryeh Leib Alter (1847-1905), the second Gerrer Rebbe.

I contacted an old roommate from my yeshivah days in Kerem B'Yavneh, Avi Katz.[98] I had heard that he had become a Breslover chassid, but I hadn't had much contact with him since 1971—almost twenty-five years.

> "By my community standards, you went off the deep end."

I phoned Avi and basically said, "I know that you're a Breslover chassid. I have seen that you have long *peyot* and wear a long coat. By my community standards, you went off the deep end. But I know that Breslov is famous for its *simchah* and for praying with enthusiasm. Although I'm a dentist and Modern Orthodox, is there anything that you can offer me?"

Avi was very enthusiastic and offered to teach me basic Breslov concepts and introduce me to some Breslover chassidim.

He suggested that I pray *Shacharit* in the main Breslov shul in Meah Shearim. Praying there, I felt as if I were standing in the *Bet HaMikdash* (Holy Temple). It was a feeling of tremendous inspiration and holiness. It was amazing to pray with several hundred men, many of whom arose at midnight to study Torah before immersing in the *mikveh* to prepare themselves for prayer. I had always immersed in a *mikveh* prior to Rosh HaShanah and Yom Kippur as part of my preparation for the holiness of those days, but these men prepared themselves in such an incredibly holy way *every day*.

I was used to people rolling out of bed and running to shul. Then, while still half asleep, they would mutter the prayers at breakneck speed before racing off to work. But here, in the Breslov shul, people's sole goal in life was to serve God and they sacrificed a lot, both financially and physically, to achieve this goal.

Although I was one of the only ones without long *peyot* and a long coat, I continued to pray there each morning.

---

98 Avi is the brother of Yehudah Katz, one of the Israeli soldiers still missing in action since the Battle of Sultan Yacoub in Lebanon in 1982.

After *Shacharit*, I started studying with some of the Breslover chassidim I had met in shul, including another old friend of mine from Kerem B'Yavneh, Zusha. Zusha told me that I was lucky to have finally found the gateway to an incredibly holy and joyous way to serve God, totally different from anything I had ever experienced. He had become a Breslover many years earlier.

I asked my *rosh yeshivah* what he thought about my getting involved in Breslov. He replied that I should be wary of the crazy people who attach themselves to Breslov, but that Rebbe Nachman's Torah, *Likutey Moharan*, contains many magnificent thoughts.

ALTHOUGH I WAS GROWING in my ability to pray with passion, I was afraid to accept Rebbe Nachman as my Rebbe. I was constantly playing devil's advocate with my study partners, asking them how they knew that Rebbe Nachman was greater than the other *tzaddikim*. Eventually, I came to the conclusion that we are not here to judge which *tzaddik* is greater. Instead, we should find out which approach to Judaism speaks to us and follow it with devotion and enthusiasm.

After many, many discussions and after devoting a lot of hours to *davening* with Breslover chassidim, I came to the conclusion that Rebbe Nachman's path of love, joy and cleaving to God is what most inspires me, personally, to true *avodat HaShem*.

AFTER ALMOST THREE YEARS of being involved with Breslov, I finally considered taking the big step of traveling to Uman for Rosh HaShanah. I was nervous that I would find the people there worshiping Rebbe Nachman, God forbid, rather than the Almighty, and of course, I didn't want to have any part of that.

Although my immediate family supported me completely in my decision to spend Rosh HaShanah in Uman, I faced opposition from my parents. For the last thirty-five years, I had led the Rosh HaShanah services in our local shul, and this gave my parents great pleasure. But I felt that now my soul needed Uman.

I made the trip and wasn't disappointed.

I didn't find worship of Rebbe Nachman. Instead, I found inspirational prayer and true cleaving to God. I found incredible joy and a great sharing of spiritual and material nourishment.

> Uman felt like a huge soup of the Jewish people.

Uman felt like a huge soup of the Jewish people, a *cholent* of every possible type of Jew. I never expected to see chassidim with long *peyot* and *shtreimel*s rubbing shoulders with young men with ponytails and earrings. The *mikveh* scene was outrageous—all those tattoos!

Despite the differences, a tremendous love existed between the different groups. I had always thought that most Breslovers have long *peyot* and wear long coats. In Uman, I met an entire group of clean-shaven, English-speaking, professional Breslover chassidim and saw many people of all types—non-religious, Modern Orthodox and traditional Jews—from many different countries.

During the eight days that I was in Uman, I stayed in a house with fifty English-speaking men from such diverse places as Toronto, Jerusalem, Beit Shemesh and New York. Every meal was a spiritual delight, spiced with plenty of words of Torah. We became a close-knit group as we shared our desire to become close to God. Being together with these spiritually-growing men strengthened my realization that Breslov is the best path in Torah-true Judaism to help me, personally, develop a connection with God.

My eight days in Uman were amazing. Riveting lectures by internationally-known Breslov speakers were available almost around the clock. Walking into the *tziyun* to pray, I felt as if I were in a great synagogue run by the Beitar Jerusalem soccer team. Twenty-four hours a day, loud groups of young, mainly Sephardi Jews stood around the *tziyun*, yelling and chanting songs and Psalms and reciting the *Tikkun HaKlali* with tremendous vitality and excitement. Connecting it to things I had experienced in the past, the only way I could describe it would be to say that it felt like a combination of a spiritual Woodstock festival and a Shlomo Carlebach retreat in the Catskills.

For Rosh HaShanah, I prayed in the main shul—the *kloyz*. The service was very slow, lasting from six-thirty in the morning until three-thirty in the afternoon, with an hour break. It was totally from the heart and very emotional. Although I found the service to be a bit too long for me, there were moments of extreme *deveikut* (cleaving to God).

Tashlich was unforgettable. Picture it: 25,000 people surrounding a river, doing *teshuvah*, many of them singing and dancing. There was so much joy!

Before Rosh HaShanah, I took a day trip to Reb Noson's grave in the town of Breslov. The grave is located in an old cemetery overlooking an incredibly beautiful area of the Bug River. I spent time there in *hitbodedut*; it was an amazing experience. In addition, I went to the Sofiefka Park in Uman for *hitbodedut* three or four times. One of the English-speaking rabbis took us on a special *hitbodedut* expedition to the forest, where he gave us pointers on how best to communicate with God. It was very down-to-earth, yet uplifting at the same time.

SINCE I AM NEW TO BRESLOV and new to approaching religion in such an intensive and exciting format, in many ways, I feel like a *ba'al teshuvah*. Despite my "normal" suit jacket, when I come to pray in Meah Shearim with the chassidim, I am warmly accepted.

I hope to continue studying the Torah ideas of Rebbe Nachman of Breslov and make them part of my life. I hope to strengthen my commitment to follow the Rebbe's advice to spend time in *hitbodedut*, to immerse daily in the *mikveh*, and to follow all the other guidelines he gave us to be able to serve God and increase true, deep joy in our lives.

Defining Moments

Each day has in it "thought, word and deed." God contracts His Godliness ad infinitum, to the center point of the corporeal world on which man stands. He arranges for him thought, word and deed according to the particular day, and the particular person, and the particular place, and He clothes hints for him in this thought, word and deed that He arranges for him, in order to bring him closer to serving Him.

Therefore, a person has to rigorously immerse thought, word and deed in this, and to expand his understanding—to understand what the particular hints are that are clothed in the thought, word and deed of this day that the Holy One has arranged for him—whether in physical labor or business activity. And in all this that the Holy One arranges for him each day, he has to deepen and expand his thoughts on this so as to understand the hints of God (Likutey Moharan I, 54:2).

The Gift Of Uman

Shimon Gross

*Shimon Gross (a pseudonym) is a Chassidic businessman
residing in London, England. He traveled to Uman for the first
time in the winter of 2000.*

I was invited to join a group of chassidim touring the gravesites of
the *tzaddikim* in the Ukraine. We arrived in Uman late Thursday
night. On Friday morning, we got up before dawn to pray with
the sunrise.

I remember walking down the streets of Uman at that time
of the morning. Everything was still dark, it was freezing cold
and there was snow everywhere. Before praying, we immersed
in the *mikveh* opposite the *tziyun*. I was the last one to leave the
building.

Upon leaving the *mikveh,* I heard music in the stillness. The
music grew louder as I approached the *tziyun*. I realized that
it was coming from the room of the *kohanim*, a detached room
near the *tziyun* where the *kohanim* could pray.[99] I looked in
through the window and saw a guy who looked like a hippie
sitting in front of an open book of Psalms, strumming his guitar

---

99 A *kohen* is forbidden to enter a cemetery unless certain criteria are met.
The committee that oversees the Rebbe's gravesite built a special room that
meets those *halakhic* requirements, enabling *kohanim* to pray at the *tziyun*.

and singing the words of King David at the top of his voice. He seemed to be so immersed in his prayer that he was oblivious to the world.

At that moment, I understood the gift of Uman. Uman gives each person the opportunity to connect to God, no matter his or her level of observance. That morning, I prayed differently than I had ever prayed before.

I'm not a Breslover chassid, but since then, I've traveled to Uman several times, including Rosh HaShanah. It's not easy to leave my family behind, but Rosh HaShanah in Uman is an experience that will remain with me forever.

Bridges To Judaism

Dovid Sears

Dovid Sears is a professional artist and the director of the New York-based Breslov Center for Spirituality and Inner Growth. He has authored several books, including those on Breslov Chassidut.

I discovered Chassidut when I was a little kid. My parents were members of a right-wing Conservative synagogue that had a large library. One day, when I was about eleven or twelve years old, I was exploring the library and discovered a book by Meyer Levin, an American Jewish writer in the 1930s. It was called *The Golden Mountain.* Half the book contained adaptations of Rebbe Nachman's stories; the other half, Baal Shem Tov[100] stories. As I read that book, I fell in love with Chassidut. I even started to draw pictures of the Baal Shem Tov and his chassidim. My father proudly made copies of the drawings to give to his friends.

This encounter made me realize that there was serious spirituality in Judaism. And thanks to this childhood connection I felt to Chassidut, I didn't end up in an ashram like many of my friends during the 1960s and 1970s.

---

100 See note 66, p. 125.

At my bar mitzvah, someone gave me the book, *For the Sake of Heaven*, by Martin Buber. It, too, captured my imagination. Years later, when I was attending college in Vermont, I read Buber's *Tales of the Hasidim* and the writings of Avraham Yehoshua Heschel. Although I wasn't observant, I believed in God. For me, these books were a bridge to *Yiddishkeit*.

In 1975, I noticed a secondhand bookstore in Hartford, Connecticut and went in to browse. I discovered a copy of *Rabbi Nachman's Wisdom* by Rabbi Aryeh Kaplan. It had been published the previous year. I was so excited at my find! The book was such an inspiration for me that after I finished reading it, I impulsively sent my one and only copy to friends who lived in Vermont, who had a connection with Rabbi Shlomo Carlebach.[101] When I was in college, we had lived two houses away from each other. They didn't have a telephone, so whenever Reb Shlomo wanted to speak with them, he would phone me and I would run to their house to call them to the phone.

Not long after reading *Rabbi Nachman's Wisdom*, I started to keep Torah and *mitzvot*. I am certain that *Rabbi Nachman's Wisdom* had much to do with it.

WHY DID I BECOME RELIGIOUS? For complicated spiritual and psychological reasons, I guess. Around that time—in 1973, I think—my grandmother, a remarkable woman from Chassidic stock, passed away. She had been religious, and to me, she represented the exquisite beauty of a traditional Jewish life.

After she died, I had an awesome dream. It was so powerful that it was one of the main reasons for my becoming observant. In my dream, my grandparents asked me to visit them one last time. I saw them standing at dusk on the crest of a hill on their farm. (In life, they had not lived on a farm, but had a large garden behind their house with a big grape arbor.) Everything in my dream was in shadow. It was a world without words.

---

101 See note 88, p. 75.

In that silent world, they handed me a large, two-volume set of books the size of the Oxford English Dictionary. Then we parted. The parting was very emotional, full of yearning and all sorts of indefinable feelings. Back in the carriage in which I had come, I brought the books into the light and saw the title in gold letters on a Moroccan leather binding: "THE TALMUD." I opened one volume and, much to my amazement, I was able to read it! As I read, the Hebrew letters started to peel off the page, turning into gold and then into flames, until I found myself surrounded by golden, fiery letters.

> I felt that I had received a spiritual legacy.

When I woke up, my heart was palpitating. I felt that I had received a spiritual legacy and that I had a responsibility to do something with it. I knew that I had to go to shul.

I tried the local Conservative synagogue, but it was totally different from the Conservative synagogue of my childhood. The Friday-night *kiddush* struck me as a performance; there was something about it that didn't seem real or authentic. I didn't belong there.

I tried the local Orthodox shul. The people there, mostly elderly, were overjoyed to have a young person in the *minyan*. Slowly, I became more involved in the shul, until before long, I was acting as the rabbi's assistant and joined forces with the cantor in running the NCSY[102] youth program.

In the summer of 1980, I did some temporary work in a graphic-design studio in Providence, Rhode Island. While I was staying with Lubavitcher friends there, Rabbi Aharon Waxler, a Breslover chassid from Brooklyn, came to collect money for Rabbi Gedaliah Koenig's institution in Tzefat. I asked Reb

---

102 The National Council of Synagogue Youth is a Modern Orthodox Jewish youth organization sponsored by the Orthodox Union. Founded in 1954, it has tens of thousands of members in the United States, Canada, Israel and Chile.

Aharon a lot of questions about Breslov, and told him that I had given away my only copy of *Rabbi Nachman's Wisdom* and wanted to purchase another one. He happened to have a copy in the back of his car and gave it to me. I was overjoyed to get it back. Shortly afterward, I discovered Rebbe Nachman's *Restore My Soul* in a bookshop and bought it. Now I owned two Breslov books in English (plus a Hebrew volume that I still couldn't read very well).

By this point, I was looking for something more in my *Yiddishkeit* than just a sense of community and a few like-minded friends (as important as such things are). I wanted an inner spiritual path, one that would transform me.

My study partner and I explored all sorts of Chassidic writings. Then one day, I suggested we learn *Likutey Moharan*. For me, it was like love at first sight. I was captivated! After my study partner left, I continued learning the Rebbe's book that entire night. I couldn't put it down. For two weeks I learned, intoxicated with the Rebbe's words. But soon I realized that I couldn't do this constantly. For one thing, I was working as a book illustrator and had deadlines to meet. In addition, I realized that I would have to discipline myself to understand these teachings correctly and to follow their advice in *avodat HaShem*.

A few friends and I started getting together once a week to study *Likutey Moharan*. I was on fire with Breslov. I loved it! During this time, I also met Chaim Kramer of the Breslov Research Institute in Jerusalem. I was writing and illustrating a children's version of Rebbe Nachman's parables for Artscroll and asked Chaim to check the accuracy of what I had written. I took a train to New York and we met in a little kosher restaurant in Midtown Manhattan. When I told him that in Rhode Island, there was a group of men who got together to learn Rebbe Nachman's Torah every week, he was astounded.

By the time Rosh HaShanah came around, I felt connected enough to Breslov to travel from Providence to Boro Park to participate in the American Breslov Rosh HaShanah *kibutz*.

The Rosh HaShanah services were powerful—sort of bittersweet, straight from the heart.

On *Tzom Gedaliah* (the Fast of Gedaliah), the day after Rosh HaShanah, one of the chassidim asked me, "Are you a Breslover chassid?" Without thinking, I responded, "Yes." That's when I realized that I had become a Breslover chassid. It was a milestone.

> I view traveling to Uman as an act of trust in our sages.

Later, one of the chassidim mentioned to me in a humorous vein that a person doesn't "become" a Breslover chassid; one day, he simply wakes up and realizes that that's what he is. Actually, that's what happened to me.

I VIEW TRAVELING TO UMAN as an act of *emunat chakhamim* (trust in our sages). Rebbe Nachman made a promise, and anyone who learns Rebbe Nachman's works and believes in the truth of Rebbe Nachman's promise will want to follow the Rebbe's advice. This is true whether he can afford it or not, whether he is in the mood or not, or whether it is easy or not.

The first time I traveled to Uman was in 1988. I went with my wife and two teenage children. At the time, I was learning full-time in yeshivah, so our funds were extremely limited. In order to travel, my wife had to take a leave of absence from work and we had to take our two children out of school. My elderly mother could not understand why we were so foolish as to travel behind the Iron Curtain. But by then I had been studying Rebbe Nachman's Torah for several years, and saw this as a once-in-a-lifetime opportunity. We had no idea at the time that the Soviet Union would soon topple and that the path to Uman would be open to everyone.

My family and I traveled with a small group of chassidim to the Rebbe's *tziyun*. My wife and daughter were the only two females on the trip. The journey was far from easy. The Russians did not welcome tourists. They did everything possible to hassle us.

As soon as our little group entered the Soviet Union, we were separated from the other passengers and interrogated at length. I thought that the interrogation was horrendous, but one of the other chassidim told me that in the past, the interrogations had been even worse.

Then we discovered that the airline had lost our luggage, which contained almost all of my wife and daughter's clothes and most of our kosher food. We got it back in the end—as we were leaving the country.

The money situation was terrifying. The Soviet authorities demanded that we account for every penny we brought into the country and every penny we spent. We were afraid to give *tzedakah* to a poor person on the street; after all, how could we account for it?

Even at the airport, I was vividly aware that we had entered a very different, very paranoid society. The airport was full of Soviet signs and statues, and it was no secret that our Intourist guide was a KGB agent. The bus windows were intentionally dirty to keep us from looking out and seeing how backward the country really was.

Once we were settled at the hotel in Uman, I bought a Russian-language newspaper. Before I brought it upstairs to my room, our tour guide noticed me carrying the paper and said, "I didn't know you speak Russian."

I answered, "I don't."

He looked pointedly at the paper and asked, "So what are you using that for?"

I replied, "For the bathroom."

The KGB agent responded, "Oh. That's what we use it for, too!"

(Please forgive me if this story is a little off-color, but that's what really happened!)

When we arrived in Uman, we recited *Tikkun HaKlali* at the *tziyun* and prostrated ourselves on the grave. I had expected a tremendous surge of elation upon arriving at the *tziyun*. Instead,

I felt completely numb. I was so exhausted and burnt-out from the events of the past few days that I could barely feel a thing. I remember actually pinching myself to wake myself up, but it didn't help.

Our job is to travel to the tziyun with joy.

I thought of the Rebbe's statement that reading his stories, the *Sippurey Ma'asiyot*, rouses a person from spiritual slumber. So my wife and I stood together next to the *tziyun* and read, in Hebrew, one of Rebbe Nachman's stories—the first one, about the Lost Princess. But I didn't feel any different.

It wasn't until I was on the way home that I realized I had come for a *tikkun*, not to experience a spiritual high. A spiritual experience is a gift, but it is not to be expected. By doing what I had to do, I was accomplishing my *tikkun*, even if I didn't feel any great spiritual arousal.

That in itself was a great lesson for me. Over the years, I have made many, many trips to Uman. Each trip is different— different physical obstacles, different spiritual obstacles. There were times when I had an unbelievable experience as I sat by the *tziyun* reciting Psalms, and there were other times when I just wanted to be back home in my own bed! But that's irrelevant. Our job is to travel to the *tziyun* with joy; spiritual inspiration is like the proverbial icing on the cake.[103]

THE FIRST TIME I WENT TO UMAN for Rosh HaShanah was in 1989. There were close to 1,000 people there. We prayed in a converted factory and slept in the official Soviet hotel in the middle of the town. Built in the late 1800s, this hotel was shaped like a huge

---

103 See *Likutey Moharan* II, 95 where Rebbe Nachman teaches that when a person prays, he should focus only on the words of his prayer. If the person wants to shed tears but this is not happening, he should not think about crying. For at that moment, crying is also considered a "foreign thought" during one's prayers. Here, too, our "job" is defined; all other spiritual gains are the "icing on the cake."

rectangle with an open area in the middle. On either end of the rectangle were two bathroom areas that served the entire floor.

The bathrooms smelled like horse barns and the entire floor stank. Most of the time, there was no running water. The bathtubs were filled with water, which we removed with a ladle for flushing the toilet. The rooms had high ceilings, tall windows and rows of metal-frame beds. A concierge who was also a government agent sat behind a desk near the stairs on each floor, guarding the keys and watching us carefully. For us middle-class Americans, all of this was a tremendous challenge.

As for the converted factory, I was told that during World War II, 30,000 Jews had been rounded up and kept in that factory before being slaughtered by the Germans.

The committee in charge of the Rosh HaShanah gathering had hired a crew to dig a big, square hole in the ground and pour concrete into it to make an outdoor *mikveh*. There were no walls, no fence, nothing; we had to take off our clothes and immerse in the open air, which was extremely cold first thing in the morning!

Every day, a truck came and pumped out the old water. Another truck poured boiling hot water into the pit. The water was so hot that it was impossible to immerse in the *mikveh* for another couple of hours. Then we'd crowd into the *mikveh* and jump in—about a hundred of us, grandfathers, fathers, sons, everyone together.

People were constantly coming and going. An Israeli *ba'al teshuvah* folk singer stood at the far end of the *mikveh*, strumming his guitar while surrounded by children. With the clouds of steam enveloping him, he made me think of a *tzaddik* descending into the smoke of Gehinnom to redeem lost souls as he sang, in Hebrew, "It was extremely good, it is extremely good, it will be extremely good!" This song is based on the concept that everything that happens is truly good, even if it appears to be the opposite, and it all comes from God.

Another year, they dug a *mikveh* and put a wall around it so that we had some privacy. There were also some racks with hooks to hang our clothes. But the room was still freezing and the floor was a river of mud; the

> I was beet-red from head to foot, but I survived.

whole setup was extremely primitive. This *mikveh* was used by a few thousand people every day! At five o'clock in the morning, I was there in the Ukrainian arctic darkness, trying to immerse with at least a hundred other chassidim.

One morning, I forgot the green, oversize towel that my wife had given me at the *mikveh*. When I returned the next morning, I saw that the towel had been ripped to shreds. Everyone needed a towel, and since it was assumed to be ownerless, someone tore it into small pieces and distributed it to needy bathers. (This was just before Yom Tov, so there wasn't a problem with tearing.) People were desperate for something to dry themselves with, so I guess my wife and I acquired some extra *mitzvot* that year!

Another time, I put my foot into the *mikveh* not long after it had been refilled, and the water was so hot that I thought I had burned myself. It was like a cauldron of boiling water. Then I saw a little old *chassidishe* man walk straight in, followed by another old man. I thought, *If they can do it, I can do it!* I steeled myself and—although I didn't think it was humanly possible—jumped in, dunked myself once, and ran out. I was beet-red from head to foot, but I survived.

The services that first year were incredible. In those days, we were doing outreach to the Jews who lived in Uman, and a few of them joined our *minyan*. I remember that one man in his fifties, with big silver teeth, entered the shul and screamed for joy. Then he started to dance. He was in ecstasy! For several years, he joined us for the Rosh HaShanah prayers, until he moved to Israel.

At the end of the Yom Tov, everyone danced. The dancing lasted a long time. Reb Naftali Zvi Dubinski, a frail Breslov elder who had been exiled to Siberia during Stalin's regime, danced with me in the middle of the circle. He was glowing with joy. It was a tremendous privilege to be able to dance with him.

DURING THOSE EARLY YEARS, I became friendly with one of the Jewish families living in Uman. In 1991—or perhaps it was 1992— I arrived in Uman a couple of days before most of the Americans so that I would be able to rest up from the rigors of the trip before Yom Tov. That year, the Megameter, an unused, brick factory building down the hill from the *tziyun*, had been converted into a gigantic dormitory with over 1,000 metal bunk beds. The mattresses were lumpy, and with so many people getting up at different hours of the day and night to pray, I realized that if I stayed there, I probably wouldn't be able to get much sleep. Yet I had resigned myself to spending Yom Tov there. The price was right—it was almost free—whereas a bed in an apartment cost $3 a night. That might not seem like much, but I was trying to conserve every penny.

As I walked up the path to the little house next to the *tziyun*, I encountered a local Jewish couple well in their sixties trying to carry on a conversation with an Israeli chassid. The woman, wearing a fox fur hat, asked me hopefully, "*Redst Yiddish* (Do you speak Yiddish)?"

"*A bissel* (A little)," I answered, and said that I would be happy to help her negotiate with the Israeli, who was interested in renting a room from them. In the midst of the negotiations, the woman turned to me and said that she would rather have me for a tenant! Did I need a room?

I thanked her and explained that I was trying to conserve my money. She smiled and said that she understood; her husband, who was more reserved by nature, remained impassive. They were not able to come to terms with the Israeli, and I continued walking to the *tziyun*.

A little while later, I ran into a friend of mine striding down Bilinsky Street toward the Megameter. "*Ir zucht af tzimmer?*" he asked. "Are you looking for a room?"

The more I thought about sleeping in the Megameter, the colder my feet got. I answered in the affirmative, and he directed me to an apartment at 5 Pushkina, a long, pinkish, four-story apartment building about ten minutes away. I walked up to the third floor, knocked on the door—and there was the same Yiddish-speaking man I had met before. He showed me the room, which had two beds, an Oriental rug hanging on the wall and a balcony overlooking some trees, and it looked quite clean and comfortable. But he wanted $24 per person for a week, a little higher than the standard rate. I was not willing to pay that much, and left.

> There was the same Yiddish-speaking man I had met before.

Toward late afternoon, my apprehension about staying at the Megameter increased. Just then Boris, an Uman Yid I knew from previous years, accosted me. Boris was a *pensionnaire* (retiree) with a gray beard and a few prominent silver teeth who acted as a middleman between the locals and the chassidim.

"Ich hub azah shayner tzimmer far dir mit a reicher mentch! Nit vaayt. Kum, kum," he said to me. "I have a beautiful room for you with a rich man! It's not far from here. Come, come!"

I acquiesced and tried to keep up with the elderly businessman as he hurried to 5 Pushkina—to the same apartment that I had seen before! The rate was unchanged, but now I would also have to pay Boris his $3 fee if I wanted the coveted bed. So I handed over $27. Three times in a row could not be a mere coincidence.

My hosts, Mr. and Mrs. Herschel Dibner, turned out to be wonderful people. My friends and I rented that room for several years in a row. Mrs. Dibner recited *Tikkun HaKlali* in Russian every day; her grandfather had been a Lubavitcher chassid and she still cherished his *tefilin* and *siddur*. Every day, Mr. Dibner prayed with a *minyan* of local men at the Rebbe's *tziyun*. He loved to listen to the Yiddish tapes I brought for him from America: Yom Tov Ehrlich, Yossele Rosenblatt, Theodore Bikel,

Andy Statman's early klezmer recordings. They also studied the religious books in Russian that we brought them each year, including several Breslov volumes.

After Mrs. Dibner passed away from a stroke, I urged Mr. Dibner, who suffered from a heart condition, to move with his family to Israel. He and his divorced daughter and two grandchildren eventually moved to Petach Tikvah. But it was not God's will that Mr. Dibner live to see his children put down new roots. Still grieving over the loss of his beloved wife, he died of heart failure about a month after moving to Israel, and was buried in its holy soil.

TRAVELING TO UMAN CHANGED my connection to the path of Breslov Chassidut. After all, how is a person connected to the Rebbe? Through following the Rebbe's advice and taking action, rather than just intellectually studying the Rebbe's writings. The Rebbe tells us to travel to his *tziyun*, especially on Rosh HaShanah. When we go to Uman, we are connecting with the Rebbe in a way that is beyond intellect. We are connecting to him with our entire being.

After that first Rosh HaShanah in Uman, I never wanted to be anywhere else for the Yom Tov. Although I am getting older and traveling is getting considerably harder, Uman is the place to begin the New Year. As the Rebbe himself declared, "There is nothing greater!"

Together As One

Moshe Dayan

Originally from Israel, Moshe Dayan moved to Montreal, Canada around 1980. He is a businessman who studies Torah every day.

My friends at the Breslov Centre in Montreal convinced me—and they had to work very hard to do so!—to go with them to Uman. I was amazed at the tremendous sense of *hitbatlut* (giving of oneself for the betterment of the community) that I saw there. It seemed that everyone was working for the common good and that no one was looking for self-gratification. People weren't trying to say, "Look at me! See how great I am!" It didn't matter if a person was rich or poor, learned or unlearned; we were all there together, as one group.

Although I went to Uman for Rosh HaShanah, I am not a Breslover chassid. I enjoy being with Breslover chassidim and I enjoy learning Breslov books, but I don't have the same fire that they have. Thanks to my connection with Breslov, I have begun to study Torah every day. This has a tremendous impact on how I relate to my family. Breslov has influenced me to become a better Jew.

The Very First Time

Howard Yahm

Howard Yahm is a retired psychologist living in Vermont with his wife and family.

I went to Uman because I wanted to have a Jewish religious experience. I was very close with my next-door neighbor, Nachman Futterman, and he was going that year with his eleven-year-old son.

I didn't know much about Rebbe Nachman and I viewed traveling to Uman as an extraordinary opportunity. Actually, at the beginning, my reasons for going were almost anthropological. I was going to have a foreign experience. Yes, I was raised Jewish, but in terms of practice, I was very secular and hadn't attended synagogue since my bar mitzvah.

It was a unique experience from the first moment—when I placed a *kippah* on my head as I walked out of my house. At the airport, I met a lot of amazing people. I immediately felt welcome and accepted as a brother, even though the other people were obviously very religious and I was completely unobservant and ignorant. Everyone was helpful to me; I never felt judged. Instead, I felt embraced by the Breslov community.

We traveled to Kiev via Frankfurt. I saw people praying on the plane, something I had never seen before. The first time I ever donned *tefilin* in my life was in Germany.

I loved meeting the Sephardi Jews. I had never encountered them before. Meeting Jews from all over the world was powerful to me. I had never realized how heterogeneous the Jewish world is, so full of color, from so many places in the world.

We arrived at the *tziyun* at four o'clock in the morning. That first experience was otherworldly. First there was the recital of the Ten Psalms (the *Tikkun HaKlali*) alongside so many other people who were saying it in so many different languages. Then there was getting close to the *tziyun* itself. It wasn't as if people were lined up to get there—it was a massive crush of bodies. To me, it seemed completely chaotic. But it wasn't. Each person there was trying to have his own spiritual experience, and all the people in front of him were a blockage. We inched our way forward. No one was pushing anyone else, but everyone was trying to move forward. It was a crush of bodies; the "Jewish nation" behind me, the *tziyun* ahead of me.

Once I reached the *tziyun*, no one tried to push me away. I found myself asking God to release me from the humility of things that I didn't even realize were bothering me. They were just pouring out of me.

The shul where we *davened* the Rosh HaShanah services was packed! I'm used to an American-Protestant type of service, but in Uman, it was thousands of deeply religious people having a profound spiritual experience. It all appeared chaotic at first, but then I realized that this was because I didn't understand what was going on, what was being said. The moment I stopped trying to get my mind around it, I realized that it was amazing.

Before the holiday began, I had purchased a *talit*. I stood in shul, encased in this magnificent *talit*—and then my friend, Nachman Futterman, bought an *aliyah*[104] for me! When I descended from the *bimah* after my *aliyah*, people shook my hand and congratulated me. Although I didn't understand the liturgy,

---

104 Literally, "going up"; the honor of being called to the Torah and reciting a blessing over it.

some things really moved me, such as when the people in shul said, "*HaShem Melekh* (God is King)!" Pure pandemonium broke out. It was so real; I felt God's presence at that moment in a way that I had never felt it before. It was extremely powerful.

I TRAVELED TO UMAN THE NEXT YEAR, TOO. This time, Nachman Futterman's other son, who was about eight years old at the time, came with us. So that year there were four of us—Nachman with his two sons and me. Before Rosh HaShanah, we were walking down the street in Uman when we noticed an elderly *tzaddik* with people attending to him. He was small and very, very old, and people were stopping him to ask him for a blessing. Nachman urged his sons to get a blessing. Then he encouraged me to get a blessing.

When I approached the *tzaddik*, he put his hands on my head and started sobbing. Then he hugged me close to him and continued crying on my shoulder. I was shaking. I had no idea what he was saying, but it felt to me as if he knew me from another life and was telling me something terribly important. Although I was not able to comprehend it, I welcomed it and embraced it. That was one of the most significant moments in my life. But that's Uman.

So I went to Uman twice. And then I went to Israel for Nachman's son's bar mitzvah. Although I do not keep *mitzvot*, since that bar mitzvah, I've been wearing a *kippah* all the time, because I must keep my head covered in the presence of God.

Today, I live in central Vermont. Other than the Lubavitcher rabbi in Burlington, I am the only person in central Vermont who wears a *kippah*. Everyone knows that I'm Jewish. I feel comfortable being identified as "the Jew" in a place where people don't show their Jewishness.

Traveling to Uman changed me in that I came away strenuously connected to being Jewish. Before that, I had never really thought much about it. Yes, I had read a lot of Jewish history, but I read it as history, not as my personal family history. Spiritually, I crave a connection with *Yiddishkeit*.

Here in Vermont, I volunteer at the family courts, making sure that the children's needs are being met. I do lots of *mitzvot* with my volunteer work, and I feel that through doing that, I am doing God's work.

> He hugged me close and continued crying on my shoulder.

When I was a child, I thought God was a little old man in the sky. As I got older, I rejected that idea, and then as I got even older, my perception changed completely. I really struggled with trying to define God, and finally, I came to the realization that He cannot be explained or understood, but that He exists and is All-Powerful. So although I am not a practicing Jew, I am a religious Jew with a deep belief in God.

My parents named me Chaim Shalom. I later learned that my last name, Yahm, means "sea" in Hebrew. Chaim means "life" and Shalom means "peace." So the English translation of my name is "Life, Peace, Sea." Although my parents weren't educated Jewishly, the name they gave me reflects the essence of my soul.

Search For Truth

Trevor Bell

Trevor (Yitzchak) Bell was born and raised in a Modern Orthodox family in London, England. In the early 1970s, he began searching for more meaning in Yiddishkeit. Today, in addition to his work as a legal consultant and a marriage and personal counselor, he lectures on Breslov Chassidut in the United Kingdom.

I attended public school (here in England, we call it "grammar school") and then Cambridge University, where I studied economics and sociology. After graduating university in 1967, I worked in London as an investment analyst/manager while studying to become an attorney in my "spare" time.

In the early 1970s, shortly after my marriage, a very close friend of mine lost his mother, and then in 1975, my first child was born. These two significant events impelled me to intensify my questioning the purpose of life. I asked myself:

Where am I going? What am I doing that is really meaningful?

Can those who tried to destroy the Jewish people be allowed to succeed by default?

What do I want to accomplish with my life? What do I want to leave behind after I die?

I realized that I needed something deeper in my Judaism. I was not happy with a middle-of-the-road approach and was looking for a commitment to God that would be the core of my life. I wanted a Judaism that was inspiring, authentic and vibrant.

I had begun reading about Chassidut and attending a small, Chassidic shul in London. But I still felt that something was lacking. I just didn't know what.

One of the books I read on Chassidut referred to a Chassidic rebbe who had died in the Ukraine in 1810 at the age of thirty-eight. Although he did not leave a successor, he left teachings and stories, as well as chassidim who still follow his path. His path emphasized talking alone to God, enthusiasm and joy. My curiosity was more than aroused.

I remember reading a review of a recently-published book called *Rabbi Nachman's Wisdom*. The review was not overly favorable, focusing on the fact that the book wasn't written in accordance with the modern academic and psychological theories on Rebbe Nachman. Instead of intellectually examining the Rebbe's teachings, the book had adopted the Rebbe's approach of simplicity and translated his lessons in a straightforward and uncomplicated manner for English-speaking readers.

Whilst my university education had trained me to value an intellectual approach to life, I realized that this approach did not hold the answers. This book appeared to be just what I was looking for.

I found *Rabbi Nachman's Wisdom* in a central London Jewish bookstore, but it was a hardback edition (in those days, approximately six U.S. dollars) and, being on a limited budget, I only purchased paperbacks. I decided to wait to buy the book when it came out in paperback.

Back home, I realized that it was very possible that I had made a huge mistake. After all, this might be the book that could change my life. The next day, I returned to the store and purchased the book.

IN *RABBI NACHMAN'S WISDOM*, the Rebbe states, "The only time a person can think clearly is when he is dead. When he is lying on the ground with his feet to the door,[105] he will finally see the truth."[106] That paragraph was like dynamite for me. After continuing to read more of the Rebbe's teachings, I was extremely enthusiastic and determined to find someone to teach me Breslov Chassidut.

A friend suggested that I meet an academic who wrote about Rebbe Nachman. I did so, but I felt that since the Rebbe emphasized simplicity, the professor's intellectual approach conflicted with everything the Rebbe stood for. I was searching for a simple, direct approach to God. A friend of mine had a cousin who was a Toldos Aharon[107] chassid. He had learned some of the Rebbe's Torah and was prepared to teach me.

The Toldos Aharon chassid and I started learning *Likutey Moharan* I, 4, which discusses a person's purpose in life and the importance of confession (*viduy*). I was completely bowled over. The following morning, I phoned the chassid and asked, "Do you realize what we were learning last night? Do you realize the greatness of what we were learning? It was amazing."

But he could not understand what I was so excited about. He did not appreciate the impact the material had on me.

Although the chassid and I continued to learn the Rebbe's teachings regularly, it wasn't what I was looking for. I needed contact with people who were actually committed to the Rebbe's teachings.

I carried on this way for quite a period of time. In the summer of 1979, I realized that it was impossible to become a Breslover chassid completely on my own. If I didn't find a Breslover chassid to teach me about Breslov by the end of Sukkot, I decided, I'd look to another form of Chassidut.

---

105 Immediately after death, it is customary to place the body on the ground with its feet toward the door (*Derekh Chaim*).

106 *Rabbi Nachman's Wisdom* #83.

107 A Chassidic group based in Meah Shearim, Jerusalem.

During *Chol HaMo'ed* Sukkot, I received a phone call from Rabbi Avraham Greenbaum. We had been friends at Cambridge University, and he had since moved to Israel and become involved with Breslov there. Now he was visiting England. He asked if I would be interested in learning with him—that night was Rebbe Nachman's *yahrtzeit* (anniversary of passing). It was an offer I could not refuse.

> "Do you realize the greatness of what we were learning?"

RABBI GREENBAUM INTRODUCED ME to Chaim Kramer. That same year, Rabbi Gedaliah Koenig came to England. I helped take him around London to raise money to develop the Breslov community in Tzefat. He was to me (and to many others) a very special *rav*, the likes of whom I had never met.

Rabbi Koenig traveled to Manchester for Shabbat and I joined him. That's when I first met Rabbi Elimelech Silbiger, whom I discovered had been learning the Rebbe's teachings for a number of years. I returned to London grateful to have finally found in Rabbi Koenig a mentor who fitted my conception of what a true Breslover chassid should be.

Two days later, I received a phone call informing me that Rabbi Koenig had suddenly passed away in Manchester. I was devastated; after my long spiritual search, the person I thought would guide me in the Rebbe's path was no longer there. Nevertheless, I had to pick myself up and go forward.

I began to make a much stronger connection with Chaim Kramer, who was based in Jerusalem. One day, I told him, "Chaim, I need a teacher." Sometime later, when he was visiting London, he showed up at my house with a box full of audio cassettes. It was a set of the late Rabbi Rosenfeld's recorded lessons on Rebbe Nachman's teachings. I started listening to them, and their impact on me was enormous.

I feel that I have had two foremost mentors in Breslov of the previous generation—Rabbi Koenig and Rabbi Rosenfeld, may their memories be a blessing. Although I never met Rabbi Rosenfeld (he passed away in 1978), listening to the tapes of his classes, which demonstrate his vast knowledge, and hearing his tone of certainty and authority, impacted me immeasurably.

Chaim and I became dear friends, and I feel particularly blessed that we remain very close to this day. In February 1985, my two children and I traveled with him, his wife and his son to Uman when it was still under Communist rule.

WE FLEW TO MOSCOW FROM LONDON. From Moscow, we took an internal flight to Kiev. In those days, in order to get a visa to Uman, one had to first travel to Kiev and apply for the visa there. If one was lucky, the application was approved.

We waited two days in Kiev before receiving our visas to Uman. An Intourist driver and guide (really a KGB guard) drove us there. At the entrance to the city, the police stopped us. They wanted to send us back, but our Intourist guide persuaded them to let us through.

The snow was very deep. In those days, the *tziyun* was still outside in an old lady's yard. Taking into account the wind-chill factor, it must have been minus 22 degrees (minus 30 degrees Celsius)! We remained at the *tziyun* for an hour or so. We were not sure when our guide might tell us that we had to leave. This, together with the extreme cold, made it difficult for me to have a settled mind.

Some three years later, in 1988, I moved to Manchester. I gradually reduced the amount of time I spent at my legal office and developed a close relationship with Rabbi Silbiger. We studied Breslov together almost every evening. Even after I moved back to London some eighteen years later, we continued learning together (and are still learning together) over the telephone. I am eternally grateful to him for sharing his knowledge and beliefs with me.

In 1989, the Soviets gave permission for the Breslover chassidim to gather together in Uman for Rosh HaShanah. That year, traveling to Uman was an extraordinary spiritual experience. Physically, being in Uman was extremely difficult. We were put in what was then the official Uman "hotel." It was infested with insects and the sanitation was horrific—by the end of Rosh HaShanah, there were

We were put in what was then the official Uman "hotel."

perhaps one or two toilets (without running water) for all the people staying there. There was no *mikveh*; we immersed in the cold, muddy river.

Yet this meant nothing. What was important was how I felt the Rebbe's presence in shul was almost palpable. For so many years, Breslover chassidim had yearned and dreamed of spending Rosh HaShanah in Uman, and then suddenly that dream materialized. So many people had aspired to this, but their desires had not been fulfilled. Somehow and for some reason, I and those with me were privileged to be there then. I remember sitting in shul sobbing with emotion and gratitude that we were there—in Uman, for Rosh HaShanah.

Today, it has become easier to make arrangements to travel to Uman. We just hop on a plane and go. In England, we don't even need visas to travel there. Yet because it has become easier, we tend to take things for granted. It's difficult to find the same spark we felt that first Rosh HaShanah.

I have been asked how Breslov changed my life. There is no way that I can answer that question. I cannot imagine living without it. How could I possibly survive without the Rebbe and his teachings to guide me?

My Spiritual Rebirth

Ben Zion Solomon

One of the founders of the Diaspora Yeshiva Band, Ben Zion Solomon presently resides in Moshav Me'or Modi'im, where he divides his day between playing music and Torah study. Reb Ben Zion has recorded the Breslov melodies for Shabbat, along with joyous and meditative melodies, for the Breslov Research Institute.

I was born and raised in Flatbush in the 1940s, which in those days was mostly Jewish but not very religious. One of the only religious people I knew as a child was my father's mother. She lived with my aunt, whose apartment was downstairs from us. My grandmother was *shomer Shabbat*. She attended shul every Shabbat and prayed every morning. She kept everything, but I was only semiconscious of this.

My parents were traditional. We had our yearly Pesach Seders, mostly in English with a smattering of Hebrew. My father went to shul on Rosh HaShanah and Yom Kippur; it was the same Orthodox shul that my grandmother attended. My bar mitzvah was there, too, and I attended the shul's Hebrew school for a couple of years.

I went to the neighborhood public school, where the majority of students were Jewish. After graduating Brooklyn Technical

High School (a New York City public high school that specializes in engineering, math and science), I was accepted to the United States Military Academy at West Point. Why would a Jewish boy take such a seemingly incongruous step? It was because of Mickey Marcus, my mother's cousin.

Mickey was a West Point graduate, a Word War II veteran and my personal hero. In 1948, the Israeli government brought him to Israel to train and lead the Haganah. He was killed shortly after opening up the Burma Road.[108] I wanted to be like him, but by the end of my first year at the Academy, I realized that I had made a big mistake. West Point—and the military—was not for me. After that, I bounced around a bit until I finally got a B.A. in music from New York University.

In 1964, I was accepted to the University of California at Berkeley's Graduate Music Department. That was the year that everything exploded on campus. It was the year of the Free Speech Movement[109] and political radicalism. Although I remained dedicated to my musical studies, I was very involved in university student politics and found it difficult to stay on track with everything that was going on around me. After one year of graduate school, I took an academic year off to gather my thoughts and decide if I wanted to get more involved in politics or continue with music. I decided to finish my master's degree in musicology.

---

108 This makeshift, winding path through the seemingly impassable mountains around Jerusalem was built by the Jewish forces under the direction of American Colonel Mickey Marcus to bypass the main highway and break the months-long Arab siege of Jerusalem. Named for the road built by the Allies from Burma to China during World War II, the Burma Road allowed the Jewish forces to breach the Arab siege on June 9, 1948, just days before the United Nations negotiated a cease-fire. The film, *Cast a Giant Shadow*, starring Kirk Douglas, is about Mickey Marcus and his efforts to help the fledgling Israeli army.

109 An unprecedented student protest that took place during the 1964-65 school year on the campus of the University of California at Berkeley.

Jewishly, I was anti. Berkeley was (and still is) very anti-Israel, so although I had been somewhat Zionistic in my childhood, while in Berkeley, I was totally disconnected from Judaism and Israel.

By the time I got my M.A., I was completely disenchanted with the academic world. But I loved Northern California. All the great bands were playing in San Francisco; some of my best friends were musicians in these bands. I remained in Berkeley and rented a house next to the Rose Garden—it was beautiful. I worked as a longshoreman on the San Francisco waterfront and was able to earn a large sum of money with just a few days of work. I had great friends, I was playing my music, I was happy. Life was wonderful!

Then my mother phoned to ask me to come home. My father was seriously ill.

I RETURNED TO NEW YORK, where I received a license to teach in the New York City school system. I spent the next year teaching English at a junior high school. I also got involved in theater, composing musical scores and performing in an original, off-off Broadway play. We got rave reviews and were invited to perform in London, Edinburgh and Amsterdam. Once in Europe, I decided to stay for another month to search for my family's roots in Eastern Europe.

By the time I returned to the States, my father had completely recovered, which was amazing because everyone had thought that he wouldn't. Now that he was healthy again, I went back to Northern California and joined a commune in Mendocino County. I met my wife and we were married there. It was a Jewish wedding.

We had an idyllic life. Saturday nights, I played music in a local club and earned excellent money, mainly from tips. Since we grew our own vegetables and raised chickens and goats for eggs and milk, we didn't need much money. But although I didn't feel any material lack, I was on a continuous search for spirituality.

Then all of a sudden, out of the blue, God grabbed me. I don't know why or how. One day, while meditating, it became clear to me that my roots were in Judaism. I realized that I must restrict my search for meaning to the faith to which I belonged.

Then all of a sudden, out of the blue, God grabbed me.

I came home all shaken up and told my wife that I needed to go down to San Francisco to buy myself a pair of *tefilin*. She thought that I had lost my mind. What did I know about *tefilin*? All I knew was that the one Hebrew school teacher whom I'd really liked had told me that the mitzvah of *tefilin* is the essence of Judaism.

My wife was in the final month of her pregnancy with our second child, and we were planning a home birth. She was afraid that I'd miss the birth and asked me to stay home. But I felt that I had to go. I'd only be away for less than a day, after all. I went, and that was the day our daughter was born! I viewed my daughter's birthday as the day of my personal spiritual rebirth. It was the day that I began coming close to God.

I borrowed the one and only book on Judaism from the public library and read it cover to cover three times. But nothing I read turned me on. It was just dry information, completely lacking in spirituality.

My three-year-old son, Noach, was my study partner. We learned the *aleph-bet* together. I also wrote to the Lubavitcher Rebbe, telling him my story. He sent me back a letter of encouragement with a little survival kit that included a Chabad *siddur* and some booklets. One was on *tefilin* and another was on *tzitzit*. My wife sewed me a *talit katan*[110] while I did the "macramé"—attaching the strings and tying all the knots.

---

110 A four-cornered garment worn under one's everyday clothes, to which *tzitzit* are attached.

My wife reluctantly humored me, thinking this Jewish thing would pass. Her parents were Holocaust survivors who had shed all traces of Judaism when they came to America, so she, too, knew very little about our heritage. The other people on the commune thought I was being selfish for refusing to work on Saturdays. The truth is, I had no idea how to observe the Shabbat. Since I didn't know what I could or could not do, I figured that I just wouldn't do anything!

After I received the *siddur*, I started reciting the words, although I had no idea what I was saying. I knew that *"Shema Yisrael"* is important, so I concentrated on that.

It soon became obvious to me that I needed to speak with a rabbi, but there wasn't one in the vicinity. I asked around until I found a fellow who lived in a neighboring community and who was somewhat knowledgeable about Judaism. When I asked him to recommend a rabbi to speak to, he responded, "No rabbi will speak to someone like you!" After a few minutes of thought, however, he continued, "Maybe there is *one*. He's in San Francisco right now and his name is Shlomo Carlebach." That's how I discovered the House of Love and Prayer.[111]

THE YEAR WAS 1972. I drove down to San Francisco—a four-hour drive—in my old 1949 Studebaker pickup. Once I got to the House of Love and Prayer, I pulled into the no-parking zone and got out of the truck. A man wearing a colorful knitted *kippah*, with long fringes hanging out from under his shirt, came over to me and gave me a big hug. He asked, "What can we do for you?"

I explained that I had been driving for four hours straight and would appreciate something to eat and drink. He answered, "I'm sorry. That's the one thing I can't do for you because today's

---

111 Rabbi Shlomo Carlebach (1925-1994), known as the "singing rabbi," opened a center called the House of Love and Prayer in the Haight-Ashbury section of San Francisco in the late 1960s to reach out to Jewish youths who had joined the hippie movement.

the seventeenth of Tammuz,[112] a fast day. But if you're *deeply* hungry, I can give you something better than food."

> It was obvious that he was speaking directly to me.

He led me though the basement to the backyard. There I saw Reb Shlomo sitting on a chair holding a gigantic book, the biggest book I had ever seen. People were sitting on the grass around him, listening to him teach.

I had come to San Francisco with a list of questions to ask the rabbi. I listened to Reb Shlomo learning from this book, and after fifteen minutes, I wondered what the other people were doing there. It was obvious that he was speaking directly to me and answering all my questions—every single one!

When Reb Shlomo finished teaching, I asked him for the name of the book we had been studying. It was *Likutey Moharan* by Rebbe Nachman of Breslov. He invited me to come to the House for Shabbat. It was clear that I had just met both my rebbes—Rebbe Nachman and Reb Shlomo!

The first time I spent Shabbat at the House of Love and Prayer, I went without my family. I was blown away by the whole scene there. It was amazing—Reb Shlomo's teachings, the music that bathed my soul; it was a *mikveh* of music. I returned home on fire, passionately in love with Shabbat.

I told my wife, Dina (who was then called Diane), that she should come to San Francisco to meet Reb Shlomo. We went there for Tisha B'Av. A married couple who lived on the second floor of the building where Reb Shlomo's shul was housed invited me, my wife and our two children to stay with them.

That Tisha B'Av, I met the entire *chevrah*. Everyone was my teacher; everyone had something to share. My wife really

---

112 This fast day commemorates the breach of the walls of Jerusalem prior to the destruction of the Second Temple by the Romans. It marks the beginning of the three-week mourning period leading up to Tisha B'Av, the day that both the First and Second Temples were destroyed.

connected with the women there. We were falling in love with Torah!

After that, people from the House would come up to Mendocino County to visit us at our commune. I invited them to visit on condition that they bring a *Likutey Moharan* with them. We'd sit around the fire learning Rebbe Nachman's Torah. I was really into it. Rebbe Nachman's teachings touched my soul.

DINA AND I WERE KEEPING SHABBAT TOGETHER. It was very beautiful. We'd spread a white tablecloth across a huge redwood stump. She would bake challahs; I'd run to the river to immerse. It was unbelievable, but it was just our family. We desperately needed a community.

After a year of this, I went to Reb Shlomo and told him that I had to do some serious learning. I wanted to go to a yeshivah and asked him where to go. "But please," I said, "don't tell me to go back to New York."

Reb Shlomo thought for a while. Then he took my hand and we started walking around the block. Every few minutes, he would think of something and then shake his head and mutter, "No. That's not for you." When he got back to the House, he looked me straight in the eye and said, "Ben Zion, go to Jerusalem and learn Gemara."

At the time, I didn't realize that Reb Shlomo never told people what to do; he just made suggestions. But this time, he literally commanded me to go to Jerusalem to learn.

It all happened very fast, in a matter of a few weeks. I contacted the Jewish Agency and told them that I wanted to move to Israel. When they asked me what I did, I told them that I was a teacher (after all, I did have my teaching license). They were willing to pay for my flight to Israel. Then I wrote a letter to Rabbi Mordechai Goldstein, head of the Diaspora Yeshiva,[113] one of the few *yeshivot* at the time that catered to people with

---

113 See note 7, p. 24.

no previous background in Torah learning. I told him that I wanted to learn Gemara in his yeshivah. He informed me that since I was married, not only would I not have to pay, but I would receive a monthly stipend! So we sold everything, took our kids and our musical instruments, and flew to Israel.

> It was exciting to discover God in a book.

The Jewish Agency placed us in the Mevaseret Zion Absorption Center just outside Jerusalem. On my second day in Israel, I took the bus to Jerusalem, went straight to the Breslov Yeshivah in Meah Shearim, and bought myself a big copy of *Likutey Moharan*.

Within a month of starting the absorption center's *ulpan*, I was able to understand basic conversational Hebrew. Then somebody told me that I must meet a certain Breslover chassid by the name of Rabbi Gedaliah Koenig. I attended his Thursday-night *shiur* and was completely blown away by him. Although he spoke in Hebrew and I was unable to understand much of what he said, his words went directly to my soul.

I spent the mornings studying Hebrew at the *ulpan*. In the afternoons, I would travel to Jerusalem to learn Gemara at the yeshivah. It was exciting to discover God in a book. Before this, my relationship with God had been through pondering the beauty of nature, the Pacific Ocean, the redwood trees... Living in Northern California, it's almost impossible *not* to become religious. But now God was speaking to me through a book, and I was speaking to Him through my prayers. I loved every moment of it.

WE STAYED IN THE ABSORPTION CENTER for close to a year. Originally, I had planned on spending a year or two studying Torah in Israel before returning to the United States. But when the Yom Kippur War broke out and all of Israel turned into one big family, I realized that I could never leave. Israel was, and still is, my home.

After three months in *ulpan*, the teacher said, "Up to now we've been working on conversational Hebrew. Now we're going to start learning to read an Israeli newspaper." I said to myself, *I'm getting out of here! If I'm going to learn to read Hebrew, it won't be from the newspaper—it'll be Torah.* So I left the *ulpan* and started studying full-time in the yeshivah.

Eventually, we left the absorption center and moved to Jerusalem. Every Thursday evening, I would sneak out of yeshivah to attend Rabbi Gedaliah Koenig's *shiur*. But the head of the yeshivah where I was studying was extremely anti-Breslov. When he discovered that I was leaving the yeshivah to go to a Breslov class, he called me into his office and asked, "What's this *Likutey Moharan* business?"

"I love this book," I told him, "and learning it does great things for me."

"I have a tradition from my *rosh yeshivah*," he said, "that I am authorized to teach the method of learning Gemara, Midrash and *mussar* that we learn in the yeshivah. That's what I learned from my *rosh yeshivah*, who learned it from his *rosh yeshivah*...who learned it from Reb Simcha Zissel,[114] who learned it from Rabbi Yisrael Salanter[115]..." He traced the entire *mesorah* (tradition) all the way back to Moses. Then he said, "I have an unbroken chain

---

114 Rabbi Simcha Zissel Ziv (1824-1898) was one of the leading disciples of Rabbi Yisrael Salanter and a key figure in the propagation of the *Mussar* Movement. He is also known as the Alter of Kelm, as he founded and led the Kelm Talmud Torah, a Lithuanian yeshivah that focused on *mussar* and self-development.

115 Rabbi Yisrael Lipkin (1810-1883) was a Lithuanian *rosh yeshivah*, Torah scholar, and father of the *Mussar* Movement, which promotes the study of moral teachings based on classic rabbinic works. The *Mussar* Movement, a direct response to the *Haskalah* (Enlightenment) movement which was tearing Jews away from their roots in nineteenth-century Europe, gained popularity among *litvishe*, non-Chassidic yeshivah students. The name "Salanter" was added to his name due to the influence on his thinking by his primary teacher, Rabbi Yosef Zundel of Salant (1786-1866).

to teach these things in my yeshivah. If you want to be in my yeshivah, it would be worthwhile for you to study these things. But if you want to study *Likutey Moharan*, go to the Breslov Yeshivah in Jerusalem. My suggestion, however, is that you put it on hold and concentrate on learning the sources."

> He asked, "What's this *Likutey Moharan* business?"

His advice sounded right. So although it was difficult, I stopped learning the Breslov teachings.

During this time, I was part of the group that started the Diaspora Yeshiva Band.[116] We played at public *melaveh malkah* meals in the yeshivah and were very successful. We began performing concerts. One of our songs was accepted for the competition in the Chassidic Song Festival and won first place. For several years, I supported myself by playing in the Diaspora Yeshiva Band.

From 1973 until 1976, my days were devoted to learning Gemara and my nights to playing music. In 1976, the Shlomo *chevrah* (a group of people associated with Reb Shlomo Carlebach) got together to settle Moshav Me'or Modi'im. We moved to the moshav, and I commuted to Jerusalem to study in the yeshivah.

ONE NIGHT, I RECEIVED A PHONE CALL from Rabbi Avraham Greenbaum on behalf of the Breslov Research Institute. They had heard that I was a musician and musicologist who was close to Breslov, and wondered if I'd be interested in collecting, arranging and recording the music of Rebbe Nachman and the Breslover chassidim. This offer was a dream come true.

The next day, I went to the Breslov Research Institute and met Chaim Kramer. We hit it off and I started work immediately. He arranged for me to interview some of the Breslov elders who carried the musical tradition. I would arrive with my tape recorder and tape them singing, and then listen to them talk

---

116 See note 5, p. 23.

about the Breslov melodies that were sung in Europe and in Israel. Within a few years, I had collected a massive treasury of melodies. Few of the people I taped are alive today.

In 1989, I traveled to Uman for the first Rosh HaShanah *kibutz* permitted by the Communist government. That first year in Uman was the best. Each year is great, but the first time was special. When we arrived in Uman, I went straight to the *tziyun*. I felt as if there were something pulling my heart to Rebbe Nachman. I prostrated myself on the *tziyun* and felt that my heart had completely opened. I felt inexorably connected to the Rebbe.

Traveling to Uman has brought my connection to Rebbe Nachman from the abstract and intellectual to a personal level. The prayers there are the most powerful I have ever experienced. When the thousands of chassidim cry out during the *Kaddish* prayer, "*Yehei Shemei rabbah mevorakh*—May His great Name be blessed," it seems as if the ceiling is about to be sent up into the heavens. The special atmosphere at the holiday meals with men from literally every continent nurtures an instant camaraderie. I can't imagine not spending Rosh HaShanah in Uman!

From Hollywood To Holiness

Brian Hanan

Brian Hanan is a businessman who is active in the
Los Angeles Breslov community.

Although I wasn't born Jewish, I grew up with a deep belief
in God and the truth of the Bible. My parents are Protestants,
and we attended church regularly. My mother would help me
say my prayers before going to sleep at night.

For some reason, I was always drawn to Jews. In school, most
of my friends were Jewish. When I was in high school, I read
everything that I could about the Holocaust, and Yiddish songs
literally moved me to tears.

In high school, I also started my lifelong search for meaning.
I explored the different religious philosophies, especially the
Eastern and Native American religions. But although I searched
desperately for something that would satisfy my hunger for
truth, it was never satiated.

After college, I attended the University of Southern California
in Los Angeles, where I studied screenwriting and English. It
was in Los Angeles that I met Tziporah and eventually settled
down.

Tziporah was born and raised in Israel, but when I met her in
1994, she had already been living in the United States for fifteen

years and was Americanized. Believe it or not, we met at a bar. I was with a friend of mine, an English chap who always referred to women as "birds." Before entering the bar, I told him that I hoped I would meet an interesting "bird." When I walked into the bar, I saw the woman who would become my future wife sitting at one of the tables. She looked like an interesting "bird," so I sat down next to her and we started talking—and we haven't stopped since. Her name, by the way, is Tziporah, which means "bird" in Hebrew!

A couple of months after that first meeting, Tziporah received a phone call from her family in Israel informing her that her mother was on her deathbed. Tziporah asked me if I would accompany her to Israel. Although Israel had no special significance for me, I joined Tziporah on her visit.

Tziporah's mother awoke from her coma just hours before we arrived and was sitting up, waiting anxiously to be reunited with her only daughter. The first question she asked me was "Did you have a bar mitzvah?" I lied and said, "Yes, of course," because I didn't want to hurt her. She was dying, and I didn't feel that it was important for her to know that the man her daughter was dating was not Jewish.

A few days later, we drove to Jerusalem. Climbing the hills from Beit Shemesh to the Holy City, I was overwhelmed with a strange emotion. It felt as if someone had turned on the gravity. The hills seemed so familiar to me that I started to cry.

The week before, I had dreamt that Tziporah and I were walking along an ancient road, holding hands. When we got to the Old City of Jerusalem, I recognized that road, the road from my dream. At the Dome of the Rock,[117] an Arab man came up to me and said, "You are supposed to take care of this woman."

---

117 An Islamic shrine on Temple Mount which houses the Foundation Stone (*Even Shetiyah*), the stone from which God created the rest of the world (*Yoma* 54b). Since this is the site where the Holy Temple stood, it is forbidden for Jews to ascend there due to the laws of purity and impurity.

The following day, while drinking tea in an Arab shop, the Arab shopkeeper said the exact same words that the Arab on the Temple Mount had said to me the previous day: "You are supposed to take care of this woman." It was very strange. At the *Kotel*, I was so overwhelmed with emotion that my entire body trembled. I was literally shaking like a leaf.

> I had never heard of Kabbalah and asked Tziporah about it.

TZIPORAH AND I RETURNED TO LOS ANGELES and continued with our lives. One day in 1996, as we were driving along one of the major streets, I noticed a billboard that said, "Want to know more about Kabbalah?" I had never heard of Kabbalah and asked Tziporah about it. What she said piqued my interest. A few days later, I attended an introductory lecture at the Kabbalah Centre.

I found the lecture interesting and profound. For some odd reason, I felt extremely connected to the Hebrew letters; it was a type of attachment that I had never experienced before. But we didn't go back.

A few months later, someone invited Tziporah and me to a private class in someone's home given by one of the teachers from the Kabbalah Centre. We were fascinated. It wasn't long before we started attending the Centre's Shabbat services in addition to classes during the week.

During my first Shabbat service at the Kabbalah Centre, I sat next to an Israeli who pointed to each word in the prayer book as he read it. Although I did not know how to read Hebrew, one word kept jumping out at me. I asked him about it. It was God's Name.

Soon I was immersing in the *mikveh* each morning and praying regularly in the Kabbalah Centre *minyan*, in addition to attending Shabbat services. But although we were deeply into Kabbalah, we were not observant. We did not keep kosher. On Shabbat, we drove to the Kabbalah Centre, while on Saturday night, we could be found in the Hollywood Hills, mingling with the movie stars.

I began reading anything I could find that had to do with Torah and Judaism. Torah books seemed to jump off the shelf at me—I'd go to a secular bookstore and find Torah! I'd turn on the television and there would be a rabbi speaking!

One night, I dreamt that I was standing on a rock overlooking a magnificent valley. The valley's exquisite beauty brought me to tears. It was completely covered with red, purple and turquoise strings. Then suddenly, I found myself standing inside a building that was in the process of being built. From the far end of the building, I saw a man with a long, white beard walk toward me. Looking straight at me, he said, "You are in charge of all the numbers and measurements."

"Me? How will I know what to do?" I asked.

"The spirit of God will come upon you and you will know," he replied. Then I woke up and told Tziporah about my dream.

The following month, I looked up the *parashah* that would have been my bar mitzvah *parashah* had I been born Jewish. I had been told that a person's bar mitzvah *parashah* contains an allusion to his *tikkun*, his mission in this world. My bar mitzvah *parashah* spoke about Betzalel, whom God had appointed through Moses to design the Tabernacle in the desert. The strings that were used to build the Tabernacle were the same colors as the strings I had seen in my dream, and Moses said to Betzalel that "God's spirit is upon him, and therefore he knows what to do"[118]—just as the old man had told me that the spirit of God would come upon me and I would know. As I read those words, I realized that somehow, my soul was connected with that of Betzalel.

This dream continued to impact my life. The first time I opened a Gemara, I started reading about Betzalel. Later on, when I converted, Betzalel was the Hebrew name I chose for myself (after all, Brian also starts with a *B*). Interestingly, after sitting in the same seat in our Orthodox shul for over six

118 See Rashi on Exodus 31:2-3.

months, my stepson noticed that
the name engraved on the tarnished
brass nameplate on the back of the
seat was none other than "Betzalel
something-or-other."

> Betzalel was
> the Hebrew name
> I chose for myself.

But getting back to the beginnings
of my becoming religious, after several years of heavy involvement
in the Kabbalah Centre, Tziporah and I began to notice negative
things there that we hadn't seen before. We started to look for
spirituality elsewhere. First we went to Aish HaTorah, and from
there to a Discovery seminar.[119] As a result of Discovery, Tziporah
started to believe in God. After that, we attended an Arachim
weekend.[120]

By this time, we had really become committed. We attended
Shabbat services, each time in a different Orthodox shul. I studied
regularly with an Aish HaTorah rabbi. We slowly started to keep
kosher. First we stopped eating shellfish, then non-kosher meat.
Finally, we arranged for a group of rabbis to come to our home
to *kasher* the kitchen. The first time we kept Shabbat, we loved
it. My wife's son, Michael, who was then eight years old, asked
me if we could do it again. I said yes, and from that time on, we
kept Shabbat.

With time, Tziporah and I became more and more involved
with the Orthodox community. We enrolled Tziporah's son,
Michael, in a yeshivah day school. I attended *minyan* and
studied Torah regularly, especially Breslov Chassidut with Rabbi
Elchonon Tauber. We kept Shabbat and ate only kosher. No one
dreamt that I was not Jewish and that Tziporah and I were not
married. We kept up this charade for over six years. During that

---

119 Aish HaTorah is an international Jewish educational organization founded
by Rabbi Noah Weinberg in Jerusalem in 1974. Its Discovery seminar, which
sets out to answer the question "Why be Jewish?" has been seen by 100,000
people on five continents.
120 See note 47, p. 104.

entire time, I always found an excuse not to be called up to the Torah, since as a non-Jew, it was prohibited.

I finally realized that I really, truly wanted to bind myself to *Am Yisrael* (the Jewish nation), and told the rabbis in the community my secret. To say that they were flabbergasted is an understatement! But it was obvious to them that I was a sincere in my desire to be a Jew.

FROM THE MOMENT THAT I DECIDED TO CONVERT, I had to leave the house that I shared with Tziporah. Upon becoming a Jew, I felt like a fish that was finally returned to water. Once I was a Jew, Tziporah and I got married. We even had a real Jewish wedding. It was a beautiful affair with 300 people in attendance, including my parents.

On *Shabbat Shuvah* 2006 (the Shabbat between Rosh HaShanah and Yom Kippur), Tziporah gave birth to twin girls. Shortly after the delivery, the anesthesiologist asked her if everything was all right. She responded that she couldn't feel her shoulder. A moment later, she said, "I think I'm going to die."

The doctor took one look at her and ordered me to leave the delivery room. In the waiting room, I heard the loudspeaker announce, "Code Blue, Code Blue," and watched in horror as the head of cardiology raced past me into the delivery room.

I was petrified. I felt the nurses staring at me and then turning away the moment they thought I noticed them. It was obvious that something terrible had happened.

Almost an hour later, the doctor came out of my wife's room and explained to me that Tziporah had suffered an amniotic embolism, a rare and usually fatal obstetric emergency, and that the doctors were doing their utmost to save her. Three hours later, he returned to the waiting room and told me that Tziporah had survived and was about to be transferred to the intensive care unit. "It will be another forty-eight hours before we know if she made it. Only then will we be able to assess the permanent damage. Eighty-five percent of the cases die within the hour. Of the other fifteen percent that survive, most are either brain-damaged or paralyzed."

A moment later, she said, "I think I'm going to die."

I sat next to Tziporah's bed in the intensive care unit praying with a power that I never realized I possessed. People throughout the world were also praying for her recovery.

Six days later, Tziporah was well enough to be discharged from the hospital. We experienced many, many miracles during this time. For example, there was a question if my wife would have her doctor or one of his colleagues present at the birth. Thank God, our doctor was present, since he had worked in the county hospital and had seen three amniotic embolisms, something that ninety-nine percent of all physicians never encounter during their entire career. He instantly recognized the symptoms and was able to give her immediate care, which was a major factor in her survival.

Following that miracle, I made a commitment to travel to Uman. For the last seven years, I had been studying Breslov Chassidut regularly and felt a deep connection to Rebbe Nachman. Now, in gratitude for the miracle we had experienced, I felt that I had to seal that connection with a real commitment. One year later, I traveled to Uman for the annual Rosh HaShanah *kibutz*.

THE TRIP WAS AMAZING. All sorts of Jews come to Uman: *yeshivishe, litvishe, Yerushalmi, chassidishe*, Chabad, Yemenite, Moroccan, modern American—you name it, they're there. Yet despite this diversity, there is a tremendous feeling of unity and brotherhood. It was truly messianic. The prayers were very high and profound. I have never experienced anything like it elsewhere.

Since I've returned from Uman, a week hasn't gone by that I don't think about going back there again. The blessing of Uman was material as well as spiritual. Within a month of returning home, my business started to flourish and my income quadrupled! I used some of the additional money to sponsor publication of a Breslov book, and hope to do so again this year.

It's very clear to me that Rebbe Nachman's message of hope is exactly what this generation needs to hear.

My story is still unfolding. I feel that part of the reason for my having gone through what I went through is so that I can help other Jews find their way back to Torah and help other converts find their path in Judaism. Thank God, for the last eight years, Tziporah and I have hosted a Torah class in our home and continue to share with others the gifts that we have received. Many of the people who have come through our doors have become more observant, from starting to keep kosher to wearing *tefilin* every morning to studying in a yeshivah and converting to Judaism. It's a privilege to be able to help others along the path that we have taken.

My Heart Is In The "East"

"You are wherever your thoughts are"
(Likutey Moharan I, 21:12).

*

"Jethro heard" (Exodus 18:1)—about the Splitting of the Sea, the battle with Amalek and the Exodus from Egypt (see Rashi, ad loc.). But surely the whole world heard [about these miracles]? However, Jethro heard and changed his way of life; the other nations ignored what they heard (Zohar II, 68a). This is because "Hearing depends on the heart"
(Tikkuney Zohar #58, p. 92a).

*

Rebbe Nachman once said, "When a person has a Jewish heart, he has nothing to do with space. The heart is Godliness, and God is the place of the world" (Likutey Moharan II, 56). He also taught: The essence of Godliness is in the heart, as it is written, "God is the rock of my heart"
(Psalms 73:26; Likutey Moharan I, 138).

A Spiritual Booster Shot

Shalom Bouskila

*Shalom Bouskila is a businessman and a member of
New York's Persian Jewish community.*

Shalom discovered Breslov when he was in the midst of serious personal
problems. His friends spoke about Rosh HaShanah in Uman, and he was
drawn by their sense of spiritual elevation.

I felt that God had arranged for me to be on a downslope so I
would go to Uman. If not for that descent, I wouldn't have had
the courage and stamina to travel there.

Upon arriving in the Ukraine, Shalom was overwhelmed by the stark
contrast between the Ukrainians and everything Breslov stands for.

Rebbe Nachman teaches about the importance of happiness,
but the people in the Ukraine appear half-dead. No smiles, nothing.
Just sour faces.

I was impressed by the overall level of *emunah* of the Jews I
encountered in Uman. They had completely integrated *emunah*
into their personalities. Their approach to *Yiddishkeit* was from
the heart rather than the intellect, and because it was from the
heart, it impacted my emotions. I was moved by the singing at
the *tziyun*, the sense of unity.

The one word that really sums up the experience is "phenomenal." It was absolutely amazing! The experience continues to
give light for the entire year, until the following Rosh HaShanah —
a spiritual booster shot.

There's No "Body" In Uman

Howard Kessler

Howard (Hertzel Shlomo) Kessler is a blacksmith residing in Florida since "that's where the horses are."

I grew up in a Conservative Jewish home in New Jersey. My family celebrated the Jewish holidays and went to synagogue on Shabbat. But they did not keep Shabbat or a kosher kitchen. Looking back, however, I can see little hints about the future. For example, all the other boys put on *tefilin* perhaps once or twice after their bar mitzvah. Although I was completely secular, after my bar mitzvah, I would pray in my room and put on *tefilin* every morning.

After graduating high school, I studied to be a blacksmith. In 1992, I moved to Florida because that's where the horses are. As far as Torah observance, I was beyond secular; leave that to your imagination.

My father passed away in June 1995. When that happened, something came over me and I decided to recite *Kaddish* for him. A lot of *ba'alei teshuvah* come to Torah this way. I thought that I'd go to shul once a week on Shabbat to say *Kaddish* and that would be it. But I wasn't happy with any of the shuls I went to.

Finally, I went to a more traditional shul. There they told me that I was doing it all wrong: I had to pray with a *minyan* three times a day. That's how I got started.

I was searching for more. I joined classes and started to learn. One day, in a secular bookstore, looking in the Judaica section for something meaningful, I stumbled across *The Empty Chair*. It's such a thin book—only a quarter of an inch thick—yet there, in that huge store, I discovered the only Breslov book on the shelves. I stood in the aisle and started reading. I realized that I must have this book!

I read that book over and over again. I noticed that in the back of the book there was information about the Breslov Research Institute. The next thing I knew, I was phoning the American office in Monsey to order more books.

During the next year and a half, I continued ordering books from the Breslov Research Institute in Monsey. Usually, whenever I called the office, I just left a message on their machine. One time, though, a person rather than a machine picked up the call. I was interested in purchasing a certain book and asked that person to tell me about it. He described the book for me and then he asked, "So who am I speaking with?"

When I told him my name, he said, "Oh, you've bought a lot of our books recently."

I asked whom I was speaking to. It was Chaim Kramer. We talked for a while. I told him that from everything I read, I had a strong desire to travel to Uman, but I had no idea how to get there.

Chaim responded that if I really wanted to go, then "You're going to the Rebbe" and he'd figure out the logistics together with me. He gave me his home and office numbers in Jerusalem, and his cell phone number for when he's in the United States. He said to me, "Whenever you need to speak with someone, call me."

THE FIRST TIME I TRAVELED TO UMAN, it was definitely not *ba'al teshuvah* time. It was all chassidim; the plane out of New York was totally "black hat." Although that wasn't me, I felt fine with it.

In the Frankfurt Airport (maybe it was Kiev), I noticed a chassid staring at me. It was pretty obvious that I was new to Breslov. He asked me, "What brings you to the Rebbe?" I answered, "The Rebbe speaks to me." He hugged me. With that hug, I realized that it is not the clothes that make a Breslover chassid.

In Kiev, the taxi dispatcher placed me and a few friends whom I had convinced to join me into a waiting taxi. But the driver had never been to Uman before and was unable to find the street where our accommodations were located. Finally, the driver said, "*Kaputsky*." I said to the others in the car, "I think he's throwing us out." They thought I was nuts. But I was right. The driver threw all our luggage—everything—into the street. The guys I traveled with never returned to Uman. That was their first and last trip.

I noticed a chassid walking somewhere. I was looking for the *tziyun*, and I assumed he would know how to get there. So I just left all my luggage and ran after him. "Tell me the way to the Rebbe," I said.

He pointed out the way and I ran straight there. I had left my luggage on the street, but I didn't care. It was still a few days before Rosh HaShanah, so there were only a handful of people in Uman.

After praying at the *tziyun*, I walked back to where I had left my luggage. When I was about half a block from the *tziyun*, I noticed someone walking toward me. The guy looked at me and asked, "Howard Kessler?" I said, "Chaim Kramer?" This was the first time that we actually met. The other guys had brought our luggage to the apartment where Chaim was waiting for us, and they had told him that I had gone to the *tziyun*. When I apologized for going to the Rebbe instead of to the apartment, he said, "I would expect no less from you."

Whenever I ask people who went to Uman what it was like there, they reply that it's impossible to describe it. But after I went, I realized they were telling the truth. Uman is beyond description. I feel that the Rebbe chose to be buried in Uman because if, let's say, he was buried in Israel, we would travel to Israel, stay at a fancy hotel, have hot showers and warm food, go to pray by the Rebbe, and then return home. That's it. But in Uman, it's as if the body is gone; there is no body. Washing, eating, sleeping—they all cease to exist. There is no physicality. There is only one thing, praying with the Rebbe, and your soul is completely with the Rebbe.

> There is only one thing, praying with the Rebbe.

Today, every one of my experiences is filtered through the eyes of Breslov and is taken in through the teachings of the Rebbe. I learn Chassidut every single day.

Rebbe Nachman said that even the least of his followers will have story after story about what it took for them to come to him. Each trip to Uman is such a great experience that some people are actually frightened by it. Each time they go, they wonder how the trip can be equal to the previous trip. Every year at the end of Yom Tov, I see that it was even more incredible than previous years. It's amazing. I don't understand it.

That Teshuvah Experience

Michael Caro

Born in Morocco, Michael Caro has lived in Montreal, Canada, from the age of seven. He is a businessman and a member of Montreal's Breslov Centre.

I slowly started keeping *mitzvot* after graduating high school. How did I get interested in Breslov? One of my closest friends had gotten into trouble with the law and was on probation. He was only allowed to leave the house at certain hours. When I went to visit him, I noticed the Breslov Research Institute's edition of *Tikkun HaKlali* on his dining-room table. I leafed through it and was fascinated.

Later, I discovered *Rabbi Nachman's Wisdom* and attended a few classes on Breslov. I was moved enough by what I read to want to travel to Uman for Rosh HaShanah. I was only seventeen at the time.

My parents felt I was too young to make such a journey. By Pesach, however, I was much more committed to a religious lifestyle and was determined to go to Israel—via Uman, of course—to learn Torah.

The yeshivah where I studied was not at all Breslov—actually, it was somewhat anti-Breslov. But in an amazing instance of Divine Providence, there was a Breslov *minyan* in the yeshivah's attic. I prayed with them on Shabbat.

After a year of studying in the yeshivah, I returned to Montreal, married and started a business. Every year, I travel to Uman for Rosh HaShanah. I go with *emunah peshutah* (simple faith) that if our Rebbe told us to be there, that's what we must do.

Being in Uman is an incredible experience. There's a feeling that you must do *teshuvah*. The more Torah I learn, the more I get out of the experience and the more work I put into it. I go with a sense of purpose, to grow spiritually and to repair my soul.

How has traveling to Uman impacted my life? My level of *teshuvah* is completely different. Traveling to Uman gives me the strength to continue growing in my *avodat HaShem*. I've seen people become *ba'alei teshuvah* and then give everything up. But being connected to Breslov has given me the strength to hold on, to keep at it and continue growing.

Why I Keep Coming Back

Nestor Gorfinkel

Born in Cuba, Nestor (Nachum) Gorfinkel is now a lawyer in Miami, Florida. He is married to Maria (Miriam) and has two children, Luis (Eliyahu) and Hannah.

Nestor's family fled Cuba to the United States about three years after Castro came into power. His father had survived the war years in Siberia and in the Russian army. "They were starving and unable to observe the *mitzvot*," says Nestor. When his father arrived in Cuba, he was no longer observant, so Nestor grew up in a "traditional" Conservative Jewish environment.

My wife and I began exploring our Jewish roots when I was around thirty-five years old. We started our spiritual journey at the Kabbalah Centre in Miami, but soon realized that the "religion" they were teaching had nothing to do with coming closer to God.

One Shabbat, one of the members of the community invited us for the Friday-night meal. That Friday night was December 31, 1999. The host had a Breslov brochure which piqued my curiosity, and we spent a lot of time talking about Rebbe Nachman and what it meant to go to Uman. I was very curious. It swung me spiritually.

I picked up my host's copy of *Rebbe Nachman's Tikkun* and started to read. Something clicked in me, and when I read about

Nestor Gorfinkel

Uman, I had the strange feeling that I would be going there that year.

A few weeks later, I spoke with another friend who was learning with me about some of the things which I had read in *Rebbe Nachman's Tikkun,* and this opened up a whole side of him that I had never known. He was a Breslover chassid and also a student of Rabbi Yisroel Ber Odesser. He showed my wife and me another book, *The Letter from Heaven: Rebbe Nachman's Song.* He also showed me pictures of Uman and spoke about its holiness and the concept of traveling to see Rebbe Nachman. That intrigued me even more, especially since I came from a secular yet "traditional" Jewish background. Before I started becoming religious, I never thought about such ideas as spirituality, sanctity and connection with God.

Nestor first traveled to Uman in 2000. He tried to go the following year, but was stopped by 9/11.

I travel to Uman because there's a lot that I've done in my life that I need to correct. I need to connect with this *tzaddik* to help me get through what I've done in the past and to provide me with guidance for the future. But it's not just for me—it also brings blessings to my wife and my entire family.

The first time my son and I went, I thought the journey would be highly structured, but it's not. It's like trying to get through a cafeteria; you're completely on your own. In Kiev, we stood in a huge line for an hour and a half just to get through customs. Then we learned that our luggage was on its way to Uzbekistan! The planes were called back so that we could get our bags. But by the time we had our bags, the bus to Uman had already left.

We managed to get on a different bus to Uman. But then upon arriving in Uman, I had no idea where we were supposed to go. We wandered around until we finally found an apartment to rent. It was a dump. It didn't even have running water. There were five of us in a filthy room that was less than the size of the little waiting room outside my office. I don't know how we managed to get our luggage in.

That year, Rosh HaShanah was late in the season,[121] so it was very cold—and we didn't have heat. I wore six layers of clothing and covered myself with two blankets, and I was still freezing.

We also did not have our meal cards when we arrived, even though we had paid for them in New York. We *shlepped* all the way to the old army barracks where they were serving the meals, hoping that they'd let us in without a card, but they didn't. We were starving and exhausted. In the end, a couple of kind people lent us their cards so we were able to eat something.

After eating, I went to the *tziyun*. I was completely numb by this point and wondered why I had come. And I would have to remain here for another five days!

But Rosh HaShanah was special. I prayed next to the *tziyun* with the Sephardim. It was so crowded that I don't think you could have stuck a piece of paper between the people. It was amazing and intense. The next day, I prayed in the main *kloyz*. I was astounded at the quiet; there were over 5,000 people there, yet one could hear the sound of footsteps on the gravel outside.

Musaf was very long and very powerful. Afterward, I went to the *tziyun* and recited Psalms. It felt very private and personal. By the time Rosh HaShanah was over, I understood why I had come, and I was happy that I had made the journey.

ONE YEAR, WHEN I WAS HAVING some financial problems, I considered remaining in Miami for Yom Tov. A week later, a client phoned me, a wealthy, non-Jewish man who is very spiritual and very aware that he owes his wealth to God. He had already paid for my legal services, but was so happy with my work that he handed me a check and said, "You saved me a tremendous amount of money, so here's something extra." I used that money to travel to Uman with my son.

---

121 The Jewish calendar is based on the lunar cycle, with an additional month (II Adar) added every few years to keep the holidays aligned with the seasons of the solar cycle. Therefore, Rosh HaShanah can fall anytime between early September and early October.

I've been to Uman about five times, but each year is unique and special. Since there are so many people, there are plenty of *minyanim* to choose from. The last two years, we made a *minyan* in a parking lot.

Musaf was very long and very powerful.

Don't ask yourself if it's logical to go, because if you think logically, you'll come up with a hundred and one excuses why you should stay at home. But Rebbe Nachman wants you there, and it's a huge privilege to be there. If you want to go, then even if you don't have the money, it will happen somehow. Your lifestyle will not suffer because of the financial sacrifice.

A few years ago, I met a man who told me that it was his first year in Uman. He said that it was nice, and he was happy that he'd had the experience, but he wouldn't be back next year. The following year, I met him again on the street. When I asked him what had happened, he replied, "I don't understand it myself. But I just had to come again!"

Whenever I arrive in Uman, I'm shocked at the primitive conditions. I ask myself, *What am I doing here?* When Rosh HaShanah is over, we're very grateful, because that means we're leaving the Ukraine, and the Ukraine is horrible! My son says that the best part of traveling to Uman is getting there, being with the Rebbe, and then leaving again! The first few days are great, but by the time Yom Tov is over, we're tired and ready to return home. Although we're happy to be leaving, we have no doubt that we'll be back again the following year.

Beyond Logic

Shimon Kay

Originally from London, Shimon Kay lives in Philadelphia with his wife and children. His day is divided between studying in a kollel and working as a campus rabbi.

I was raised in a religious home, but by the time I graduated high school, I was completely uninterested in religion. When my parents bribed me to spend the summer in Israel on a religious study tour, I thought, *How bad could it be?* I planned to show my face at the study sessions and enjoy the touring. By the end of the summer, I decided to remain in Israel to learn full-time.

Toward the end of that year, one of the other students at the yeshivah lent Shimon a book about Breslov.

I couldn't put it down and started looking for additional books about Breslov.

That summer, the student who had lent Shimon the book told him that he was going to Uman for Rosh HaShanah. At first, Shimon assumed that he was going to Russia to help the Jews there. But after hearing more about it, he decided to join him.

But the teachers at the yeshivah soon talked me out of it. Instead, I prayed in the Breslov shul in Meah Shearim. It was the best service that I have ever experienced, extremely powerful.

The following year, Shimon was determined to travel to Uman for Rosh HaShanah, "no matter what." With some financial assistance from a generous benefactor "who wanted the merit of being in Uman but was physically unable to travel," he purchased a ticket to Kiev.

About a month before Yom Tov, as a courtesy, I informed the *rosh yeshivah* that since I was traveling to Uman for Yom Tov, I would be leaving the yeshivah two days before Rosh HaShanah and returning two days after. The *rosh yeshivah* responded, "If you travel to Uman for Rosh HaShanah, don't bother returning to the yeshivah." I explained that I had already purchased a ticket and finalized all the arrangements. He retorted, "You can still do *teshuvah* and change your mind."

I continued learning at the yeshivah until two days before Rosh HaShanah, when I left for Uman. But I was very distracted. I had no idea where I would be learning after Yom Tov. I was very close with the yeshivah's *mashgiach ruchani* (spiritual supervisor), who put a lot of pressure on me not to go. He spoke with me countless times and even promised that if I remained in the yeshivah for Rosh HaShanah, then the following year, he would personally drive me to the airport.

My study partner was also upset with me. He didn't want to lose me and tried every possible means to stop me. But I went.

One of my most difficult challenges was my inability to explain to my friends and teachers my desire to travel to Uman. When it came to Torah learning, I had no difficulty explaining why something was right or wrong. But here it was a matter of emotions. It was beyond logic. People thought I was crazy for jeopardizing my future, and I was incapable of giving a logical reason to explain my actions.

The actual trip to Uman was, and always is, crazy—lots of pushing, which is especially difficult for someone brought up in England. The moment I arrived in Uman, I went straight to the *tziyun* to recite Psalms. That night, we woke up in the middle of the night to recite *Selichot*. It was so cold that my teeth were chattering. A modest-looking chassid was standing next to me.

He had a wispy beard and rosy cheeks. He noticed that I was shivering and gently placed his coat over my shoulders. The cold didn't bother him; he was completely immersed in the prayers.

That first trip to Uman was overwhelming. Prior to the shofar-blowing on Rosh HaShanah morning, I was overcome with emotion. The following year, I was expecting it to happen again, but it didn't. A Rabbi Lichter explained to me that emotional prayer is like a wet fish—if you try to grab it, it will jump away!

Another highlight of the trip was visiting Reb Noson's grave in Breslov. That summer, I had read Reb Noson's biography, *Through Fire and Water*. It gave me a lot of strength, because whatever difficulties I was encountering, Reb Noson had also encountered—only worse!

I remember sitting on a little hill overlooking Reb Noson's grave and praying. It was beautiful, so peaceful, without the hustle and bustle of Uman. Simple peasants, horses pulling carts—it was as if I had traveled back in time. As I sat on that hilltop, praying and looking at this scene, I felt a tremendous connection with Reb Noson and with the Rebbe.

People had drummed into my head that Breslover chassidim spend their entire day in prayer, that they never learned and were ignoramuses. But after seeing the caliber of the people who went to Uman, I felt vindicated. I met tremendous Torah scholars whose every action was infused with a sense of royalty and honor of the Torah.

Since that first trip to Uman, I've gone every year, except the year that my daughter was born right before Rosh HaShanah.

"If Breslov Can Do That, Be A Breslover Chassid"

Avi Winter

Avi Winter (a pseudonym) comes from a prominent Orthodox family. A product of America's finest yeshivot, he was groomed for greatness in the non-Chassidic world—until he decided to travel to Uman for Rosh HaShanah.

Everyone was fighting me, telling me to stop this craziness, but I felt that I had to go to Uman, so I went. As a result, I was thrown out of my yeshivah.

Another excellent yeshivah immediately accepted me, but it had one condition—that I sever all ties with Breslov and that a senior *rosh yeshivah* sign a letter attesting to that. My father was heartbroken. He couldn't understand why I was doing this to myself, and went to speak with a senior *rosh yeshivah*. He begged the *rosh yeshivah* to speak with me and tell me to stop this *mishugas* (craziness) that I had with Breslov. The *rosh yeshivah* agreed to speak with me.

When I came to see him, he said, "When I learned in Barano-witz,[122] I noticed that there was one group of *bachurim* that excelled

---

122 One of the most prestigious *yeshivot* in prewar Europe, under the leadership of Rabbi Elchonon Wasserman (1874-1941), a disciple of the Chofetz Chaim.

in everything they did. Everyone in the yeshivah learned with *hasmadah* (diligence), but these boys learned with even more *hasmadah*. Everyone in the yeshivah took their prayers seriously, but these boys took their prayers even more seriously. There was something special about them. They had a burning desire for spiritual growth that drove them to attain tremendous heights. I wondered what was the source of that burning desire. Eventually, I discovered that they were Breslover chassidim. If that's what Breslov can do, then be a Breslover chassid. I cannot prevent a boy from taking a spiritual path that can lead him to greatness."

The *rosh yeshivah* spoke with my father. That was the end of my family's opposition to Breslov. And yes, every year I travel to Uman for Rosh HaShanah.

An Extra Dimension

Michael Lowe

A resident of Manchester, England, Michael Lowe works in high tech.

I grew up in a traditional, but not Orthodox, family. I went to Sunday school every week and attended the Orthodox shul three times a year. I only started becoming religious after I got married. It was a slow and steady process. Over the last twenty-six years, I have grown in both knowledge and observance.

We lived in London for the first six years of our marriage and belonged to a middle-of-the-road Orthodox shul where most of the members were not observant. When we moved to Manchester in 1988, we joined a small, Chassidic *shtiebel*. It was the type of shul that encouraged religious and personal development. I started attending Torah classes and was really growing in my *Yiddishkeit*.

The *shtiebel's rav* was a typical *litvishe* Torah scholar whose main focus was on learning Talmud and Jewish law. One Shabbat afternoon, while we were talking during the Third Meal, I confided to him that I felt something lacking in my *Yiddishkeit*. He said that I should get in touch with Trevor Bell. The amazing thing was that the *rav* didn't really know Trevor. The previous week, he and Trevor had been seated at the same table at a wedding. Trevor had enthusiastically spoken to the *rav* about Breslov, and the *rav* was impressed enough to suggest that I speak to Trevor to find out more.

TREVOR BELL AND I STARTED LEARNING TOGETHER once a week. This continued for six years until he moved back to London. We have since continued our learning over the phone. After a couple of years of learning together, Trevor convinced me to travel to Uman for Rosh HaShanah. Since then, I've gone six times.

I have a love-hate relationship with Uman. On a spiritual level, Uman is extremely intense. But physically, it's tough. Every year, it becomes more crowded, and that makes it even more difficult. We English Jews are very polite, but the Israelis have a totally different style. It took me a while to get used to the pushing and shoving. But after being there three times, my shoulders grew wider and my elbows stronger.

I was shocked by the poverty that I saw in the Ukraine. I also had difficulty coping with the lack of organization. Everything there is total chaos! The first night that I stayed at the "Waldorf Astoria,"[123] I tried—unsuccessfully—to sleep on an uncomfortable bed while people (loudly!) went in and out of the room. Eventually, I got used to it.

On the other hand, being in Uman is a chance to contemplate life and review the year. The services are very different from what I'm used to. They're slower, with a higher level of devotion.

Many people oppose Breslov because they are ignorant of what it's all about. When I first got involved with Breslov seven years ago, one of the senior members of my shul asked me, "Are you a Breslover chassid?" The way he said it, I felt as if I were being asked if I were a Communist.

I responded, "Do I look like one?" Actually, I prefer to avoid labels—I'm just Jewish. I learn the *daf yomi*,[124] attend a class in Mishnah, go to shul three times a day, and try to fulfill the Torah as best I can. But Breslov adds an extra dimension to my *Yiddishkeit*.

---

123 See Publisher's Foreword for the explanation of this fanciful sobriquet.

124 Literally, "page of the day," a system of learning through all sixty orders of the Gemara by studying one folio page each day. Under this system, it takes seven-and-a-half years to complete the entire Gemara.

Uman Gives Me Hope

Rabbi Elchonon Tauber

Rabbi Elchonon Tauber grew up in the very Orthodox neighborhood of Williamsburg in New York City. Today, he is the Rav of Congregation Beis Yehudah, a prominent shul in Los Angeles, California.

When I was a fifteen-year-old yeshivah student, someone showed me a book written by Rebbe Nachman. I had been raised to believe that a rebbe is born perfect, with no ups and downs, so I was shocked to read about Rebbe Nachman's vulnerability. Here was someone who struggled, just as I was struggling! Rebbe Nachman was willing to talk about his personal struggles and that each person's *avodat HaShem* is constantly changing, never stagnant. We're not all the same; each of us is an individual, with individual struggles to overcome.

The realization that a *tzaddik* as great as Rebbe Nachman had to struggle to perfect himself gave me tremendous comfort. Until then, I viewed my teachers and rabbis as being somewhat like machine *matzot*, all completely uniform. I thought that spiritually, they were all doing exactly the same thing, that they were completely perfect. Now I realized that they, too, had their ups and downs. Like handmade *matzot* that are bumpy and never alike, each of them was unique, with their own unique challenges. Their connection with God was constantly changing and never stagnant.

THE NEXT TIME I ENCOUNTERED BRESLOV was two years later. I was seventeen years old, and traveled to Skver[125] to spend a Shabbat with the chassidim there. The rabbis I met there warned me to stay far away from Breslov and not to learn the Breslov books since they would make me crazy. When I heard that, I felt that I *must* get hold of a Breslov book. I said to myself, *Do they really think that I am so weak and vulnerable that a book can make me nuts? I'll show them!* I got hold of a copy of *Likutey Moharan*. Although at first, I didn't understand much of what the Rebbe wrote, I found it fascinating and had a strong desire to learn it.

THE THIRD TIME I ENCOUNTERED BRESLOV was a few years later. I was twenty years old, married, living in Lakewood, New Jersey, and studying in the *kollel* there. I had a regular study session in *Tanya*[126] with a close friend of mine, a Gerrer chassid. When we completed the *Tanya*, he suggested that we study Rebbe Nachman's *Likutey Moharan*, explaining that it's "even more challenging than the *Tanya*."

My friend and I began studying *Likutey Moharan* together, and once I started, I would never give it up! It was—and still is—amazing. As I studied the Rebbe's teachings, I began to consider myself a student of Rebbe Nachman—a Breslover. I never hid that affiliation, although in those days, Breslov was looked upon with disdain.

Once people knew that I was a Breslover, they asked me questions about it. I answered honestly that I didn't know the answers. I'd tell them that most people who fly in an airplane have little, if any, knowledge of aerodynamics. Although they don't understand why the plane flies, they know that it takes them where they want to go. I, too, don't understand everything about Breslov. But although I have lots of questions, I know that Breslov is taking me where I want to go.

---

125 The town of New Square, in Rockland County, New York, was incorporated by the Skverer chassidim of Eastern Europe, a sect that was strongly opposed to the Breslover chassidim.

126 See note 96, p. 188.

After completing his studies in Lakewood, Rabbi Tauber moved to Los Angeles to become a *dayan* (rabbinical judge) and pulpit rabbi. There he met Rabbi Gedaliah Koenig, who had come to Los Angeles to raise money for the Breslov community in Tzefat. In those days, Rosh HaShanah in Uman was still an impossible dream. Rabbi Gedaliah told Rabbi Tauber that until it became possible to travel to Uman for Rosh HaShanah, he should travel to Meron instead.

> I know that Breslov is taking me where I want to go.

The first time I traveled to Uman was in 1989. Just thinking about that trip makes me nauseous! The country was still under Soviet rule, so we had to travel there on an official tour. In Uman, they put us up in a horrible hotel. It was completely infested with roaches and there was just one toilet—that didn't flush!—for our entire floor. The stench was so bad that we questioned whether it was permissible to make a blessing in our hotel room. The smell made me feel too sick to eat. In addition, this was the first time we were traveling to Uman for Rosh HaShanah, so we had no idea what type of food to bring with us. We survived on *matzot*.

The *davening*, however, was unbelievable. There was such a tremendous feeling of joy that we had actually made it, that we were really in Uman! All the people who came that Rosh HaShanah were dedicated Breslovers. Most had dreamed for years of being able to fulfill the Rebbe's directive and spend Rosh HaShanah in Uman. Now they were finally realizing that dream. The excitement was palpable.

On the plane taking us to the Soviet Union, we met two Orthodox rabbis. They were shocked that we were leaving our wives and children to spend Rosh HaShanah in Uman. When I asked them where they were going, they said that the Agudath Israel[127] had sent them to lead Rosh HaShanah services in Lemberg (Lvov). They were not earning money from the trip; they were traveling there solely for the mitzvah, to help their fellow Jews.

---

127 A political organization which represents Orthodox Jewry.

This is just one example of how, when it comes to traveling to Uman for Rosh HaShanah, people are illogical. These rabbis were upset that we were leaving our families for Yom Tov, yet they were doing the exact same thing. But they viewed what they were doing as legitimate, because it was not Uman.

IT'S NOT ALWAYS CONVENIENT for me to travel to Uman for Rosh HaShanah. I'm the rabbi of a prominent congregation. It can be difficult leaving the community at such an important time of the year.

In 2001, Arab terrorists attacked the Twin Towers on Tuesday, September 11, exactly one week before Rosh HaShanah. Normally I would have left Los Angeles on Wednesday night, but I decided to travel on Monday instead, so that I would have time to visit my elderly parents in New York before leaving to Uman. I arrived in New York the day before 9/11. After the attack on the Twin Towers, the Los Angeles airport was closed for several days and I would never have made it to Uman. Thank God, I was already in New York when it all happened.

From New York, I was supposed to fly Lufthansa to Kiev, but that flight was canceled. It was possible to fly Uzbekistan Airways to Kiev, but I was extremely nervous about the safety of traveling with them. Who knew what type of plane they'd be flying? Besides, the flight was scheduled to arrive in Kiev on Erev Yom Tov, so if there were any delays, I would end up spending Yom Tov in some crazy place other than Uman.

I phoned Rabbi Elazar Mordekhai Koenig, the leader of the Breslov community in Tzefat, to ask for his advice. He told me to go, and added that if worst came to worst, I'd end up spending Yom Tov in the airport.

It was frightening to fly so soon after the terrorist attack. We were afraid that the plane might be blown up. We arrived in Uman on Erev Rosh HaShanah at three o'clock in the afternoon. I barely had time to take a quick shower and get dressed before Yom Tov began.

That Rosh HaShanah, an ominous cloud of fear hung over us. With the attack on the Twin Towers, our sense of security had been demolished in one fell swoop.

It was frightening to fly so soon after the terrorist attack.

EVERY TIME I TRAVEL TO UMAN, I find it humbling to be among so many people who are true *ovdei HaShem* (servants of God). In Los Angeles, I am the rabbi of a community. But in Uman, I am just one of the chassidim, part of the whole. I am free to express my emotions, to really pray with every fiber of my being. It's a feeling of newness and rejuvenation for the entire year. But most important of all, traveling to Uman gives me hope.

There is a famous story about the Holocaust that illustrates what I'm trying to say. A father and son miraculously managed to remain together in one of the concentration camps. Prior to Chanukah, the father set aside his tiny margarine ration and, pulling a few threads out of his ragged camp uniform, he was able to fashion a candle to light on the first night of Chanukah.

"Wouldn't it be better to use that margarine to nourish our bodies?" the son asked. "Isn't it a mitzvah to do everything we can to survive?"

"Yes, my son, it is a mitzvah to nourish our bodies, but it is also a mitzvah to nourish our souls. Lighting the Chanukah candles gives us hope, and hope is what we so desperately need now."

Traveling to Uman gives us hope. Just by being there with the Rebbe for Rosh HaShanah, we have attained a *tikkun*. Yes, we messed up during the year—after all, we are human. When we remember all the things we've done wrong, we are disappointed with ourselves. It weighs us down and makes it hard for us to continue. But the Rebbe states that being in Uman for Rosh HaShanah is a *tikkun* for our shortcomings. Not only are we forgiven, but the damage is repaired and we are able to start anew. Thanks to Uman, we are able to pick ourselves up and continue on.

Pathway To The Heart

Dr. Julian Ungar-Sargon

*Originally from London, England, Dr. Julian Ungar-Sargon is
a neurologist living in Chicago, Illinois.*

I was born in London in 1950 and attended an Orthodox Jewish
school where my mother was the principal. I spent my post-
high-school year in Israel at Yeshivat Merkaz HaRav.[128] Despite
my traditional Orthodox upbringing, I was plagued by questions
and doubts. For the next twenty years, I continued on my path
in traditional Judaism, resigned to the fact that I would not get
any answers.

During the year that I spent at Merkaz HaRav, I developed a
love for the teachings of Rabbi Avraham Yitzchak Kook and his
creative genius (little did I know then of his deep connection to
Rebbe Nachman). At the end of the year, I returned to England
to get my diploma from the Royal Academy of Music (in piano)
and to attend the London Hospital Medical College. A few years
later, in 1972, I won the Duke scholarship to study medicine in
the United States. While there, I fell in love with neurology and
decided to pursue my postgraduate training in the U.S.

---

128 A national-religious yeshivah founded in Jerusalem in 1924 by Rabbi
Avraham Yitzchak Kook, the first Ashkenazi Chief Rabbi of Israel.

In 1977, I married into a prominent *litvishe* family. After completing my fellowship at the Neurological Institute of New York, we went to Israel, where I learned in a yeshivah in Bnei Brak. My father-in-law, a Torah scholar and pulpit rabbi, took a sabbatical that year to join me in Israel and teach me "how to learn." I owe him all my skills in *nigleh*.[129]

We returned to the United States and settled in Philadelphia, where I learned with the legendary Reb Mendel Kaplan, a student of the Brisker Rav, Rabbi Yitzchak Zev Soloveitchik.[130]

In 1984, I joined the faculty of the Harvard Medical School in Boston. The Rav, Rabbi Yoshe Ber Soloveitchik,[131] was still alive, and I jumped at the opportunity to attend his lectures and *daven* in his shul for the last few remaining years of his life. He articulated the schizophrenia that I had always felt existed in *Yiddishkeit* and presented a *"Torah im derekh eretz"* approach to Judaism that appealed to me.[132]

Two years later, I decided to deepen my knowledge of *Tanakh* and history and enrolled at Harvard Divinity School, where I graduated with a master's in theology. From there, I went on to Brandeis University to work on a PhD in Midrash.

We moved to Israel in 1990. I learned half-day in the Volozhin *kollel* and worked on my PhD during the other half. During this time, I was going through an intense midlife crisis. I could no longer ignore the conflict I saw between Western values and

---

129 The "revealed" parts of the Torah—e.g., the Talmud and the Codes.

130 Rabbi Yitzchak Zev Soloveitchik (1868-1959) was the son and successor of Rabbi Chaim Soloveitchik, *rav* of the Lithuanian city of Brisk. He fled the Holocaust and re-established the Brisker Yeshiva in Israel.

131 Rabbi Yoshe Ber Soloveitchik (1903-1993), known as "the Rav" to his thousands of students, was *rosh yeshivah* of the Rabbi Isaac Elchanan Theological Seminary at Yeshiva University in New York. He was a grandson of Rabbi Chaim Soloveitchik of Brisk.

132 Rabbi Soloveitchik emphasized the synthesis between Torah and secular scholarship in the Western world, which became a basis for the philosophical framework of Modern Orthodoxy.

strict Orthodoxy, as well as other theological and moral issues, especially concerning the Holocaust.

I also felt unfulfilled in both my personal and professional life. My children constantly forced me to evaluate my value system, and I often fell short. I found it a real challenge to raise children who would remain committed to our tradition without losing their critical thinking abilities in the process. I felt that the Judaism they were being taught was being spoon-fed to them in neat sound bites, with trite and banal answers.

IT WAS IN 1994, a year after the death of Reb Shlomo Carlebach,[133] that I came across a collection of Reb Shlomo's teachings entitled "*Lema'an Achai Vere'ai* (For My Brothers and Friends)." Suddenly, I was exposed to a new way of thinking. His Torah was sweet! It included references to the teachings of Rebbe Nachman and Rabbi Tzadok HaKohen.[134]

Reading this book, I felt something inside me open up. I had been raised in a very strict, "German" home[135] and had been taught the *litvishe*, analytic methods of learning. There was almost no connection between my emotions and my intellect. In Reb Shlomo's book, I discovered a synthesis of the two, something I had never experienced before.

Over the next few years, I immersed myself in this new approach, studying it on both an academic and personal level. These new (for me) concepts of serving God with the heart, and all that this entailed, radically altered my perspective on *davening* and learning.

I had never really known the art of *davening*. I never really grasped the meaning of Divine Providence at the personal

---

133 See note 88, p. 175.

134 Rabbi Tzadok HaKohen Rabinowitz (1823-1900) was the scion of a *litvishe* rabbinic family who became a *chassidishe* rebbe. He was a prolific writer in all areas of Judaism, *halakhah*, Kabbalah and *mussar*.

135 Jews originating from Germany (sometimes called "*Yekke*") are famously punctual and known for an attention to detail that manifests in an exacting adherence to Jewish laws and customs.

level. In fact, I had never really had a personal relationship with God! I was never taught these things. It was as if I had been given the road map, but had never been shown how to drive.

> I had been raised in a very strict, "German" home.

In my new course of study, I discovered, on the one hand, a brilliant analysis of the human soul in the unique psychological style of the Polish rebbes, while on the other, an insistence on the "broken heart" as a prerequisite to *avodat HaShem*. I realized that although I had been able to master the texts, I had never learned to control my emotions.

But although I had discovered the problem, I was not given practical steps to solve it. How could I reach balance and harmony with these disparate and opposing drives and feelings? I had seen the diagram, but now I needed a practical manual. So while I changed my method of learning, there was no real change in my behavior or relationships.

IN 2003, AS I WAS TRYING TO UNDERSTAND the difference between Rabbi Chaim Volozhin's *litvishe* understanding of certain esoteric concepts and the *chassidishe* approach of Rabbi Shneur Zalman of Liadi, founder of the Chabad-Lubavitch movement, someone showed me Lesson 64 in *Likutey Moharan*, which discusses these ideas. As I read it, I literally found myself falling off of my chair. It was amazing! In these few paragraphs, Rebbe Nachman articulates a position that somehow includes all the paradoxes of life and the questions that can and cannot be answered.

Here were answers to the deepest questions of my life. The Rebbe articulates the issues of God's goodness and justice, free choice, and all the philosophical questions I had piled up in the course of my *"schizofrumkeit."* His words resonated deeply within me, and it dawned on me that after studying the Torah of Rabbi Kook and Rabbi Tzadok HaKohen, I had finally come to *their* rebbe—Rebbe Nachman!

I began learning *Likutey Moharan* intensively, as well as other works by the Rebbe and Reb Noson. I discovered that instead of focusing on externalities such as dress, rituals, *nusach* (order of prayers) or family customs, Breslov really required from me only three things—three difficult things.

The first is that I learn *Shulchan Arukh*[136] every single day. Although I had never formally "left" the practical observance of *halakhah*, it had become habitual. By nature, I am rebellious, and I don't like being told what to do every minute of the day. What I saw as the focus on outward behavior and the superficiality of modern *frumkeit* (religiosity) made it difficult for me to see any meaning in the endless repetition of ritual practice. The lifeless *davening* I encountered in shul contributed to my impression that *frumkeit* was in fact "brain-dead" (according to the Harvard criteria, of course!).

Once I started studying Breslov books, I felt the Rebbe pushing me to return to learning the *Shulchan Arukh* and the *daf yomi*,[137] something that I had stopped doing some years earlier out of all sorts of resentments. Instead, I had studied anything else but that! Now Rebbe Nachman, who had shown me the "heart" in *Yiddishkeit*, was instructing me to return to learning it. The Rebbe insisted on both *halakhic* observance as well as the fire of enthusiasm. How could I refuse? And the gifts were not long in coming. With my commitment to the Rebbe, I found my resentments melting.

The second thing Breslov Chassidut requires is that I speak with God directly—*hitbodedut*. I found it extremely difficult to talk to God as if He is really there, as close to me as a father. As the child of a Holocaust survivor, I had been taught that God was an entity to be feared above all and that strict *halakhic* observance did not include any sense of intimacy with the Divine.

This would prove to be (and remains as) the single most difficult challenge for me in my time-strapped lifestyle. Along with *hitbodedut* came the Ten Psalms (the *Tikkun HaKlali*) and

---

136 See note 51, p. 106.
137 See note 124, p. 258.

the notion of *Tikkun HaBrit* (sexual purity). Although other Chassidic dynasties emphasize different aspects of *avodat HaShem* (for instance, Chabad emphasizes the intellectual approach which is then supposed to "inflame the heart," while Ger focuses on service of the heart), Rebbe Nachman insists that the way to holiness begins with *Tikkun HaBrit*. Over the course of time, *hitbodedut* combined with the *Tikkun HaKlali* and spiritual purification in the *mikveh* began to influence my imaginative soul and cleanse it of its impurities.

> I found it
> extremely difficult
> to talk to God.

The third aspect of Breslov Chassidut, which I had yet to fulfill, was traveling to Rebbe Nachman's *tziyun* in Uman for Rosh HaShanah.

IN THE SUMMER OF 2003, I TRAVELED TO ISRAEL. I stopped by the Breslov bookstore on Meah Shearim Street to ask if they had any books that clarify Lesson 64 in *Likutey Moharan*, the teaching that had first brought me to Breslov. They didn't, but they suggested that I speak to Chaim Kramer of the Breslov Research Institute. That was how I first met Chaim.

On Rosh Chodesh Elul, I traveled to Tzefat to ask Rabbi Elazar Mordekhai Koenig, the leader of the Tzefat Breslov community, to clarify certain points for me. At the end of the conversation, Rabbi Koenig turned to me and said, "*Nu?*"

I had no idea what he was referring to, so I remained silent.

He looked at me again and repeated, "*Nu?*"

Again I remained silent.

This repeated itself several times until someone in the room whispered to me, "Uman."

Rabbi Koenig wanted to know if I would be traveling to Uman for Rosh HaShanah.

A voice inside me prompted me to reply, "All right," although at that point, I had no idea what Uman was all about. But since I had given him my word, that was it. I would be traveling to Uman.

When my wife heard about it, she couldn't believe what I was proposing. "Uman? On Rosh HaShanah?" We hadn't been apart from each other or from our six kids for decades on the High Holidays! *Oy vey*, you can imagine the discussions that went on!

I BOARDED A PLANE FOR MUNICH a couple of days before Rosh HaShanah. I had a ten-hour layover before my connecting flight to Kiev, so I decided to rent a car and drive to Dachau.

Dachau is a neat little town with photo shops and restaurants, café houses and beer halls. Amidst the quaint village scenery, you suddenly see a looming presence: barbed wire heralding the entrance to another world, a sinister reminder of another, darker reality. Although the overwhelming majority of Dachau's victims were Jewish, the Jews are barely mentioned in the recordings for tourists. Instead, you hear about "man's inhumanity to man." What an erasure of memory! Disgusted, I returned to the airport to catch my flight to Kiev.

Kiev and the Ukraine reminded me of the dark world of Communism. Outside the airport, the Breslovers argued with the taxi drivers while remaining wary of the very real danger posed by the local mafia. Every five or ten miles, we were stopped by "police" and the driver had to bribe them to let us go further.

By the time we arrived in Uman, it was dark, the streetlights few and far between. With the kind help of Eliyahu Reiter, I found Chaim Kramer. I was jet-lagged and depressed, but his warm welcome and bear hug gave me hope! He showed me to the apartment where I would be staying.

I barely slept that night. The following day, Erev Rosh HaShanah, I attempted to get to the *tziyun*, but it was too crowded and I was unsuccessful. All around me, I saw Israelis pouring into the town, *shlepping* suitcases and trying to get settled before Yom Tov began. It was chaotic and disorderly and felt a bit like the *arba'ah minim shuk* in Jerusalem right before Sukkot.[138]

His warm welcome and bear hug gave me hope!

With the start of Yom Tov, the hustle and bustle came to an abrupt stop as everyone rushed to shul to *daven*. From there, I joined the group eating in a tent set up in the courtyard of Chaim's house. Over the last five years, this festive meal has become the center for me and many other English-speakers in Uman. Chaim's warmth and unconditional love make for a great collegial spirit.

The following morning, I *davened Musaf* together with more than 10,000 men! During the *Amidah*[139] prayer, it was so quiet that one could hear a pin drop. The *chazzan*, Rabbi Moshe Bienenstock, prayed with an incredible sweetness until he finally broke down sobbing. (It was worth traveling to Uman just to hear that heartfelt cry.) The shofar's shrill notes pierced my heart; they sounded like the bawling of an infant. Most surprising was the clapping as we recited "*HaMelekh HaKadosh* (The Holy King)," crowning God as our King. It was liberating. I felt as if we were actually coronating the King of kings!

Immediately after Yom Tov was over, the place exploded with dancing and unrestrained joy. I felt that we were celebrating the miracle of Jewish survival! Throughout the generations, nations have tried to annihilate us, yet we are very much alive. Perhaps that is one of the reasons why Rebbe Nachman chose to be buried in Uman, the site of the Gonta massacre.[140] Here we

---

138 A busy marketplace set up in several areas of the city, where vendors sell *lulavim* (palm fronds), *hadasim* (myrtle leaves), *aravot* (willow branches) and *etrogim* (citrons), which are used to fulfill the mitzvah of the Four Species (*arba'ah minim*) on the festival of Sukkot.

139 See note 83, p. 161.

140 In 1768, the Ukrainian Haidamak army, under the leadership of Ivan Gonta, massacred tens of thousands of Jews in Uman. Before his death, Rebbe Nachman said, "The souls of the martyrs [slaughtered by Gonta] await me."

were, 235 years later, nearly sixty years after the Nazis and also a decade and a half after the fall of Communism, and we were dancing on the streets of Uman under the very eyes of the local National Guard that was standing on every street corner. What historical irony! It was as if the Rebbe were tapping his finger to our singing. Rebbe Nachman's prophecy about his legacy was finally justified as his message was getting through to the Jewish nation. Having woken up from a spiritual coma, we needed the Rebbe like never before.

THE ANNUAL TRIP TO UMAN has impacted my life in so many ways. My year now revolves around Rosh HaShanah and *Shabbat Zakhor*,[141] the two times of the year when I visit the Rebbe. Each time, I prepare myself weeks in advance, and the effects linger long after my return.

My *avodat HaShem* has also changed. My prayers and Torah learning are more balanced, something I had never even thought about in my younger years. Rebbe Nachman taught me the art of *davening*—slowly and with intention.

Each year, I try to be of service to the newcomers who join the meal at Chaim's table, to help them in their struggles and spiritual journeys. The conversations and the bonds that we Breslovers share extends to my service at the emergency medical clinic in Uman, as well making the chassidim who visit Chicago feel less alienated.

I hope to become a better chassid. To me, this means following the path of others before me—like Rabbi Yitzchak Breiter, who gave us guidelines to follow on a daily basis.[142] It means deepening my understanding of the Rebbe's Torah and of Reb Noson's *Likutey Halakhot*. It means using the tools of Breslov to

---

141 The Shabbat preceding Purim, when the Torah portion of "*Zakhor et asher asah lekha Amalek*—Remember what Amalek did to you" is read.

142 Rabbi Breiter authored *Seder HaYom*, a work which provides clear directives on how to apply the Rebbe's teachings to one's daily life.

help me in my continuing struggles, like going to the *mikveh* and learning *Likutey Halakhot. Sefer HaMidot, Hishtapkhut HaNefesh* and *Meshivat Nefesh*, all of which are part of my daily "quota" that must be completed

> Rebbe Nachman taught me the art of *davening*.

before my day begins. It means helping disseminate the Rebbe's Torah to my own community, whether through classes or personal conversation or our weekly *hitbodedut* group.

Above all, it means living with a connection to the *tzaddik*, realizing that I must live a life consistent with his teachings and demands.

Yes, Breslov is a very demanding spiritual path, but for broken souls like me, it is a lifesaver.

True Magic

David Menaged

*David Menaged is a New York-based businessman, a member
of the Sephardi community of Brooklyn, and a member of the
Carlebach Shul in New York's Upper West Side.*

America chased me and my three brothers from *Yiddishkeit.*
The 1970s were a difficult time; a lot of kids from my
generation got lost. I was one of them. We thought Judaism was
cultural—something nice, but that's about it.

In my search for meaning, I traveled around the world with
my brothers and some friends. I tried all kinds of different
philosophies, the "here and now," different levels of consciousness.
I spent a lot of time in Southeast Asia and Morocco; I saw Sufis,
Black Magic, White Magic, all sorts of things, very far-out things.
I was trying to figure out who I was and what made me tick, but
I was not successful.

My eldest brother went to Israel after meeting someone in
Europe who said, "You're almost thirty and you've never been
to Israel?" Another brother and I decided to surprise him and
come to Israel for his thirtieth birthday. We arrived in Jerusalem,
rented a room at the King David Hotel, and spent two days
walking through the city, searching for our brother. We found
him in a pastry shop.

The three of us spent a week running around Israel. Although we enjoyed ourselves immensely, at the end of the week, we were ready to return to the United States and get on with our lives.

On the Friday night before our trip home, we went to the *Kotel* for *Kabbalat Shabbat*. But it didn't mean too much to us—we were all very far from Judaism at that point.

At the *Kotel* that night, we met an acquaintance from the Sephardi community in Brooklyn. He insisted that we visit a Breslov yeshivah located in the Muslim Quarter[143] before returning home.

After *Kabbalat Shabbat*, we entered the Muslim Quarter to look for the yeshivah. It was in a crumbling, old Arab building. It was drafty—there were no windows—and the ceiling looked as if it were about to cave in. The room was dim; just a few lights were on. The moment we walked in, one of the yeshivah students jumped up to greet us and asked if we spoke English. Food magically appeared in front of us.

Then the man sitting next to me started talking, and I was blown away. He spoke about ideas in Judaism I never knew existed. I had been searching the world for consciousness and self-awareness, and here was this man talking to me about these ideas, but in terms of Judaism!

I had always thought of Torah as a nice cultural thing—that I'm part of this great people, and that's wonderful—but nothing deeper than that. Now this religious Jewish man was talking and my jaw literally dropped open in amazement.

That night, my brothers and I decided to cancel our return trip to America and remain in Israel for another ten days. We spent every waking moment with the Breslover chassidim. When we left, the *rav* there told us that he was positive we'd return in another seventy days. We thought that was ridiculous.

---

143 See note 85, p. 167.

My brothers and I are businessmen. That summer, when we weren't involved with our business, we were reading the only Breslov books available then: *Rabbi Nachman's Stories, Advice* and *Azamra*. The more we read, the more we became determined to return to Israel in time for the High Holidays. So seventy days to the day that my brothers and I left Israel, we boarded a plane back to Israel, but this time, we went with a few friends.

WE RENTED AN APARTMENT in the Old City. Every morning, we got up before sunrise to pray and then spent the entire day immersed in Torah. The six of us became very close, and we still are. For several years, we rented that apartment in the Old City for Yom Tov and spent almost every waking minute with the Breslovers in Jerusalem.

So of course, when Uman opened up in the early 1990s, I was eager to travel there. The first time I went, we were seven men packed into a tiny room for the entire holiday. We brought all our water and food—duffel bags of peanut butter and bottled water—and were able to go to the *tziyun* whenever we wanted. It was an amazing experience, an experience of true bonding and a spiritual high.

After spending three Rosh HaShanahs in Uman, I decided that I needed some private time there, and went again in October. I was able to spend hours alone at the *tziyun*, which was very special.

Uman has had a positive impact on my life. I am a firm believer that whatever happens—from my kidney stones to my wonderful family—is all for my ultimate benefit. Thank God, I have a teacher who is able to take Rebbe Nachman's teachings and simplify it to a level where I can understand it and grow from it.

I have had the privilege of traveling with unaffiliated Jews to Uman. Each time I am there, I am humbled by the experience and grateful that I was blessed with the tools that enable me to become who I've become.

On Fire With Breslov

Yehudah Levinson

Yehudah Levinson practices law in Toronto, Canada.

I grew up in a traditional home and became religious through God's compassion. I was searching for spirituality for as long as I can remember. Even as a young kid—before my bar mitzvah—I spoke to a rabbi about Judaism and meditation. As a teenager and college student, I read a lot of Jewish books, including Herbert Weiner's *Nine and a Half Mystics: The Kabbala Today* and Rabbi Aryeh Kaplan's *Jewish Meditation: A Practical Guide*, but nothing clicked. In college, I delved into Buddhism and ended up with two degrees in comparative religion.

At age thirty, I decided to go into law. I saw it as mankind's attempt to reconcile its highest aspirations with the chaos of day-to-day life. That's the way I practice law today.

I attended law school in Halifax, Nova Scotia. My first Chanukah there, I had an urge to light Chanukah candles. I didn't even own a menorah, so I just placed the candles on a piece of aluminum foil and lit them.

It was the eighth night of Chanukah. I sat in front of the candles until they went out. Somehow, the light burned through all the layers that separated me from acting like a Jew so that I could begin to return to God. When my father saw my interest in Judaism, he connected me with Shalom and Judy Brodt, a Montreal couple that teaches Judaism to seeking Jews (they now live in Jerusalem). They brought me to Reb Zalman Shechter's center in Pennsylvania for Shavuot. After that experience, I decided to start keeping Shabbat.

The summer following my second year of law school, I had a position as a legal assistant at the Canadian Human Rights Commission in Ottawa. I spent my evenings at a small Jewish library in the house of one of the Lubavitchers who lived there. I spent a lot of time there just reading.

One evening, I came across a book called *The Divine Conversation*. It was about *hitbodedut*. I remember thinking, *Finally, someone is talking to me.* Although theoretically, I always knew that meditation exists in Judaism, this was the first time I read something that actually addressed it. I was so inspired that I went running out right then and there for *hitbodedut* along the Rideau Canal, one of Ottawa's beautiful parks. After finishing the book, I started doing *hitbodedut*, although not regularly.

AT THE END OF THE SUMMER, I returned to law school in Nova Scotia. My wife and I married a few months later. Together we grew in our observance, although we didn't have anyone to teach us formally. Still, by the time we moved to an Orthodox community, we were already quite knowledgeable.

My wife and I had very different approaches in our journey to full Torah observance. I was extremely enthusiastic, rushing head-on to become more and more observant, while she was more reserved. However, once we decided on something, she was the strong one who resolutely kept us from falling back. Today, we laugh about it, but I remember the time she was very upset because I wanted to add yet another stringency to my observance. In an attempt to calm her, I promised, "Don't worry, dear. We'll always be Modern Orthodox." Thank God, I was wrong!

A couple of years later, I came across the book, *Outpouring of the Soul*, in a bookstore and realized that it was very similar to *The Divine Conversation*. To Chaim Kramer's eternal credit, his name and the phone number of the American branch of the Breslov Research Institute were written inside the book.

"This is Yehudah Levinson. *IS ANYONE THERE?*"

I wanted to learn more, so I called the number and left a message on the answering machine saying that this is Yehudah Levinson, I'm interested in this book, and could someone please get back to me? I must have called at least four times. The last time I phoned, I said in frustration, "This is Yehudah Levinson. *IS ANYONE THERE?*"

Chaim happened to be in the United States at the time. On his way to the airport to catch a flight back to Israel, he had stopped by the office to pick up the phone messages. When he heard my call, he called me to let me know that he was about to leave the country, but that he would contact me when he returned. Six weeks later, he was back in America, and my wife and I traveled to New York to meet him. It was the beginning of a long and very dear friendship.

The next year, 1988, Chaim convinced us to join the American Breslover chassidim at the annual Rosh HaShanah *kibutz* in Boro Park. Travel to Uman was not yet an option.

THE FOLLOWING YEAR, 1989, travel to Uman for Rosh HaShanah became possible. Chaim convinced my wife to let me go. After seeing how the trip impacted our lives, my wife was more than happy to let me travel in subsequent years.

The spiritual impact was obvious. In traveling to Uman, I had followed my Rebbe's advice, tying my connection to him. In my daily *hitbodedut*, I thank God for giving me the gift of being able to follow the Rebbe's advice.

Although we had anticipated the spiritual ramifications of traveling to Uman, we were not expecting a change in our material circumstances. Before Uman, my law firm was foundering, and I was seriously considering closing it. But after returning home from Uman, business started to pick up.

The trip to Uman was a real adventure. In Moscow, we waited hours until the pilots were sober enough to fly the plane! In Kiev, a tractor took the luggage from the plane and then unceremoniously dumped it on the floor of the terminal. The buses from Kiev to Uman were ancient. The roads were full of enormous potholes. The hotel in Uman was ridiculous—$75 a night for a rickety bed with a straw mattress and a horsehair blanket. We had running water for just one hour a day. Forget about showers, they were nonexistent! The hotel had installed flush toilets, but there wasn't enough water pressure to operate them. The *mikveh* was nothing more than a hole in the ground lined with garbage bags.

But the prayers, the *achdut* (unity), the whole atmosphere—it was amazing. Some old men came to shul who had not seen a Torah scroll in fifty years (since before the Nazi invasion). They broke into tears at the sight of it. The dancing at *Tashlich* was incredible! The whole thing was an unbelievable experience.

When we traveled to the town of Breslov, we saw people in rickety, horse-drawn wagons pulling buckets of water up from the well. It was a completely different world, like a scene from Rebbe Nachman's time. Who would have believed that the Soviet state, this major world power that put men in space and that we were so afraid of, was so primitive?

SINCE THAT FIRST ROSH HASHANAH, I've traveled to Uman every year, except for one time when my wife and son were very sick. I felt so bad about not going that year that now I travel there twice a year, once for Rosh HaShanah and once in the middle of the year.

One year right before Rosh HaShanah, my wife miscarried and the doctors had to operate to save her life. I wanted to stay in Toronto with her, but she insisted that I travel to Uman. "When my life is in such danger, this is the most important thing you can do," she said.

Each year, I have the unbelievable *nachat* of standing with my three sons in the *kloyz*, while a few seats away are others from our small group. The Rebbe told us to be there, so that's where I am. After all, how could I not travel to the Rebbe who lights my heart on fire?

Appendix A

List of Contributors

(Numbers in parentheses refer to page numbers.)

Abeles, Dovid (16). Originally from Toronto, David Abeles is presently studying in a yeshivah in Tzefat, Israel.

Beilinson, Guillermo (90). Guillermo Beilinson lives in La Plata, Argentina, where he heads the Breslov Research Institute's Spanish branch. In the past seventeen years, he has translated nearly thirty of BRI's books into Spanish.

Bell, Trevor (214). Trevor (Yitzchak) Bell was born and raised in a Modern Orthodox family in London, England. In the early 1970s, he began searching for more meaning in Yiddishkeit. Today, in addition to his work as a legal consultant and a marriage and personal counselor, he lectures on Breslov Chassidut in the United Kingdom.

Ben-Yishai, Yaakov (178). Yaakov Ben-Yishai lives in Montreal, Canada. He divides his time between running his jewelry business and studying Torah.

Bergman, Ozer (110). Raised in a Modern Orthodox home, Ozer Bergman's search for truth brought him to Breslov. He has spent the past thirty years teaching Breslov Chassidut to Jews of every stream, in English, Hebrew and Yiddish, on three continents. He is also a writer and editor for the Breslov Research Institute.

Bouskila, Shalom (241). Shalom Bouskila is a businessman and a member of New York's Persian Jewish community.

Burton, Tanchum (32). Originally from Brooklyn, New York, Tanchum Burton is now a practicing psychotherapist, rabbi and educator in Jerusalem.

Caro, Michael (246). Born in Morocco, Michael Caro has lived in Montreal, Canada, from the age of seven. He is a businessman and a member of Montreal's Breslov Centre.

Cohen, Eliyahu (161). Eliyahu Cohen is a businessman and a member of Montreal's Breslov Centre.

Dr. D. (187). Married with ten children, Dr. D. has a thriving dental practice in the center of Jerusalem. He devotes his mornings to Torah study and his afternoons to taking care of patients.

Dayan, Moshe (209). Originally from Israel, Moshe Dayan moved to Montreal, Canada around 1980. He is a businessman who studies Torah every day.

Elkaslai, Shimon (104). Originally from Montreal, Shimon Elkaslai became religious after attending an Arachim seminar. He teaches at Montreal's Breslov Centre.

Emergy, Moshe (167). Born in Israel, Moshe grew up in both Spain and the United States. Today, he lives in Montreal, Canada and is one of the co-founders of the Breslov Centre.

Fleischman, Bob (169). Bob Fleischman is a successful businessman in Miami Beach, Florida.

Friedland, Huna (81). Huna Friedland lives in Jerusalem with his family. He is director of the Kesher Institute, a yeshivah program designed for "at-risk" young men, and maintains a private practice offering therapy, counseling and consulting for individuals and institutions.

Futterman, Nachman (174). Nachman Futterman is in the textile import-export business. Today, he lives in Jerusalem with his wife and children.

Goldschmidt, Danny (157). Danny Goldschmidt is an active member and Trustee of Manhattan's Carlebach Shul. An attorney by training, he presently works as a financial advisor at a major brokerage house.

Gorfinkel, Nestor (248). Born in Cuba, Nestor (Nachum) Gorfinkel is now a lawyer in Miami, Florida. He is married to Maria (Miriam) and has two children, Luis (Eliyahu) and Hannah.

Gross, Shimon (195). Shimon Gross (a pseudonym) is a Chassidic businessman residing in London, England. He traveled to Uman for the first time in the winter of 2000.

Hager, Zvi (50). Originally from Brooklyn, New York, Zvi Hager is presently studying in the Lakewood Kollel in Lakewood, New Jersey. His parents are Breslover chassidim.

Hamburg, Moshe (99). Moshe Hamburg lives in Ramat Beit Shemesh, Israel, where he studies part-time and works in high-tech sales. He is currently studying to become an Israeli tour guide.

Hanan, Brian (231). Brian Hanan is a businessman who is active in the Los Angeles Breslov community.

Herman, Menachem (23). Menachem Herman is a popular rock guitarist and songwriter. He lives in Ramat Beit Shemesh, Israel.

Jackson, Yaron (119). Yaron Jackson lives with his family in Tzefat, Israel. Yaron studies full-time in a yeshivah.

Katz, Yossi (107). Originally from Toronto, Canada, Yossi Katz resides in Lakewood, New Jersey, where he is studying to be a rabbi.

Kay, Shimon (252). Originally from London, Shimon Kay lives in Philadelphia with his wife and children. His day is divided between studying in a *kollel* and working as a campus rabbi.

Kessler, Howard (242). Howard (Hertzel Shlomo) Kessler is a blacksmith residing in Florida since "that's where the horses are."

Kosoy, Eliezer (60). Originally from Toronto, Eliezer Kosoy presently lives in Jerusalem. He is a talented musician who devotes most of his day to his yeshivah studies, while playing for weddings and other events in the evenings.

Kramer, Chaim (64). Founder and head of the Breslov Research Institute, Chaim Kramer travels throughout the world spreading the teachings of Rebbe Nachman. He came to Breslov through his *rebi* and father-in-law, Rabbi Zvi Aryeh Rosenfeld.

Levinson, Yehudah (277). Yehudah Levinson practices law in Toronto, Canada.

Lipshutz, Yonatan (94). Yonatan ("Yoni") Lipshutz lives in Tzefat. He is the violinist for the Simply Tsfat Band.

Lowe, Michael (257). A resident of Manchester, England, Michael Lowe works in high tech.

Mann, Chaim (13). Chaim Mann lives in Montreal, Canada, where he is a member of Montreal's Breslov Centre.

Menaged, David (274). David Menaged is a New York-based businessman, a member of the Sephardi community of Brooklyn, and a member of the Carlebach Shul in New York's Upper West Side.

Moskowitz, Simcha (123). Simcha Moskowitz (a pseudonym) is married with four children. He lives in Jerusalem, where he studies full-time in a *kollel*.

Reiter, Eliyahu (163). Originally from Manhattan, New York, Eliyahu Reiter presently resides in Tzefat, Israel, where he is a member of the Simply Tsfat Band, teaches in a women's yeshivah and studies Torah.

Rietti, Rabbi Jonathan (51). Originally from London, England, Rabbi Jonathan Rietti presently resides in Monsey, New York, where he works as a senior lecturer for Gateways, a Jewish outreach organization.

Sanders, Gavriel (131). A former Christian missionary, Gavriel Sanders now lectures internationally as a "missionary" for Judaism. He lives in Far Rockaway, New York.

Sears, Dovid (197). Dovid Sears is a professional artist and the director of the New York-based Breslov Center for Spirituality and Inner Growth. He has authored several books, including those on Breslov Chassidut.

Shapiro, Dovid (38). Originally from Paterson, New Jersey, Rabbi Dovid Shapiro presently resides in Jerusalem, where he edits Hebrew manuscripts.

Solomon, Ben Zion (220). One of the founders of the Diaspora Yeshiva Band, Ben Zion Solomon presently resides in Moshav Me'or Modi'im, where he divides his day between playing music and Torah study. Reb Ben Zion has recorded the Breslov melodies for Shabbat, along with joyous and meditative melodies, for the Breslov Research Institute.

Spring, Rabbi Chaim (185). Rabbi Chaim Spring does fine book-binding and restoration of old books. He lives in Ginot Shomron, a settlement in Judea and Samaria.

Stubbs, Gershom (181). Gershom Stubbs resides in Scranton, Pennsylvania, where he works with children with behavioral disabilities.

Tauber, Rabbi Elchonon (259). Rabbi Elchonon Tauber grew up in the very Orthodox neighborhood of Williamsburg in New York City. Today, he is the *Rav* of Congregation Beis Yehudah, a prominent shul in Los Angeles, California.

Ungar-Sargon, Dr. Julian (264). Originally from London, England, Dr. Julian Ungar-Sargon is a neurologist living in Chicago, Illinois.

Winter, Avi (255). Avi Winter (a pseudonym) comes from a prominent Orthodox family. A product of America's finest *yeshivot*, he was groomed for greatness in the non-Chassidic world—until he decided to travel to Uman for Rosh HaShanah.

Yahm, Howard (210). Howard Yahm is a retired psychologist living in Vermont with his wife and family.

Zagury, Gil (171). Gil Zagury owns a clothing manufacturing company in Montreal, Canada. He is married with two children, and is a member of Montreal's Breslov Centre.

Appendix B

Breslov Biographies

Reb Avraham b'Reb Nachman

Reb Avraham Chazan (1849-1917) was the son of Reb Noson's prime disciple, Reb Nachman Chazan of Tulchin (thus, he was known to all as "Reb Avraham b'Reb [the son of Reb] Nachman"). He was the bridge between the founders of Breslov Chassidut and the followers to come, recording many of the stories and oral traditions that he received from his father in *Kokhavey Ohr*, *Sichot VeSippurim* and other works.

Reb Shimshon Barski

A direct descendant of Rebbe Nachman, Reb Shimshon Barski (1873-1935) was an important and influential Breslover chassid in Uman prior to World War II. He authored *HaEtzot HaMevu'erot* (Explained Advice), which expands and clarifies *Likutey Etzot*, and brought many Jews close to Breslov Chassidut, especially Polish Jews. He was known for his clear, rational thinking and calm demeanor.

Rabbi Levi Yitzchok Bender

Rabbi Levi Yitzchok Bender (1897-1989) came to Uman in 1915 as a penniless war refugee from Poland and became a close student of Reb Avraham b'Reb Nachman. He remained in Uman for the next twenty years, living and teaching Breslov Chassidut.

He was selected to be the *chazzan* for the morning prayer service at the annual Rosh HaShanah *kibutz*. In 1935, he and Rabbi Eliyahu Chaim Rosen were arrested and imprisoned by the NKVD (predecessor of the KGB) for soliciting international relief for local Jews during the Ukrainian famine of the early 1930s. Granted a conditional reprieve, Reb Levi Yitzchok fled Uman. He spent World War II in Siberia and immigrated to Israel in 1949. The recognized head of the Breslov community in Jerusalem, he became a spiritual guide for many *ba'alei teshuvah* who joined Rebbe Nachman's following in large numbers in the 1970s and 1980s.

Rabbi Moshe Bienenstock

Born in Germany after World War II, Rabbi Bienenstock is a contemporary Breslov elder and the *chazzan* for the *Musaf* prayers in Uman for Rosh HaShanah. He resides in Jerusalem.

Rabbi Yitzchak Breiter

Rabbi Yitzchak Breiter (1886-1943) discovered Rebbe Nachman's works as a yeshivah student in Poland and made his first trip to Uman the following Rosh HaShanah. He continued traveling to Uman until 1917, when the Russian Revolution closed the border. He established a Rosh HaShanah *kibutz* in Lublin and composed a moving prayer asking to be able to travel to Rebbe Nachman's gravesite, which was recited by Breslover chassidim for some seventy years until the gates finally reopened. Rabbi Breiter succeeded in increasing the ranks of Polish Breslover chassidim to several thousand, and authored several books. A recognized elder in the Warsaw Ghetto, he was deported and murdered by the Nazis in Treblinka, may God avenge his blood.

Reb Moshe Burstein

Reb Moshe Burstein (b. 1914) is one of the leading figures in the contemporary Breslov world. Born in Poltosk, Poland, he came to Jerusalem with his wife and infant son in 1935 and founded the daily Breslov *minyan* in the Old City. During the Israeli War of Independence, he was captured by the Jordanians and spent nine months as a civilian hostage in Jordan together with eight other Breslover chassidim. After his release, he was resettled in the Katamon neighborhood of Jerusalem, where he bought, rebuilt and administered the Breslov shul there. Later, he built a newer, larger shul in Jerusalem's Givat Moshe neighborhood, naming it *Or Avraham* (Light of Abraham) after his *rebi*, Rabbi Avraham Sternhartz. Reb Moshe was the *chazzan* for the annual Rosh HaShanah *kibutz* in Meron. For fifty years, he longed to be worthy of praying at Rebbe Nachman's *tziyun*. When he finally reached the *tziyun* in 1988, he recited the *Shehecheyanu* blessing.

Reb Shmuel Chechik

Reb Shmuel Chechik (d. 1999) was renowned among Breslover chassidim for his outstanding scholarship, keen wit and unyielding devotion to the teachings of Rebbe Nachman.

Reb Michel Dorfman

Born in Kiev, Reb Yechiel Michel Dorfman (1913-2006) became a Breslover chassid in his early teens. He married Rabbi Avraham Sternhartz's granddaughter, Mariasah. Escaping the Stalinist purges of the Ukraine in the late 1930s, he fled to Moscow, where he survived the war only to be arrested by the NKVD (predecessor of the KGB) and exiled to Siberia for nearly seven years. Following Stalin's death, his sentence was commuted and he returned to Moscow. Reb Michel was a key figure in maintaining the annual Rosh HaShanah *kibutz* in Uman despite the Communist ban on religious gatherings. He was willing to place himself in great danger to escort American Breslovers to Uman and show them Rebbe's Nachman's *tziyun*. In 1971, he and his family received permission to immigrate to Israel, where he was appointed honorary *rosh yeshivah* of the Breslov Yeshivah in Jerusalem.

Reb Naftali Zvi Dubinski

Reb Naftali Zvi Dubinski (d. 1993) came to Uman when he was seventeen years old and joined the group of *ovdim* (devotees) who spent their nights in *hitbodedut*, their mornings in prayer and their days in Torah study. His wife died in childbirth, leaving him with one son. In 1937, Reb Naftali Zvi was arrested and sentenced to eight years in a Siberian slave labor camp for the "crime" of convincing a Jewish boy to stop working on Shabbat. Completely isolated during this period, he had no idea what happened to his six-year-old son during World War II. In fact, his son was being raised by Reb Yochanan Galant. He was finally reunited with his son in 1954, when they met in Uman for Rosh HaShanah. He immigrated to Israel in 1971, at the same time as his son and grandchildren.

Gedaliah Fleer

Reb Gedaliah Fleer (b. 1940) is a contemporary, English-speaking Breslov teacher. He was the first Westerner to penetrate the "forbidden city" of Uman in more than thirty years, since Rabbi Shmuel Horowitz stole across the border around 1929. His attempts to reach the Rebbe's *tziyun* are detailed in *Against All Odds*, published by the Breslov Research Institute.

Reb Yochanan Galant

A joyful and vibrant Jew, Reb Yochanan Galant (1901-1979) was one of the eleven Breslover chassidim who traveled to Uman for the first Rosh HaShanah *kibutz* after the Holocaust. Although he had no children of his own, Reb Yochanan showed tremendous self-sacrifice to raise and teach Reb Yaakov, the son of Reb Naftali Zvi Dubinski, when the latter was exiled to Siberia. He and his wife immigrated to Israel in 1964, where he taught the Israeli Breslover chassidim many traditional tunes that had been sung in Uman.

Avraham Greenbaum

Reb Avraham Greenbaum (b. 1949) is a contemporary Breslov writer, translator and teacher. He is the author of over two dozen books on Torah spirituality, Chassidut, Kabbalah, preventive healthcare, healing and environmental responsibility, and is the founder and director of the Azamra Institute, a global outreach network.

Rabbi Shmuel Horowitz

Born in Tzefat, Israel, Rabbi Shmuel Horowitz (1913-1989) began practicing *hitbodedut* after reading Reb Alter Tepliker's *Hishtapkhut HaNefesh* (*Outpouring of the Soul*). Around 1929, he traveled to Poland and smuggled himself into Russia to visit Rebbe Nachman's *tziyun*. He remained in Uman for two and a half years, studying with Rabbi Avraham Sternhartz and participating in the Rosh HaShanah *kibutz* three times before he was discovered and arrested by the Soviets for illegal entry into Russia. He spent three months in a Russian prison and was released with the intervention of the Chief Rabbi of Israel, Rabbi Avraham Yitzchak Kook, in 1933. He spent the rest of his life in Meron near the gravesite of Rabbi Shimon bar Yochai, where he spent his nights in the mountains practicing *hitbodedut*.

Rabbi Aryeh Kaplan

Rabbi Aryeh Kaplan (1934-1983) was a prolific writer and translator whose works on Jewish thought, practice, mysticism and Chassidut are regarded as a significant factor in the growth of the *ba'al teshuvah* movement. Born in Bronx, New York, Rabbi Kaplan earned an M.A. in physics and studied at the Mir Yeshivah and Yeshiva Torah Vodaath in New York. There he was influenced by Rabbi Zvi Aryeh Rosenfeld, who single-handedly effected a revival of Breslov Chassidut among American yeshivah students. Rabbi Kaplan wrote the first-ever translation of *Rabbi Nachman's Wisdom* along with *Outpouring of the Soul, Rabbi Nachman's Stories* and *Until the Mashiach*.

Rabbi Elazar Mordekhai Koenig

Rabbi Elazar Mordekhai Koenig (b. 1945) is the leader of the Breslov community in Tzefat, Israel. He heads the Nachal Novea Mekor Chochma Institutions, which include Kiryat Breslov (a religious housing complex), a *kollel*, the Magen Avot Yeshivah, the historic Trisk Synagogue, and a five-story Torah Center. He founded the New York-based Breslov Center for Spirituality and Inner Growth in 1997 in order to make Rebbe Nachman's teachings accessible to the American public.

Rabbi Gedaliah Koenig

Rabbi Gedaliah Koenig (1921-1980) was born in the Old City of Jerusalem. Originally a Lubavitcher chassid, he was drawn to Breslov by Rabbi Avraham Sternhartz and eventually became one of his leading disciples. He was the driving force behind the establishment of the Breslov community in Tzefat, which is headed by his son, Rabbi Elazar Mordekhai Koenig. He authored *Chayey Nefesh*, a treatise in response to Rabbi Chaim Volozhin's work, *Nefesh HaChaim*, on the topic of what it means to bind oneself to the *tzaddik*, and numerous other, unpublished manuscripts, including commentaries on *Likutey Moharan*.

Yisrael Korsonski

Reb Yisrael Korsonski (d. 1985) lived in Moscow after World War II and, with great self-sacrifice, traveled to Uman under the Communist regimes despite the ban against religious gatherings. He immigrated to Israel in 1973.

Moshe Mykoff

Originally from New York, Reb Moshe Mykoff (b. 1951) is a Breslov writer, editor and translator based in Jerusalem. He is the author of several important Breslov books, including *The Empty Chair*, *The Gentle Weapon*, *Seventh Heaven: Shabbat with Rebbe Nachman* and the English translation of Rebbe Nachman's *Sefer HaMidot* (*The Aleph-Bet Book*). Since 1984, he has been involved in the ongoing English translation of the *Likutey Moharan* by the Breslov Research Institute; thirteen of the projected fifteen volumes of this monumental work have been published.

Reb Noson

Reb Noson Sternhartz (1780-1844) was born in Nemirov, a small town near Breslov. A promising Torah scholar, he was drawn to

Chassidut over the objections of his father and father-in-law and became the foremost disciple and scribe of Rebbe Nachman in 1802. After the Rebbe's passing, Reb Noson single-handedly shaped the Breslov movement into the vibrant force it is today, despite the fact that there is no "living" Rebbe. Using his formidable talents in learning and a phenomenal memory, he preserved the lessons, stories and everyday conversations of Rebbe Nachman; published all of the Rebbe's works; and wrote his own commentaries, *chidushim* and prayers based on the Rebbe's lessons. He also established the first Rosh HaShanah *kibutz* at the Rebbe's *tziyun* in 1811 and built the first Breslov synagogue in Uman in 1834.

Rabbi Eliyahu Chaim Rosen

Rabbi Eliyahu Chaim Rosen (1899-1984) was the founder and dean of the Breslov Yeshivah in Jerusalem. Born in Potolsk, Poland, he was orphaned as a very young boy. As a yeshivah student, he found a copy of *Tikkun HaKlali* and met a Breslover chassid who convinced him to travel to Uman in 1914. He became the student of Reb Avraham b'Reb Nachman and remained in Uman for the next two decades. In 1935, he and Rabbi Levi Yitzchok Bender were arrested and imprisoned by the NKVD (predecessor of the KGB) for soliciting international relief for local Jews during the Ukrainian famine of the early 1930s. Granted a conditional reprieve, Rabbi Rosen escaped Uman and immigrated to Israel. He established the Breslov Yeshivah in the Old City of Jerusalem in 1936 and founded the Breslov Yeshivah in Meah Shearim in 1953, where he taught generations of students until his passing.

Rabbi Zvi Aryeh Rosenfeld

A modern-day pioneer of the Breslov movement, Rabbi Zvi Aryeh Rosenfeld (1922-1978) brought the Chassidut to American shores and nurtured its growth among American-born students for more than three decades. A scion of Breslover families dating back to Rebbe Nachman's time, he was born in Gydinia, Poland and grew up in Brooklyn, New York. He studied at Yeshiva Torah Vodaath and received his rabbinical ordination at the age of twenty-three, after completing the entire Talmud for the second time. Rabbi Zvi Aryeh pioneered the translation of Rebbe Nachman's teachings into English, beginning with *Rabbi Nachman's Wisdom*, which Rabbi Aryeh Kaplan translated at his behest. Rabbi Zvi Aryeh also devoted himself to strengthening Breslov Chassidut in Israel, collecting funds to build the Breslov Yeshivah in Meah Shearim, publish Rebbe Nachman's works in Hebrew, and support needy Israeli Breslover families.

Reb Avraham Yehoshua Rosenvald

Reb Avraham Yehoshua Rosenvald (d. 1970), commonly known as Reb Shika, displayed much dedication and ingenuity to keep the flame of Yiddishkeit alive in Russia. For example, when the Jewish cemetery in Moscow was completely full and the Soviets began to cremate bodies or bury them next to crosses, Reb Shika persuaded his former friends in the Communist Party to reallocate several acres of a planned garbage dump for a new Jewish cemetery. He performed many *mitzvot* with self-sacrifice, including *davening* in a shul on Shabbat (the nearest one was a three hours' walk away) and reciting *Tikkun Chatzot* and *Tikkun HaKlali* every night.

Rabbi Yaakov Meir Schechter

Rabbi Yaakov Meir Schechter (b. 1931) is one of the foremost and fiery leaders on the Breslov scene today. He was born in the Old City of Jerusalem, where he learned from the leading Breslover chassidim of the past generation, particularly Rabbi Avraham Sternhartz. In addition to his leadership of the Breslov community, he is one of the *roshei yeshivah* of Sha'ar HaShamayim Yeshivah, a school which emphasizes the study of Kabbalah, also in Jerusalem.

Rabbi Shmuel Shapiro

Rabbi Shmuel Shapiro (1913-1989), one of the most outstanding students in the Etz Chaim Yeshivah headed by Rabbi Isser Zalman

Meltzer, was drawn to Breslov by Rabbi Shmuel Horowitz and became a Breslover chassid in 1934. Known as "the *tzaddik* of Jerusalem," Reb Shmuel would spend the nights practicing *hitbodedut* in the fields and then put in a full day's Torah study. His one great desire, that seemed to perpetually elude him, was to visit Rebbe Nachman's *tziyun* in Uman. He finally made it in 1973, and was able to spend Rosh HaShanah with the Rebbe in 1988. He passed away shortly afterward, having suffered from Parkinson's disease for nearly thirteen years.

Rabbi Avraham Sternhartz

Rabbi Avraham Sternhartz (1862-1955) was the great-grandson of Reb Noson and a grandson of the Tcheriner Rav, Rabbi Nachman Goldstein. Orphaned at a young age, he was raised by his illustrious grandfather. He married at age sixteen after having completed the entire Talmud. Following his marriage, he received his rabbinical ordination from the Rogotchover Gaon. At the age of nineteen, he was appointed *Rav* of Kremenchug. At twenty-two, he was appointed *chazzan* for the Rosh HaShanah *kibutz*, a post that he held both in Uman and in Israel for a total of seventy years. Rabbi Avraham arrived in Jerusalem's Old City in 1936, where he was received and recognized as the outstanding Breslov elder of his generation. In 1940, he established the Rosh HaShanah *kibutz* in Meron.

Reb Alter Tepliker

Reb Moshe Yehoshua Bezhilianski (1860?-1919), known as Reb Alter Tepliker after his birthplace in Teplik, Ukraine, was a leading Breslover chassid in Uman at the turn of the century and the brother-in-law of Reb Avraham b'Reb Nachman. Author of ten works on Breslov Chassidut, Reb Alter pioneered the publication of Breslov teachings in a topical format, such as *Hishtapkhut HaNefesh* (on *hitbodedut*), *Meshivat Nefesh* (on inner strength), *Or Zorei'ach Haggadah* (on the Pesach Hagaddah), and *Mili de-Avot* (on *Pirkey Avot*). He was murdered during a pogrom while studying in the shul in Teplik.

Appendix C

Breslov Bibliography

All Breslov books in English translation are published by, and available from, the offices of the Breslov Research Institute.

Advice—A translation of *Likutey Etzot*, the compiled advice from *Likutey Moharan* and other works of the Rebbe.

The Aleph-Bet Book—A translation of Rebbe Nachman's *Sefer HaMidot*, containing epigrams and practical advice, organized alphabetically.

Azamra!—A translation of Likutey Moharan I, 282, the Rebbe's lesson about finding good in others and in oneself, with additional commentary and prayers by Reb Noson.

Crossing the Narrow Bridge—A practical guide to Rebbe Nachman's teachings exploring a broad range of topics, from joy, peace and charity to earning a living, taking care of one's health and raising children, this book answers many of the practical and technical questions that puzzle those who are making their first acquaintance with Breslov.

The Empty Chair—A treasury of wisdom and advice for living joyously and spiritually, based on the teachings of Rebbe Nachman.

The Gentle Weapon—Prayers for everyday and not-so-everyday moments, based on lessons in *Likutey Moharan*.

Hishtapkhut HaNefesh—see *Outpouring of the Soul*

Likutey Etzot—See *Advice*

Likutey Halakhot—Reb Noson's monumental, eight-volume work on Breslov thought and Kabbalah following the order of the *Shulchan Arukh*

Likutey Moharan—Rebbe Nachman's main work of teachings. An authoritative English translation with facing Hebrew text, full explanatory notes, source references and supplementary information is underway; thirteen of the planned fifteen volumes have been published by the Breslov Research Institute.

Meshivat Nefesh—See *Restore My Soul*

Outpouring of the Soul—A translation of *Hishtapkhut HaNefesh*, a collection of teachings on *hitbodedut* from Rebbe Nachman's and Reb Noson's writings, compiled by Reb Alter Tepliker.

Rabbi Nachman's Stories—A translation of *Sippurey Ma'asiot*, the thirteen tales of Rebbe Nachman, with additional stories and parables. Translated and annotated by Rabbi Aryeh Kaplan.

Rabbi Nachman's Tikkun—An introduction and commentary to Rebbe Nachman's *Tikkun HaKlali*, a set of ten specific Psalms whose recitation serves as repentance for all sins, particularly the sin of wasted seed.

Rabbi Nachman's Wisdom—A translation of *Shevachey HaRan* and *Sichot HaRan*, translated by Rabbi Aryeh Kaplan and annotated by Rabbi Zvi Aryeh Rosenfeld. A revised edition by Rabbi Ozer Bergman is being readied for press.

Restore My Soul—A translation of *Meshivat Nefesh* by Reb Alter Tepliker, presenting Breslov teachings on how to combat hopelessness and depression, and draw from the wellsprings of joy and spiritual strength.

Sefer HaMidot—See *The Aleph-Bet Book*

Sichot HaRan—See *Rabbi Nachman's Wisdom*

Shemot HaTzaddikim—Reb Noson's compilation of the names of the *tzaddikim* throughout the generations, the recital of which arouses powerful spiritual forces and can even alter the forces of nature.

Sippurey Ma'asiyot—See *Rabbi Nachman's Stories*

Through Fire and Water: The Life of Reb Noson of Breslov—A thoroughly-researched biography of the man who preserved all of the Rebbe's lessons and devoted his life to bringing the Rebbe's message of faith, hope and joy to the world.

The Treasury of Unearned Gifts: Rebbe Nachman's Path to Happiness and Contentment in Life—Insights from *Likutey Moharan* II, 78, the Rebbe's lesson on the concepts of connecting to the *tzaddik*, the need for Torah study, lovingkindness and the "concealed Torah," the path to the Holy Land, simplicity, and never giving up hope.

Tzaddik—A translation of *Chayey Moharan* (The Life of Rebbe Nachman) by Reb Noson, containing conversations, sayings, stories, dreams and visions of the Rebbe.

Until the Mashiach—A definitive account of Rebbe Nachman's life, tracing his career day by day and year by year, including an historical overview, detailed maps, and anecdotes about Rebbe Nachman's family, followers and other contemporary figures.

Glossary

Aleph-bet—the Hebrew alphabet

Avodat HaShem—Divine service

Avraham Avinu—the Patriarch Abraham

Ba'al teshuvah (pl. *ba'alei teshuvah*)—lit., "master of return"; a Jew who has returned to the path of Torah Judaism

Bachur (pl. *bachurim*)—a young man; usually refers to a young man who is studying in a yeshivah

Ben—son of

Berakhah (pl. *berakhot*)—blessing

Bimah—pulpit at which the Torah is read in synagogue

Bubbe and Zeide (Yiddish)—Grandma and Grandpa

Challah—a braided bread served on Shabbat, Yom Tov and other special occasions

Chanukah—eight-day holiday celebrated in winter, commemorating the rededication of the Holy Temple after its defilement by the Greeks

Chassid (pl. *chassidim*)—a member of a Chassidic group

Chassidishe (Yiddish)—one who follows the Chassidic customs (as opposed to the *litvishe* customs)

Chassidut—a Jewish revival movement founded in Eastern Europe in the eighteenth century by the Baal Shem Tov, Rebbe Nachman's great-grandfather. One of its core teachings is that God's presence fills all one's surroundings, and one should strive to serve God in every word and deed.

Chazzan—cantor

Chevrah—group

Chidush (pl. *chidushim*)—something new; usually refers to a novel Torah idea

Chol HaMo'ed—the intermediary days of the holidays of Pesach and Sukkot

Cholent—a slow-cooking stew traditionally served as the main course at the Shabbat-morning meal

Daven (pl. *davening*) (Yiddish)—pray

Emunah—belief; faith in God

Erev—eve of

Gehinnom—hell

Geirut—conversion

Gemara (Aramaic)—the redaction of the Oral Law which forms the second part of the Talmud, redacted in the fourth through fifth centuries by Rav Ashi and his student, Ravina

Haggadah—liturgy of the Pesach Seder

Halakhah (pl. *halakhot*)—Jewish law

Hitbodedut—lit., "self-seclusion"; Rebbe Nachman uses the term to refer to a daily practice in which one sets a time and place to speak to God. In a certain sense, hitbodedut is prayer; in another sense, it is unstructured, verbal meditation.

Kabbalah—body of Jewish esoteric wisdom

Kabbalat Shabbat—Friday-night prayer heralding the onset of Shabbat

Kaddish—prayer recited daily in shul and by mourners

Kashrut—Jewish dietary laws

Kibutz—lit., "gathering"; specifically, the Breslov Rosh HaShanah gathering

Kiddush—the blessing pronounced over wine at Shabbat and Yom Tov meals; a reception after Shabbat-morning services

Kippah—skullcap or head covering worn by Jewish males; also called "yarmulke"

Kloyz (Yiddish)—synagogue

Kohen (pl. *kohanim*)—a member of the Jewish priestly class, a patrilineal descendant of Moses' brother, Aaron

Kollel—a group of married men who learn together following the same approach or system, usually receiving a subsidy

Kotel—the Western Wall, the last remnant of the Holy Temple in Jerusalem

Lag Ba'Omer—the thirty-third day of the Omer, referring to the fifty-day counting period between Pesach and Shavuot in memory of the Omer-offering that was brought in the Holy Temple

Litvak—a *litvishe* Jew

Litvishe (Yiddish)—one who follows the Lithuanian Jewish customs (as opposed to the Chassidic customs)

Ma'ariv—evening prayer service

Ma'aser—lit., "tenth"; a tithe given to charity

Mamash (Hebrew)—really

Mashiach—Messiah

Matzah (pl. *matzot*)—unleavened bread

Melaveh malkah—lit., "escorting the queen"; a festive meal eaten after the conclusion of Shabbat

Menorah—an eight-branched candelabra kindled on each night of Chanukah

Mezuzah (pl. *mezuzot*)—a small parchment containing the verses from Deuteronomy 6:4-9 and 11:13-21, which is affixed to the doorposts of a Jewish home

Midrash—homiletical rabbinic teachings

Mikveh—a special pool of water used for ritual purification

Minchah—afternoon prayer service

Minhag—custom

Minyan (pl. *minyanim*)—quorum of at least ten men required for a communal prayer service

Mishnah—the redaction of the Oral Law which forms the first part of the Talmud, redacted in the second century C.E. by Rabbi Yehudah HaNasi

Mitzvah (pl. *mitzvot*)—a Torah precept or commandment; a meritorious act

Musaf—the "additional" prayer service conducted after *Shacharit* on Shabbat and Yom Tov

Mussar—ethical lessons for personal and spiritual growth

Nachat—pleasure

Niggun (pl. *niggunim*)—melody

Parashah (pl. *parshiyot*)—Torah portion

Pesach—the Jewish Passover, a biblical festival commemorating the Exodus from Egypt, occurring in spring

Pesach Seder—the festive meal conducted on the first two nights of Passover (first night only in the Land of Israel), with a prescribed order of rituals and symbolic foods that recall the Exodus from Egypt

Peyot—sidelocks

Posek—one who renders decisions in Jewish law

Purim—holiday commemorating the salvation of the Jewish people from the edict promulgated by Haman in Persia, in the time of Mordekhai and Esther

Rav—rabbi

Reb—title of respect given to a fellow Jew

Rebbe—leader of a Chassidic group

Rebi—lit., "my master"; the rabbi-teacher from whom one receives his primary direction in Torah

Rosh Chodesh—the first day of a Jewish month

Rosh HaShanah—the Jewish New Year

Rosh kollel—head of a *kollel*

Rosh yeshivah (pl. **roshei yeshivah**)—dean of a yeshivah

Segulah—propitious remedy

Selichot—prayer recited in the Hebrew month of Elul and during the Ten Days of Repentance between Rosh HaShanah and Yom Kippur, including verbal confession of one's misdeeds in the past year and a plea for God's forgiveness

Shabbat—the Jewish Sabbath

Shabbosdik (Yiddish)—of a Sabbath nature

Shacharit—morning prayer service

Shavuot—biblical festival commemorating the Giving of the Torah at Mount Sinai, occurring in early summer

Shema Yisrael—a declaration of faith in the oneness of God and a commitment to fulfilling His commandments, comprised of verses from Deuteronomy 6:4-9 and 11:13-21, and Numbers 15:37-41. Recited daily during morning and evening prayers, and before going to sleep.

Shemoneh Esrei—lit., "Eighteen"; the silent devotional prayer which is the focus of the three daily obligatory prayers. So named because it initially consisted of eighteen blessings; an additional blessing was added later.

Sheva berakhot—lit., "seven blessings"; festive meals celebrated with a bride and groom on each of the seven days following their wedding, during which seven blessings are appended to the Grace after Meals

Shiddukh—marriage match

Shiur (pl. **shiurim**)—Torah class or lecture

Shlep (Yiddish)—drag

Shofar—ram's horn, traditionally blown during Rosh HaShanah morning prayer services

Shomer Shabbat—Sabbath-observant

Shtiebel (Yiddish)—lit., "little house"; a room or small building set aside for prayer services, lectures and communal gatherings such as a shared Third Meal of Shabbat

Shtreimel (Yiddish)—a fur hat worn by married Chassidic men on Shabbat, Yom Tov and other special occasions

Shul (Yiddish)—synagogue

Siddur—prayer book

Simanim—lit., "signs"; foods eaten on Rosh HaShanah whose Hebrew or Yiddish names hint to blessings for a good and sweet new year

Simchah—joy; celebration

Simchat Torah—festival celebrated after Sukkot by dancing with the Torah scrolls

Sukkot—biblical festival commemorating God's benevolent care of the Jewish people during their forty-year sojourn in the desert and His continuing providence over material blessing, occurring in autumn

Talit (pl. **talitot**)—prayer shawl

Talmud—the Jewish Oral Law, expounded by the rabbinical leaders between approximately 50 B.C.E. and 500 C.E. The first part of the Talmud, called the Mishnah, was codified by Rabbi Yehudah HaNasi around 188 C.E. The second part, called the Gemara, was edited by Rav Ashi and Ravina and completed around 505 C.E.

Tanakh—an acronym for *Torah, Nevi'im, Ketubim* (Torah, Prophets, Writings); the twenty-four books of the Bible

Tashlich—lit., "you will cast away"; a prayer recited next to a natural or man-made body of water on the first day of Rosh HaShanah, after *Minchah*, as a means of symbolically "casting away" one's sins

Tefilin—mitzvah of wearing special leather boxes on the head and the arm during morning prayers (except on Shabbat and Jewish festivals); the boxes themselves, which contain biblical verses declaring the oneness of God and the miracles of the Exodus from Egypt

Teshuvah—repentance

Tikkun—rectification; remedy

***Tikkun Chatzot*—**the Midnight Lament over the destruction of the Holy Temple

***Tikkun HaKlali*—**lit., "General Remedy"; a set of ten chapters of Psalms selected by Rebbe Nachman, whose recitation serves as repentance for all sins, particularly the sin of wasted seed

Tisch (pl. ***tischen***) (Yiddish)—lit., "table"; a gathering of chassidim around their rebbe which usually includes singing, Torah discourses and refreshments.

***Tisha B'Av*—**the Ninth of Av, a fast day commemorating the destruction of both the First and Second Temples in Jerusalem

***Torah*—**lit., "teaching"; the Jewish Written Law, given by God to Moses at Mount Sinai; a piece of Torah wisdom

***Tzaddik*—**righteous person; one who has spiritually perfected himself

***Tzedakah*—**charity

***Tzitzit*—**mitzvah of attaching tassels to a four-cornered garment; the tassels themselves

***Tziyun*—**gravesite

***Ulpan*—**Hebrew-language immersion course

Yarmulke (Yiddish)—skullcap or head covering worn by Jewish males; also called "*kippah*"

Yeshivah (pl. ***yeshivot***)—lit., "sitting"; a school for the study of Talmudic and Torah texts

***Yetzer hara*—**evil inclination

Yiddishe nachat (Yiddish)—Jewish pleasure from seeing the achievements of a child or student

Yiddishkeit (Yiddish)—Judaism

***Yom Kippur*—**the Day of Atonement

***Yom Tov*—**Jewish festival

***Zohar*—**the greatest classic of Kabbalah, a mystical commentary on the Torah authored by the school of Rabbi Shimon bar Yochai, a Mishnaic Sage and leading disciple of Rabbi Akiva, during the second century C.E.

www.ingramcontent.com/pod-product-compliance
Lightning Source LLC
LaVergne TN
LVHW051727080426
835511LV00018B/2914

9 781928 822295